THE SPIRIT IN GALATIA

SOCIETY
OF BIBLICAL
LITERATURE

DISSERTATION SERIES

edited by
Howard C. Kee

Number 49
THE SPIRIT IN GALATIA
PAUL'S INTERPRETATION OF *PNEUMA* AS DIVINE
POWER
by
David John Lull

David John Lull

THE SPIRIT IN GALATIA
PAUL'S INTERPRETATION OF
PNEUMA AS DIVINE POWER

Scholars Press

Distributed by
Scholars Press
101 Salem Street
Chico, California 95926

THE SPIRIT IN GALATIA
PAUL'S INTERPRETATION
OF *PNEUMA* AS DIVINE POWER
David John Lull

Ph.D., 1978
Claremont Graduate School

Supervisor:
Hans Dieter Betz

Library of Congress Cataloging in Publication Data

Lull, David John.
   The Spirit in Galatia

   (Dissertation series—Society of Biblical Literature ;
no. 49 ISSN 0145-2770)
   Originally presented as the author's thesis,
Claremont Graduate School, 1978.
   Bibliography: p.
   1. Spirit—Biblical teaching. 2. Holy Spirit—Biblical
teaching. 3. Bible. N.T. Galatians—Criticism,
interpretation, etc. I. Title. II. Series: Society of Biblical
Literature. Dissertation series ; no. 49.
BS2655.H67L84   1980   231'.3   79-26094
ISBN 0-89130-367-7
ISBN 0-89130-368-5 pbk.

Printed in the United States of America
1 2   3   4   5
Edwards Brothers, Inc.
Ann Arbor, Michigan

TABLE OF CONTENTS

PART II
THE HISTORICALITY OF THE SPIRIT

TABLE OF ABBREVIATIONS

AGJU	Arbeiten zur Geschichte des antiken Judentums und des Urchristentums
BAG	W. Bauer, W. F. Arndt, and F. W. Gingrich, *A Greek-English Lexicon of the NT and Other Early Christian Literature*
BDF	F. Blass, A. Debrunner, and R. W. Funk, *A Greek Grammar of the NT and Other Early Christian Literature*
BFCT	Beiträge zur Förderung christlicher Theologie
BHT	Beiträge zur historischen Theologie
BJRL	*Bulletin of the John Rylands University Library of Manchester*
BZNW	Beihefte zur Zeitschrift für die neutestamentliche Wissenschaft
EvT	*Evangelische Theologie*
FRLANT	Forschung zur Religion und Literatur des Alten und Neuen Testaments
HR	*History of Religions*
HKNT	Handkommentar zum Neuen Testament
HNT	Handbuch zum Neuen Testament
HNTC	Harper's NT Commentaries
HTKNT	Herders theologischer Kommentar zum Neuen Testament
HTR	*Harvard Theological Review*
HTS	Harvard Theological Studies
ICC	International Critical Commentary
IDB	G. A. Buttrick (ed.), *Interpreter's Dictionary of the Bible*
JB	A. Jones (ed.), *Jerusalem Bible*
JBL	*Journal of Biblical Literature*
JSSR	*Journal for the Scientific Study of Religion*
KJV	*King James Version*

LCL	Loeb Classical Library
MeyerK	H. A. W. Meyer, Kritisch-exegetischer Kommentar über das Neue Testament
MNTC	Moffatt NT Commentary
NEB	*New English Bible*
NovT	*Novum Testamentum*
NovTSup	Novum Testamentum, Supplements
NTD	Das Neue Testament Deutsch
NTS	*New Testament Studies*
PSTJ	*Perkins (School of Theology) Journal*
RGG	*Religion in Geschichte und Gegenwart*
RSR	*Recherches de science religieuse*
RSV	*Revised Standard Version*
SBT	Studies in Biblical Theology
SD	Studies and Documents
SEÅ	*Svensk exegetisk årsbok*
SJLA	Studies in Judaism in Late Antiquity
SJT	*Scottish Journal of Theology*
TDNT	G. Kittel and G. Friedrich (eds.), *Theological Dictionary of the New Testament*
THKNT	Theologischer Handkommentar zum Neuen Testament
TU	Texte und Untersuchungen (zur Geschichte der altchristlichen Literatur)
TF	Theologisches Forschung
TZ	*Theologische Zeitschrift*
WMANT	Wissenschaftliche Monographien zum Alten und Neuen Testament
WUNT	Wissenschaftliche Untersuchungen zum Neuen Testament
ZNW	*Zeitschrift für die neutestamentliche Wissenschaft*

PREFACE

The initial conception of the topic for this investigation
came from two projects that began at about the same time: a
seminar paper for Professor Betz on Rom 8:1-11, which was later
revised for a seminar with him on "Hellenistic discussions of
inspiration"; and papers that I wrote for seminars on "Process
Thought and Biblical Studies," which were sponsored by the
Center for Process Studies (at the School of Theology at Claremont) under the direction of Professor Cobb. I became interested in questions about Paul's "theology of the Spirit" in
itself, and also in relation to possible "backgrounds," on the
one hand, and in relation to conceptions of the Spirit in recent theology, especially in "process theology." The original
conception of the study, therefore, included Paul's statements
about the Spirit in the four main letters, Hellenistic "backgrounds," and a theological interpretation from the perspective
of "process theology."

After the preparation of the first draft of the chapter on
the use of the term πνεῦμα in the first of the main letters of
Paul, Galatians, my original project underwent major revisions.
Methodology required that I begin with an internal analysis of
Paul's use of πνεῦμα in Galatians. This proved to be a major
undertaking by itself: since the Spirit plays such a primary
role in the letter, I was led into virtually all the problems
of writing a commentary on Galatians. Although I freely borrowed ideas from Betz's articles on Galatians, I made no effort
to consult Professor Betz's commentary manuscript, which is now
available in the Hermeneia series of Fortress Press (Philadelphia, 1979), a copy of which Professor Betz kindly made
available to me before publication for the preparation of the
second draft of the dissertation. The length of this chapter,
together with the exigencies of a doctoral program, required
the study to have a narrow, rather than broad, scope. What was
to be the first chapter, therefore, became the dissertation.

As an internal analysis of Paul's statements about the
Spirit in the letter to the Galatians, it lacks a full-length

discussion of the question of developments in Paul's thinking about the Spirit between Galatians and Romans; and it lacks an indepth treatment of possible "backgrounds." Instead, it represents a "first step." The advantage is that Paul's statements about the Spirit in Galatians are understood first of all, clearly, in their origin in Christian experience in the Galatian churches, and in Paul's polemic with his opponents in Galatia.

Also, from a hermeneutical standpoint, this is an advantage, because a hermeneutic primarily interested in the *conceptual content* of texts often neglects, in its search for *literary* "backgrounds," the *concrete events* of which particular texts are abstractions, and from which they originated.[1] But a hermeneutic developed from the perspective of "process thought," in which events are primary, should begin with the immediate, concrete experiences, of which particular texts are relatively abstract expressions, and out of which they emerged. This, then, is the emphasis reflected in the study.

Finally, since I wanted to attend to the process of understanding "in front of" the text, as well as "behind it," so to speak, my initial interest in a dialog between Paul and contemporary theology is reflected in the dissertation. Bultmann's existentialist interpretation of the NT in his *Theology of the NT* represents the most important interpretation of the Spirit in theology today.[2] But W. Norman Pittenger,[3] a process theologian, and Wolfhart Pannenberg[4] represent similar attempts to go beyond the conceptual limitations of Bultmann's existentialist interpretation of the Spirit. These, then, together with Paul, are dialog partners in the study, especially in the final chapter. My own theological perspective is that of process theology, somewhere between Schubert M. Ogden,[5] and John B. Cobb, Jr.[6] The dialog will be satisfying to the extent that each perspective is creatively transformed by the others.

In short, this investigation seeks to contribute to the understanding of Christianity in the churches of Galatia, of Paul's message to the Galatians, and of theology in our own day.

NOTES

PREFACE

[1]Cf. the discussion of the relation between "the real-life situation" of the Jewish people and literary traditions in the search for the origins of "Jewish millenarism" in Sheldon R. Isenberg's "Millenarism in Greco-Roman Palestine" (*Religion* 4 [1974] 26-46, esp. 35): "the origins of Jewish millenarism are to be sought in the real-life situation of the people. The search for causes in the prophetic literature or in Iranian religion confuses the channels for expression of millenarian impulses with the total phenomenon. Ultimately millenarism involves behaviour as well as myths as well as institutions. It arises in a society following on particular historical events that normally go beyond the re-reading of traditional texts and the collection of extraneous literary allusions." (Cf. also his comments about the quest for the origins of apocalypticism in the history of ideas and religions primarily by means of literary analyses, on p. 27).

[2]Rudolf Bultmann, *Theology of the New Testament* (2 vols. in 1; trans. Kendrick Grobel; New York: Scribner's Sons, 1951, 1955) 1.330-40.

[3]Cf. W. Norman Pittenger, *Life in Christ* (Grand Rapids, MI: William B. Eerdmans, 1972) 35-46, 62-73; and idem, *The Holy Spirit* (Philadelphia: United Church, 1974).

[4]Cf. Wolfhart Pannenberg, "The Working of the Spirit in the Creation and in the People of God," pp. 13-31 in *Spirit, Faith, and Church* (ed. Edward P. Echlin, SJ; Philadelphia: Westminster, 1970); idem, "The Doctrine of the Spirit and the Task of a Theology of Nature," *Theology* 75 (1972) 8-21; idem, *The Apostles' Creed in the Light of Today's Questions* (trans. Margaret Kohl; Philadelphia: Westminster, 1972) 128-43; and idem, *Faith and Reality* (trans. John Maxwell; Philadelphia: Westminster, 1977) 20-38.

[5]Cf. Schubert M. Ogden, *Christ Without Myth: A Study Based on the Theology of Rudolf Bultmann* (New York/Evanston/London: Harper & Row, 1961); and idem, *The Reality of God, and Other Essays* (New York/Evanston/London: Harper & Row, 1963).

[6]Cf. John B. Cobb, Jr., *A Christian Natural Theology Based on the Thought of Alfred North Whitehead* (Philadelphia: Westminster, 1965); *The Structure of Christian Existence* (Philadelphia: Westminster, 1967); and *Christ in a Pluralistic Age* (Philadelphia: Westminster, 1975).

ACKNOWLEDGMENTS

It is a pleasure to acknowledge the assistance I have received while the dissertation was in the making. I would mention especially H. Dieter Betz and John B. Cobb, Jr., whose insights not only gave rise to the conception of the study, but are a constant source of stimulation to me.

A special debt of gratitude is due my friend and conversation partner since our days as seminary students, Ronald F. Hock, who read each draft of the work in very considerable detail. His comments and criticisms were more helpful to me than he knows.

Just as important during the writing was my wife's support and constant encouragement. Without these, my work would have been far more difficult, if not impossible. Because she also led her own creative life, and allowed me to share in it while I led mine, my experience as a graduate student has been full of joy, rather than the usual drudgery. As one who works slowly, I have been particularly fortunate!

CHAPTER I

INTRODUCTION

Reasons for the Investigation

An investigation of the term πνεῦμα in Paul's letter to
the Galatians is needed, from the side of NT scholarship, because debate continues over the question about the nature of
the crisis in the churches of Galatia and, therefore, about the
historical occasion of Paul's statements about the Spirit. The
focus of this debate is the character of Paul's opponents in
Galatia. Currently, the consensus is limited to a single
point: that someone was engaging in a circumcizing campaign in
the Galatian churches. But on the other points no agreement
exists. What was the significance of circumcision to these
people and to Paul's converts in Galatia? Were they also
considering obedience to the law of Moses? Who were Paul's
opponents? Were they Jewish (-Christian), or Gentile-
Christian? Did they come from the churches of Galatia, or
were they outside agitators? And what is the relationship
between, on the one hand, Paul's polemic against obedience to
the law of Moses and, on the other, such statements as 3:10,
5:3, 6:13; and the discussion about corruptions of the flesh
in 5:13-24? Were the churches of Galatia having problems with
flagrant libertinism? Did Paul have to deal with a misunderstanding of his gospel without obedience to the law of Moses?
Or did his ethics based on the Spirit leave his converts without ways of dealing with problems of the flesh?

The view that Paul's opponents in Galatia were "Judaizers"
presupposes such antitheses as law and gospel, wrath and grace,
merit and faith. F. C. Baur gave this view its classical expression, which included the view that Paul's opponents in
Galatia were sponsored by the church in Jerusalem. Significantly different, however, is J. B. Lightfoot's view that the
opponents were Pharisaic Judaizers who were as much at odds
with the Jerusalem church as with Paul. More recently, this
view has been defended by F. F. Bruce, who defines the problem
in the Galatian churches as an identity crisis: Christians in

1

Galatia thought they would be mere Gentile "God-fearers," but
not "full Jews," unless they accepted circumcision and other
Jewish customs.[1]

     As soon as it is assumed, however, that Paul's statements
in the letter can be used simply as a mirror of the beliefs and
behavior of his opponents and/or his converts in Galatia, the
characterization of Paul's opponents as "Judaizers" becomes
questionable. On this assumption, 5:13-24 and 6:13 are taken
as the reason for 3:10 and 5:3; that is, these statements are
seen as having their Sitz im Leben in problems with flagrant
libertinism in the churches of Galatia. Since a legalist cannot be an antinomian, but both can be (or claim to be) a pneumatic, the issue becomes how to reconcile Paul's polemic
against obedience to the laws of Moses with his polemic against
libertinism. Three solutions are (1) to deny the Galatian
churches were having problems with libertinism,[2] (2) to deny
the Galatians were becoming legalists,[3] and (3) to identify two
problems in the churches of Galatia: legalism and libertinism.[4]
A fourth view challenges both assumptions behind the first
three attempts to reconcile Paul's statements against nomism
with those against libertinism. In this view problems with the
flesh do not follow only from libertinism and, therefore, are
not necessarily inconsistent with nomism; and, secondly, Paul's
statements cannot be taken simply as mirror images of the beliefs and behavior of Paul's converts and opponents in Galatia.[5]

     At issue between these four solutions to the problem of
Galatians--that is, four different ways of understanding the
controversy in the Galatian churches that prompted Paul's
letter--is how to reconstruct the experiences of the Spirit in
the churches of Galatia. According to the first and fourth
views, Christians in Galatia may have experienced the Spirit as
liberating them from the flesh, but also as requiring "works of
the law" to make their liberation legitimate and fully effective in keeping them from problems with the flesh. Experiences
of the Spirit, according to the second view, had led to sarkic
behavior, rather than to freedom from it, either because of
their deliberate self-understanding as libertinists, or because
in their initial enthusiasm they did not have ways of dealing

with problems with the flesh.[6] The third view attributes one
kind of pneumatic experience to one part of the Galatian
churches and the other to another part.

In order to place my view within this discussion, I turn
now to Schmithals, who criticizes the two positions available
at the time of his article; namely, on the one hand, the view
that the Galatians were having problems with Judaizers and, on
the other, the view that they were having two problems with
Judaizers and libertinists.[7] Next I turn to Betz, who represents a methodological advance, which moves the discussion beyond the impasse of the previous definition of the problem of
Galatians.[8] Then, finally, I clarify my own position.[9]

In his article, "The Heretics in Galatia,"[10] Schmithals
revised Lütgert's theory by denying that any Judaizers actually
existed in the churches of Galatia. Schmithals argued that
Paul may have *thought* Judaizers were behind the Galatian conflict, but that he was wrong: the Galatians were considering
following Jewish-Christian Gnostics, who practiced circumcision
as a rite that symbolized the emancipation of the pneuma-self
from the prison of the flesh, and who had definite libertine
tendencies. Schmithals then interprets Paul's statements about
the Spirit in Galatians as Paul's use of the Gnostic opponents'
own phrases and self-understanding; but because Paul was un-
informed, or misinformed, about his opponents' views, instead
of turning these pneuma-expressions against them, Paul un-
wittingly plays into the antinomian, libertine tendencies of
the Jewish-Christian Gnostics in Galatia. In this way Schmithals attempts to explain why πνεῦμα opposes both law and flesh
in Galatians.

Schmithals' solution is unpersuasive for at least two
reasons; one has to do with his documentary evidence, the other
with his method of exegesis. In a footnote, he makes a statement with regard to his documentary evidence, or the lack of
it, which should have been a clue that he was mistaken. He
says:

> That the custom of circumcision among Jewish Christian
> Gnostics in the Syrian-Palestinian territory was com-
> mon and was still practiced in Galatia is *just as*

> *likely* as the fact that it was given up as the progress
> of the Gnostic mission advanced toward the West. Thus
> the church's heresy fighters cannot in fact report of
> any of the later Gnostics that they practiced circum-
> cision.[11]

This argument, however, is reversible: that "the church's heresy fighters cannot in fact report of any of the later Gnostics
that they practiced circumcision" is *prima facie* evidence that
Gnostics *had not* practiced circumcision, not that they "gave
it up." Texts like Col 2:9ff.; Eph 2:11; Gos. Phil., Log. 123;
Hippolytus, *Phil.* 5.7; and Gos. Thom., Log. 38,[12] do not necessarily give evidence of the *practice* of circumcision among Gnostics; more likely they represent the *allegorical interpretation*
of the rite, which was not practiced by them. Less radical
wings of Gnosticism might at first allegorically interpret circumcision, and then later drop all references to it. But circumcision is so closely associated with obedience to the law
of Moses that it is improbable that a group so opposed to
obedience to the law of Moses would *practice* the rite that
epitomized it. In other words, Schmithals does not provide
convincing evidence that what is historically improbable actually occurred at all, let alone occurred in the Galatian
churches.

Schmithals' thesis is also methodologically questionable.
On the one hand, he correctly points out that not all that Paul
says in the letter to the Galatians accurately reflects either
the views actually held by the Galatians and the Gnostic missionaries, or their actual behavior. But then, on the other
hand, the only discernible criteria for attributing certain
views or behavior to the Galatians are Schmithals' theory about
Paul's "misunderstanding" of the situation in Galatia and his
thesis about the identity of Paul's opponents in Galatia as
circumcizing, libertinistic, Jewish-Christian Gnostics. Behind
1:11-24 he sees the Gnostic charge that Paul was not a "pneumatic" but a mere "sarkic," a charge that allegedly is reflected
in 4:12-16.[13] But Paul gives no evidence that he faced this
charge in Galatia. Rather, in these verses it is more likely
that Paul is on the *offensive*, not on the defensive; that is,
Paul argues that while the "gospel" of his opponents is only

"from men," and therefore is no real gospel at all, his is
"from God." This also is reflected in 3:1-5, 19 and 4:21-31.
In other words, 1:11-24 and 4:12-16 cannot be used as a mirror
for the Galatians' and Paul's opponents' views. Schmithals
also takes 4:10 as evidence of actual practices in the Galatian
churches, which allegedly shows that they practiced *Gnostic*
worship, not the observance of the law of Moses.[14] But 4:8-10
is a stereotyped description of the "superstitious" and "religiously scrupulous"[15] and, therefore, cannot be taken without
further ado as evidence of actual practices in the Galatian
churches. Schmithals also takes 6:12 as evidence of the real
motives of Paul's opponents; namely, the avoidance of persecution.[16] But this too is a *topos* in the exposure of "charlatans" and, therefore, cannot be used as a mirror of the opponents' real motives and intentions. The same can be said of
5:13-6:10, which Schmithals considers to be the section of the
letter in which Paul is best informed of the real situation in
Galatia, and which is evidence that they were becoming *libertinistic Gnostics*, not legalistic Jews.[17] Finally, he denies
that 4:21 reflects the actual desire of the Galatians;[18] but he
takes 5:3 and 6:13 as reflections of Paul's opponents' goals
and intentions to practice circumcision without observing the
law of Moses.[19] But 6:12-13 is full of *topoi* from the exposure
of "charlatans": they are charged with being self-seeking
lovers of fame,[20] cowards,[21] and antinomians.[22] On the other
hand, 4:21 is the clearest reflection of the Galatians' desire
in the whole letter. It confirms that 3:1-5 is based on the
Galatians' consideration of going the way of righteousness of
the law of Moses,[23] of which circumcision is the epitome.[24]
This leaves Schmithals with 5:3 (and 3:10, which he does not
discuss), which in any case is a problem for those who see in
Paul's letter a mirror of the Galatians' opinions and behavior.
The only evidence that the Galatians did not intend to obey the
law of Moses, into which obedience circumcision would have ini-
tiated them, and of which it was inextricably symbolic, would
be if they indeed were *self-confessing libertinists*. The crux
of the problem, therefore, is 5:13-6:10. And on this problem
hangs the question whether the statements about the Spirit in

Galatians, and the experiences of the Spirit in the churches of
Galatia to which these statements refer, arose in the context
of libertinism or "religious scrupulosity."[25]

Betz proposes another interpretation of the situation in
Galatia, and of Paul's message to the Galatians. For Betz, the
Galatians were considering circumcision, and the way of righteousness of the law of Moses, precisely *because* they were having "problems with the flesh," as an effort to reintroduce a
"code of ethics," of which they had none after beginning Christian existence with a period of "initial enthusiasm." He,
therefore, sees Paul's statements about the Spirit, which "defend the Spirit," as part of an effort to restore the Galatians'
confidence in the Spirit's ability to keep them from falling
back into slavery to the flesh without any "code of ethics"
bound to particular national or ethnic customs.[26] In Betz's
view, therefore, Paul's statements about the Spirit are to be
placed in the context of a polemic against the Galatians' de-
pendence on "religious scrupulosity" as a means of avoiding
"problems with the flesh," and of maintaining freedom.

Both Betz and Schmithals agree that the Galatians were
having problems with "flagrant wrongdoing." While Schmithals,
however, considers the Galatians' "sarkic" problems as being
due to their freedom in the Spirit, Betz leaves open the possibility that they were having "problems with the flesh" *in
spite of* their life in the Spirit. The difference between
their views of the Galatian situation is in their understanding
of the role of circumcision for the Galatians and for Paul's
opponents. Both Betz and Schmithals try to explain the conjunction of circumcision and "problems with the flesh."
Schmithals attributes *both* the practice of circumcision *and*
"sarkic" behavior to Paul's opponents in Galatia. Betz, however, attributes only the *former* to Paul's opponents, but *the
former and the latter* to the Galatians. For Schmithals, the
Galatians took circumcision as a symbol of freedom from the
flesh, which they turned into license for "sarkic" behavior.
But for Betz the Galatians were seeking circumcision in order
to *prevent* falling into "problems with the flesh."

The advantage of Betz's view is that it does not have to
resort to a theory that Paul had misunderstood the nature of
the crisis in the Galatian churches. Methodologically it is
more sound, insofar as it understands Paul's statements in the
letter first in terms of their rhetorical and compositional
function before drawing from them inferences about the beliefs,
motives and behavior of the nomists in Galatia. And it does
not depend on an historical anomaly, for which documentary evidence must be found. On the contrary, the *Kerygmata Petrou*
provides evidence that some Jewish-Christians in the second
half of the third century A.D. engaged in a "Judaizing" campaign among Gentiles.[27] Justin Martyr's *Dial. c. Tryph.* (46-
47) is evidence that some Gentile Christians in the second
half of the second century A.D. took a position between con-
servative Jewish-Christians, who demanded circumcision for
salvation, and radical Gentile-Christians who completely rejected the OT and Judaism, as in the case of Marcion: that is,
he argues that circumcision was *sufficient* for salvation but
not *necessary*. Further, Josephus (*Ant.* 20.38-48) provides
evidence that some Gentiles in the first century A.D. desired
to be circumcised following conversion to Judaism in order to
be "genuine Jews"; and that Jewish opinion was divided on the
question whether circumcision was required before Gentile converts could become "genuine Jews." And 2 Cor 6:14-7:1 seems
to be an "anti-Pauline fragment," which reflects the views of
some Jewish Christians in the Pauline churches who advocated
separation from uncircumcised Christians because they identified the latter as belonging to the forces of evil.[28]

The weakness of Betz's position, however, is that a
theoretical model of developing religions seems to be laid over
Paul's letter. The theoretical model seems to be that of Max
Weber, according to which a "charismatic movement" is marked by
a period of "initial enthusiasm," during which the needs and
interests of "daily life" (*Alltagsleben*) are ignored; but when
that period is over, the community settles down to the business
of dealing with the realities of daily life (*Veralltäglichung
des Charisma*).[29] The problem is not so much Weber's theoretical model, but whether it fits the evidence of Paul's letter to

the Galatians. While Betz does not argue that the Galatians
had stopped experiencing pneumatic phenomena,[30] he does think
that the period of "initial enthusiasm" was over, in the sense
that the problems of daily existence, in particular "problems
with the flesh," had caused the Galatians to doubt that they
were πνευματικοί, and to look to Christian nomists in Galatia
for ways of dealing with these problems. This view, however,
does not fit the evidence of Paul's letter. First of all, the
letter provides no evidence that either Paul or the Galatians
had come to *doubt* that his converts were still πνευματικοί.
In 6:1 Paul does not *assure* the Galatians that they really
were πνευματικοί; rather, *assuming* they still regarded themselves as πνευματικοί, as he does, he recommends that they
deal with "transgressors" in a manner consistent with their
status and self-understanding as πνευματικοί (that is, ἐν
πνεύματι πραΰτητος). Secondly, the letter gives no indication
that either Paul or Christians in Galatia were *surprised* by
"problems with the flesh" in their communities; rather, all
the evidence points to the contrary, that they *expected* these
problems to arise, as they would in any human community. This
is to be inferred from the fact that Paul had instructed them
about the dangers of "the works of the flesh."[31] The third
point is that the letter does not describe the Galatians'
"problems with the flesh" as instances of "*flagrant* wrongdoing"; rather, in the only passage that seems to make concrete
reference to these problems (6:1), Paul speaks of a *fortuitous*
"transgression."[32] Furthermore, 6:1 emphasizes the proper way
of dealing with "transgressors," not the presence of "problems
with the flesh" in the Galatian communities. And, finally, the
letter gives evidence that already during the period of "initial enthusiasm" the Galatian communities had some forms of
social order, which Weber's theoretical model holds for later
stages of "routinization"; included are Paul's own ethical instruction, that is, a "code of ethics," from which they could
learn right from wrong,[33] ceremonies,[34] and even an "educational institution."[35] The fact that Paul wrote to the
"church*es* of Galatia" seems to imply that Christian communities
in Galatia already enjoyed a level of political, social and

economic organization (3:28) not typical of the period of
"initial enthusiasm" described by Weber's theoretical model.

When we follow the evidence in the letter without a Weber-
ian theoretical model, another reconstruction of the situation
in Galatia results. In this study it is argued that the Galatians took seriously "problems with the flesh," and that they
found Paul's missionary preaching attractive because it offered
a solution to these problems. Then, because they considered
their conversion to Christian faith a conversion to Judaism,
they were receptive to the argument that they would not be
"*genuine* Jews" unless they became circumcized. They regarded
this as a way of completing what Paul had begun (3:3): Paul had
provided them with a "code of ethics" (5:19-23), but now they
wanted from the law of Moses rites of repentance, forgiveness
and atonement to deal with "transgressions." Paul's counter-
argument is that this is nothing but "superstition" and "religious scrupulosity" (4:8-10), and that it is "apostasy" (1:6-
7). He reminds them that without the ceremonial laws of Judaism ("works of the law") they already were "genuine Jews"
("sons of Abraham" and "heirs"), and were free from the flesh
and the law of Moses. And he points out to them that his missionary preaching, including his ethical teaching, was not
simply identical to Christian preaching that included a place
for the law of Moses, and that the point of the difference was
precisely with the ceremonial laws which the Galatians were
considering taking up.[36] As evidence he appeals to their experiences of the Spirit,[37] to Scripture, tradition and history,[38] and to his own ethical teaching, with which they were
already familiar.[39]

In other words, this study argues that, while 6:1 is evidence that the Galatians were having "problems with the flesh,"
5:13-6:10 does not provide evidence of "*flagrant* wrongdoing" in
the Galatian churches. In these verses Paul confronts the
Galatians' consideration of going the way of righteousness defined by the law of Moses, that is, of "religious scrupulosity,"
as the correct approach to ethics. Paul's argument is that the
Galatians' experiences of the Spirit prove that without the intervention of the divine Spirit they were neither free nor able

to live in accordance with the divine "will"; that the way of
righteousness of obedience to the law of Moses is based on the
contrary assumption; and that Scripture and tradition foretell
the end of the law of Moses with the coming of Christ and of
his Spirit received by faith.[40]

The reconstruction of the Galatian situation presented
here lends support to the view that Schmithals criticizes;
namely, the view represented by F. C. Baur, that Paul opposed
"Judaizers" in Galatia. But it also differs significantly from
that view. In the first place, I prefer to speak of Paul's
opponents as Jewish-Christian "nomists"[41] instead of
"Judaizers." The latter is bound up with the view that Pauline
Christianity already stood off from Judaism, which stood *over-
against* the former; the situation in Galatians, however, presupposes a different relationship existed between them. The
line between Judaism and Christianity was not yet clear;
neither Christian faith nor circumcision marked the difference.[42] Paul speaks of his converts without circumcision as
true "sons of Abraham,"[43] as "heirs of the kingdom of God,"[44]
and as members of the "heavenly Jerusalem" and the "Israel of
God."[45] Furthermore, the term "Judaizer" is associated with
the identification of Paul's opponents with "Petrinism" and the
Jerusalem church. While Paul wants the Galatians to see the
nomists in Galatia as *aligned* with the "false brethren" in
Jerusalem,[46] the "men from James," who came to Antioch, and the
"circumcision party,"[47] and with Peter,[48] he does not *identify*
the Galatian nomists with any of these. Rather, Paul in 2:7-10
indicates that his disagreement with the nomists in Galatia was
not a disagreement with the Jerusalem church. The implication
is that the Galatian nomists were at odds with the Jerusalem
church, but Paul was not. Finally, the presupposition that
Paul's opponents in Galatia were *outsiders*, associated with the
"Judaizer" view, is a conjecture which this study neither sup-
ports nor questions. Paul addresses the Galatians as a homoge-
nous group, distinguishing neither between Jews and Gentiles,
nor between nomists and Paulinists--and neither between nomists
and libertines, nor between "sarkics" and pneumatics: all are
addressed as οἱ πνευματικοί, who are all in danger of the

"apostasy" of nomism.[49]   And yet Paul seems to distinguish
between the "agitators" and the addressees of the letter.[50]
Although this tends to support the "outside agitators" view,
these two characteristics of Paul's letter also fit the view
that the nomists were members of the Galatian churches,[51] but
that Paul had already "read them out" of the Christian communities, so that the portrayal of the agitators as "outsiders"
is both rhetorical and, in Paul's mind, real.[52]   As Josephus
(*Ant.* 20.38-48) shows, a converted Gentile can provide the
motivation to seek circumcision without *outside* "agitators";
all it takes to carry out his desire is one Jewish travelling
merchant. Or, in the case of the Galatians, why not one
travelling merchant from *within* the Christian communities, who
returned from having had contact with Jews or Jewish Christians? Who knows; the letter is vague about the source and
identity, as well as the number, of the "agitators." This
study does not try to settle this question.

     A profile of the nomists does emerge in the course of
argument: Paul's opponents were Christians,[53] for whom circumcision played a decisive role without, in their minds, contra-
dicting the Christian faith that salvation is in Christ.   Perhaps they regarded circumcision as a rite required of *genuine*
Jews, that is, of "sons of Abraham," "heirs of the kingdom of
God," participants in the "heavenly Jerusalem," and members of
the "Israel of God," which status would make available to them
the Mosaic ceremonial system of repentance, forgiveness and
atonement provided for "transgressions." Although it is difficult to distinguish between Paul's rhetoric and the "agitators'"
actual views, such terms as ἐνάρχεσθαι and ἐπιτελεῖν, and the
phrase ἐπιθυμίαν σαρκὸς οὐ μὴ τελεῖν may have been associated
in their view with circumcision and obedience to the law of
Moses;[54] and perhaps the slogan ἃ ἐὰν θέλητε ποιεῖν,[55] and ἡ
ἀνάγκη τοῦ περιτέμνεσθαι were part of their views.[56]   The burden of this study, however, does not rest on a more precise
identification of Paul's opponents in Galatia, nor does it
propose one.

     The second reason for this study, from the standpoint of
NT scholarship, is that the present consensus, according to

which early Christians, including the Galatians, received the
gift of the Spirit at baptism,[57] has no basis in Paul's letter
to the Galatians, nor in the rest of the *corpus Paulinum*. This
study argues that the initial experience of the Spirit, as well
as subsequent ecstatic experiences, had their Sitz im Leben in
hearing Christian proclamation in the Galatian churches.[58]

The need for a study on the Spirit in Paul's message to
the Galatians also arises from two contemporary theological
options. The existentialist interpretation of the Spirit in
Rudolf Bultmann's *Theology of the New Testament*[59] correctly
points out the inappropriateness of speaking of the Spirit as a
"nonworldly" *material*.[60] But, at the same time, his existentialist interpretation tends to eliminate the concept of the
Spirit as a discrete entity, insofar as it identifies the Spirit
as a new possibility of human existence, rather than as the
power that makes the new structure of human existence possible,
despite Bultmann's desire to speak of the Spirit as a power.[61]
This leaves Bultmann without a conceptuality for expressing the
Spirit's efficacy in human existence.[62] This study seeks to
overcome these limitations of the existentialist interpretation
of the Spirit, by adopting the conceptual framework of the process philosophy of Alfred North Whitehead, in which one can
speak of entities in nonsubstantialist categories, and of non-
coercive causal efficacy.[63]

Today theologians interested in developing a "theology of
nature"[64] consider inadequate the interpretation of the Spirit
represented by Bultmann's existentialist theology, because of
its unnecessary and illegitimate parochial and ecclesiastical
emphasis on the Spirit's soteriological role in the new life of
faith. In order to liberate theology from this self-imposed
"ghetto," and to open up theology to other concerns, Pittenger
and Pannenberg emphasize the role of the Spirit as the origin
of all life, and as the creative activity of the Spirit in the
world, including "nature." In this view, the Spirit who is the
origin of the new life of faith is the same Spirit who is present in the creation of the world, who speaks through the prophets of Israel, and who today is active in the whole cosmos.
While I share these concerns, I question whether this theology

of Spirit can be attributed to Paul, particularly in Galatians.[65] In Part II of this study, therefore, I present Paul's
theology of the Spirit in Galatians under the heading of "the
historicality of the Spirit," which includes three aspects: the
soteriological (Chapter IV), christological (Chapter V), and
eschatological (Chapter VI). Whether and how theology today
can move beyond Paul's "theology of the Spirit" to a "theology
of nature" is a task of theology, which requires a reexamina-
tion of the use of the term πνεῦμα in Paul's letter to the
Galatians.[66]

Summary of the Theses Developed in the Study

In principle, the two parts of this study are distinguished
in that the first part deals with the historical context of
Paul's statements about the Spirit in Galatians: that is, the
events because of which Paul wrote the letter, and the nature
and social setting of experiences of the Spirit in the life of
the Galatian churches; and the second part deals with the theology of the Spirit in Paul's message to the Galatians, which
has three aspects--soteriology, christology and eschatology--
under the heading of "the historicality of the Spirit." Although this distinction does describe the nature and scope of
the chapters that comprise each of the parts of the study, in
practice this distinction is an abstraction. We cannot reconstruct the historical situation in the Galatian churches except
through Paul's conceptual expressions that comprise the theology of the Spirit in the letter, and vice versa.

Although Christians in Galatia were having the typical
problems with the flesh that trouble every human community,
they were not *libertinists*; rather, they were considering practicing circumcision and following the way of righteousness of
the law of Moses. They had begun Christian existence with ecstatic experiences, which they continued to enjoy; but, because
they wanted to be "genuine Jews," they were receptive to Jewish-
Christian nomists (Chapter II). Against this development, Paul
argues, appealing to the Galatians' pneumatic experiences on the
occasion of Christian proclamation (Chapter III), on soteriological, christological and eschatological grounds: that only

πνευματικοί are free, and only they live in accordance with the
divine "will," that is, only they fulfill "the Law" of Scripture, which is identical with "the 'law' of Christ" (Chapter
IV); that the Spirit received by faith, which brings new life,
is identified neither with an eternal Spirit-in-the-world, nor
with the performance of the rites of the law of Moses, but
rather with God's Son, whose coming brought an end to the law
of Moses (Chapter V); and that the new life begun by the Spirit,
not circumcision, nor any other "work of the law," is the Galatians' assurance of, and their unity with, the future righteousness and eternal life (Chapter VI).

The final chapter of the study develops a doctrine of the
Spirit in dialog not only with Paul's theology of the Spirit in
Galatians, but also with Bultmann's existentialist theology,
and with the theologies of nature of Pannenberg and Pittenger.
Paul and Bultmann agree that human existence is not static but
genuinely historical, in the sense that new possibilities are
opened up by historical events. While they agree here, at
other points they disagree. Paul regards human existence as
subject to the incursion of external powers, which are real,
discrete, purposive entities, whereas Bultmann tends to eliminate this aspect of Paul's concept of the Spirit by interpreting the Spirit in terms of a new "self-understanding." Bultmann correctly criticizes Paul's substantialist concept of the
Spirit as a "nonworldly material"; and he rightly sees a tension between Paul's thinking of the Spirit as a power that
works by compulsion, and the role he attributes to the believer's decision between moral alternatives. But Bultmann goes
too far when he denies to the Spirit the real efficacy Paul
affirms. From this discussion is derived a concept of the
Spirit which takes account of the major concerns of both Paul
and Bultmann, while creatively transforming their concepts.
The Spirit is a discrete, purposive, but nonsubstantial entity,
whose real efficacy is not coercive but persuasive, and whose
aim is the creative transformation of human existence toward a
more intense and complex appropriation of the personal presence
of God.

Paul's theology of the Spirit in Galatians and Bultmann's
existentialist interpretation of the Spirit emphasize the soteriological activity of the Spirit in the new life of faith,
and the origin of the Spirit's activity in the death of Christ
on the cross. Pannenberg and Pittenger, however, are concerned
with the development of a theology of nature and, therefore,
emphasize the role of the Spirit as the origin of all life and
its creative activity in the world, including "nature." That
the soteriological activity of God did not *begin* with the event
of Christ's death on the cross is more clearly stated by Pannenberg and Pittenger than by Bultmann, although the latter does
not deny this. Paul agrees that the love of God did not *begin*
with the death of Christ, for he too speaks of the love of God
in history *before* the Christ-event. Bultmann, more clearly
than Pannenberg and Pittenger, however, brings out Paul's emphasis in Galatians on the role of the Spirit as creator of a
decisively new life of faith, and its origin in the death of
Christ on the cross. It is possible, therefore, to think of
the Spirit as God's special act of love, in the sense that it
seeks to bring about a creative transformation of human existence in which, by sustained attention to the creative presence
of God in the world, primacy is given to God's lures toward
self-realization; and in the sense that this creative transformation of human existence has its origin in the historical
event of the death of Christ on the cross.

Further, Pannenberg and Pittenger take account of the divine creative activity in "nature," whereas Bultmann tends to
deny this aspect of Paul's understanding of God-in-the-world.
Paul's phrase "a new creation" connotes more than "a new humanity" or a new "self-understanding," phrases which restrict
God's creative activity to human affairs. While Rom 8:18-23
speaks more fully and directly of the redemption of "nature"
and humanity--that is, of creation--this aspect of Paul's theology is implicit in Galatians in the phrase "a new creation."
If Paul, Pannenberg and Pittenger are in agreement at this
point in a theology of nature, they are in disagreement at
others. For in Galatians Paul almost puts "nature"--that is,

the στοιχεῖα τοῦ κόσμου, flesh, and the world--on the side
opposed to God. He does not see "nature" as something inherently endowed with the eternal, creative activity of God; rather, he almost sees "nature" as something from which God sets
humanity free. And yet by naming God's soteriological activity
as an act of new *creation*, Paul implicitly affirms God's redemptive activity in "nature" as well as in human affairs. For
Paul these two cannot be separated, since he sees human existence as inextricably bound up with and in "nature," as his
language about the flesh indicates. For Paul "Spirit" names
the soteriological activity of God to set the Christian believer free from the destructive aspects of "nature" in human existence. From this discussion is derived a concept of the Spirit
in which the major concerns of Paul, Bultmann, Pannenberg and
Pittenger are taken into account, and in which each of their
concepts of the Spirit is also creatively transformed. The
Spirit known in the new life of Christian faith is the same God
that is the constant, creative ground of all things. The
Spirit, therefore is a *particular*, but not an *exclusive*, mode
of God-in-the-world.

NOTES

CHAPTER I

[1]Cf. his article, "Galatian Problems, 3. The 'Other' Gospel," *BJRL* 53 (1970-71) 271. For the view that this identity crisis arose among Paul's converts, from a misunderstanding of Paul's message about the role of the Jerusalem church and of the Septuagint, but without Jewish-Christian missionaries from the Jerusalem church or from the local synagogues, see Johannes Munck (*Paul and the Salvation of Mankind* [Richmond, VA: John Knox, 1959] 87-134). Although I do not think sufficient evidence exists in the letter to settle the differences between these two views, I also argue that the problem in the Galatian churches is in part an identity crisis (see below, pp. 9, 11, and Chapter II).

[2]Cf. Klaus Wegenast, *Das Verständnis der Tradition bei Paulus und in den Deuteropaulinen* (WMANT 8; Neukirchen-Vluyn: Neukirchener, 1962). Wegenast identifies the opponents as Ebionites. Although I do not attempt to identify precisely Paul's opponents in Galatia with known Jewish-Christian groups, I agree that libertinism was not a problem in the Galatian churches (see below, pp. 7-10, and Chapter II).

[3]This view was expressed by Frederic R. Crownfeld ("The Singular Problem of the Dual Galatians," *JBL* 64 [1945] 491-500). For a discussion of this view, and its most articulate representative, Walter Schmithals, see below (pp. 3-6, and Chapter II). Robert Jewett ("Agitators and the Galatian Congregation," *NTS* 17 [1971] 198-212) also argues that the problem in the churches of Galatia included libertinism, but he identifies the agitators as Zealots from Judea, rather than as Gnostics (as Schmithals does); he, therefore, attributes legalism to the agitators, but libertinism to the Galatians, who were interested only in certain ceremonial laws (e.g. circumcision and calendar cults).

[4]Cf. Wilhelm Lütgert, *Gesetz und Geist: Eine Untersuchung zur Vorgeschichte des Galaterbriefes* (BFCT I/22/6; Gütersloh: C. Bertelsmann, 1919); and J. H. Ropes, *The Singular Problem of the Epistle to the Galatians* (HTS 14; Cambridge: Harvard University, 1929).

[5]This is the approach taken here, and in the Hermeneia commentary on Galatians by H. Dieter Betz. For a discussion of Betz's view, see below, pp. 6-10, and Chapter II.

[6]The latter is also possible in the fourth view, as Betz's position illustrates (see below, pp. 6-10, and Chapter II).

[7]Cf. below, pp. 3-6.

[8]Cf. below, pp. 6-9.

[9]Cf. below, pp. 9-11.

[10]W. Schmithals, "The Heretics in Galatia," *ZNW* 47 (1956) 25-67; appeared in revised form in *Paulus und die Gnostiker* (TF 35; Hamburg: Herbert Reich, 1965) = *Paul and the Gnostics* (trans. John Steely; Nashville/New York: Abingdon, 1972) 13-64.

[11]Cf. Schmithals, *Paul*, 59 n. 134 (emphasis added).

[12]Ibid., 39.

[13]Ibid., 49-51.

[14]Ibid., 44.

[15]Cf. Heinrich Schlier, *Der Brief an die Galater* (MeyerK 7; 14th ed.; Göttingen: Vandenhoeck & Ruprecht, 1971) and H. D. Betz, *A Commentary on Paul's Letter to the Churches in Galatia* (ed. Helmut Koester; Philadelphia: Fortress, 1979) ad loc.

[16]Cf. Schmithals, *Paul*, 39-40, 55 (cf. also Betz, *Commentary on Paul's Letter*, ad loc).

[17]Cf. Schmithals, *Paul*, 34 n. 51, 48, 52-54.

[18]Ibid., 34.

[19]Ibid., 19, 26-27, 33, 39-40, 52.

[20]Cf. Ὅσοι θέλουσιν εὐπροσωπῆσαι ἐν σαρκί, and ἵνα ἐν τῇ ὑμετέρᾳ σαρκὶ καυχήσωνται (cf. also 4:17, 5:26 and 6:3).

[21]Cf. ἵνα...μὴ διώκωνται (cf. also 2:12).

[22]Cf. οὐδὲ...νόμον φυλάσσουσιν (cf. also 1:7, 2:13, 4:17, 5:7, 10b, 11, 19-21).

[23]Against Schmithals, *Paul*, 41-42.

[24]Cf. 5:3.

[25]This term is better than "legalism" (cf. below, Chapter II).

[26]Cf. Betz's commentary (*Commentary on Paul's Letter*, passim) and his earlier articles: "Spirit, Freedom, and Law: Paul's Message to the Galatian Churches," *SEÅ* 39 (1974) 145-60; and "In Defense of the Spirit: Paul's Letter to the Galatians as a Document of Early Christian Apologetics," pp. 99-114 in *Aspects of Religious Propaganda in Judaism and Early Christianity* (University of Notre Dame Center for the Study of Judaism and Christianity in Antiquity 2; ed. Elisabeth Schüssler-Fiorenza; Notre Dame, IN: University of Notre Dame, 1976).

[27]For a discussion of the Jewish-Christian character of the *Kerygmata Petrou*, and of the Gentile character of its audience, see Georg Strecker in Walter Bauer (*Orthodoxy and Heresy*

in Earliest Christianity [2nd German ed.; Philadelphia: Fortress, 1971] 257-71). Strecker argues that the anti-Paulinism of the *Kg. Pt.* is merely literary; i.e., that no actual anti-Pauline controversy existed in the community of the *Kg. Pt.* (cf. pp. 263-264).

[28]Cf. H. D. Betz, "2 Cor 6:14-7:1: An Anti-Pauline Fragment?" *JBL* 92 (1973) 88-108. For the other texts mentioned above, see Betz (*Commentary on Paul's Letter*, "Appendices").

[29]Cf. Max Weber, *The Theory of Social and Economic Organization* (New York: Free Press, London: Collier-Macmillan, 1947) 358-73, esp. 364, 367, 370. This is Weber's widely discussed theory about the "routinization of charisma."

[30]For Betz's view that pneumatic phenomena continued to occur at the time of the letter, see his comments in his commentary on 3:5. For the view that Weber's theory does not preclude the possibility that the "enthusiasm" of the initial period would continue into the later stages of "routinization," see John G. Gager (*Kingdom and Community: The Social World of Early Christianity* [New Jersey: Prentice-Hall, 1975] 67-68, 89 n. 2).

[31]Betz suggests 5:21b refers to baptismal instruction, which included 5:19-23 (cf. his *Commentary on Paul's Letter*, ad loc.).

[32]Cf. προλημφθῇ in this verse (cf. also 5:7).

[33]For evidence that Paul's missionary preaching in other churches, e.g. in Thessalonica, included ethical instruction, see 1 Thess 2:7, 11-12, 3:2, 4:1-8, 9, 11, and 5:11.

[34]Cf. 3:1-5, 26-28 and 4:6.

[35]Cf. Betz (*Commentary on Paul's Letter*) on 6:6.

[36]Cf. 1:12-2:21 and 5:1-12.

[37]Cf. 3:1-5 and 4:6.

[38]Cf. 3:6-4:31.

[39]Cf. 5:13-6:10.

[40]Cf. especially Chapter II below; but also see Chapters IV and VII.

[41]This phrase is not my own invention (see, e.g., Jewett, "Agitators").

[42]In 2:13-15, οἱ Ἰουδαῖοι refers to Jews *and* Jewish-Christians, as the context makes clear. The contrast in 2:14 is not between Jew and Christian, but between Jew and *Gentile*.

[43]Cf. 3:6-4:7 and 4:21-31.

[44]Cf. 5:21b.

[45]Cf. 4:26 and 6:16.

[46]Cf. 2:4.

[47]Cf. 2:12. Paul and they do not criticize each other, but Peter (cf. Betz, *Commentary on Paul's Letter*, "Introduction, 2.C. The Anti-Pauline Opposition").

[48]Cf. 2:11-14.

[49]Paul makes no distinction between the addressees of 1:6-7, 3:1-5, 4:21 and 6:1.

[50]Paul refers to the "agitators" in the third person, but to the addressees of the letter in the second (cf. 1:6-9, 3:1, 4:17, 5:7, 10, 12, and 6:12-13).

[51]Although the church in Corinth was divided by factions, unlike the churches of Galatia, nevertheless evidence that "*outside* agitators" were responsible for the Corinthian problems is lacking.

[52]In 4:30, Paul recommends that the Galatians do what he had already done (cf. 1:8-9 and 6:16).

[53]Otherwise Paul's struggle to distinguish their views from his, and his polemical caricature of their "gospel" as no gospel at all, but a "perversion" of it, would be inexplicable (cf. his phrase in 1:6, "a different gospel," which he corrects in 1:7 by saying, "not that there is another gospel").

[54]In 3:3, Paul is certainly twitting them and their position; the question is whether he uses some of their own terms.

[55]For a discussion of this phrase in 5:17, see below, Chapter IV (pp. 122-23).

[56]In 6:12, Paul could have injected the motif of necessity himself in order to contrast nomism and freedom (cf. also 2:3). That Jewish-Christians did favor circumcision for other Jewish-Christians without demanding it of Gentile-Christians is evident from 2:7-10; for the same attitude among Gentile-Christians, see Justin (*Dial. c. Tryph.*, 46-47), and for this interpretation of the Gnostic Cerinthus, see Jewett ("Agitators," 199). In 3:10 and 5:3, which also employ the concept of necessity or obligation, the relationship between Paul's statements and the nomists' views is even less clear (cf. also 6:13).

[57]For a representative Roman Catholic view, see Schlier's commentary (*Brief an die Galater*, passim); and for a representative Protestant view, see James D. G. Dunn (*Baptism in the*

*Holy Spirit: A Re-Examination of the NT Teaching on the Gift of
the Spirit in Relation to Pentecostalism Today* [SBT 15, 2nd
Series; London: SCM, 1970] and *Jesus and the Spirit: A Study of
the Religious and Charismatic Experience of Jesus and the First
Christians as Reflected in the NT* [Philadelphia: Westminster,
1975]). Betz's commentary, despite his anti-sacramental
polemic with Schlier's commentary, does not completely give up
this view (cf. on 3:2, 26-28 and 4:6).

[58]Cf. below, Chapter III.

[59]Bultmann, *Theology*, 1.330-40.

[60]Ibid., 1.333, 334.

[61]Ibid., 1.330, 335, 336, 337.

[62]Ibid., 1.336.

[63]Cf. below, Chapter VII (pp. 195-99).

[64]Cf. Pannenberg, "Working of the Spirit," "Doctrine of
the Spirit," *Apostles' Creed* (128-43), and *Faith and Reality*
(20-38); Pittenger, *Life in Christ* (35-46, 62-73) and *The Holy
Spirit*.

[65]Pannenberg and Pittenger both appeal to "*the* biblical"
concept of the Spirit, but Pannenberg also specifically attributes this view to Paul, although he cites only 1 Cor 15:45
(cf. *Faith and Reality*, 20). Cf. below, pp. 167 n. 65, 185.

[66]Cf. below, Chapter VII, pp. 199-201.

PART I

THE SPIRIT IN THE CHURCHES OF GALATIA

INTRODUCTION

In the letter to the Galatians, Paul gives the term πνεῦμα a prominent position; one might say, the *most* prominent position. Each time Paul uses the term πνεῦμα, it denotes an experienced reality among the Galatians, of which Paul not only approves, but also of which he reminds the Galatians with many and complicated arguments. He uses it in interrogatives,[1] in arguments from Scripture and tradition,[2] and in parenesis;[3] that is, he uses it in each of the rhetorical forms used in the exposition of his argument in 3:1-6:10.[4] As a term πνεῦμα is contrasted with ἔργα τοῦ νόμου[5] (or simply νόμος[6]) and with ἐπιθυμία σαρκός,[7] ἔργα τῆς σαρκός[8] (or simply σάρξ[9]).

These uses of the term πνεῦμα by Paul in the letter to the Galatians raise many questions, of which two are the concern of Part I of this investigation. The first is: What were the historical events in the life of the churches of Galatia that gave rise to Paul's uses of the term πνεῦμα in the letter? And the second, which in some ways is a narrowing of the first, is: What were the experiences of the Spirit in the churches of Galatia to which Paul refers by his use of the term πνεῦμα?

By answering these questions, two things will be achieved. We will have gained an understanding of the *concrete experiences*, of which the *concepts* of the Spirit in the Galatian letter are relatively *abstract* expressions. As such, secondly, we will have begun to explain the *historical reasons* for Paul's uses of πνεῦμα in Galatians. For, the historic origins of Paul's uses of the term πνεῦμα in the letter to the Galatians are to be sought in the *real-life situation* of the Christians in the churches of Galatia, *as well as* in the history of *ideas*.[10]

Part I, therefore, concerns the origins of Paul's uses of πνεῦμα in his letter to the Galatians. We begin in Chapter II with the polemical situation in the churches of Galatia that provides the historical occasion of the uses of the term πνεῦμα in Paul's letter. Then in Chapter III we turn to the specific experiences of the Spirit, to which Paul's use of πνεῦμα refers.

In this way we will have placed Paul's uses of the term
in their proper historical context.[11]

NOTES

PART I. INTRODUCTION

[1]Cf. 3:1-5.

[2]Cf. 3:6-14, 4:1-7, 21-31.

[3]Cf. 5:1-6:10.

[4]The term πνεῦμα is not used in 1:1-2:21. It is used in 6:11-18 only in 6:18 where it stands for the human, rather than the divine, πνεῦμα.

[5]Cf. 3:2, 5.

[6]Cf. 4:5-6 and 5:18.

[7]Cf. 5:16-17, 24-25.

[8]Cf. 5:19-23.

[9]Cf. 3:3 and 6:8.

[10]For a discussion of the relation between "historical event" and "the history of ideas," on the one hand, and the relation between concrete experience and conceptual expression, on the other, see above, "Preface," p. x.

[11]For the reasons why this study lacks a discussion of the "background" of Paul's uses of πνεῦμα in Galatians in the history of ideas, see above, "Preface," pp. ix-x.

CHAPTER II

THE HISTORICAL OCCASION OF PAUL'S USE OF
PNEUMA IN THE LETTER TO THE GALATIANS

Introduction

The purpose of this chapter is to establish the historical
occasion of the letter to the Galatians and the relationship of
Paul's use of πνεῦμα to that occasion. First it is necessary
to determine the "cause" of the letter.[1] This leads to the
question, why the Christians in Galatia were considering accepting circumcision.[2] Then it will be possible to state the
relationship between the Spirit and the historical occasion of
the letter to the churches of Galatia.[3]

Section 1. The Historical Occasion of the Letter

Following the "prescript" (1:1-5), Paul begins with a
statement of the cause of the letter in 1:6-7.[4] The "post-
script" (6:11-18), a recapitulation of the main points of the
argument of the letter, begins with a statement that is related
to the cause of the letter, namely, 6:12-13. From these verses
it can be seen that the cause of the letter is the Galatians'
readiness to accept a "gospel" which includes circumcision;
for the Galatians were about to turn to "another gospel" (1:6)
brought by those who would impose circumcision on them (6:12-
13). This is confirmed by the rest of the letter: Paul's
single[5] preoccupation is with the desire of the Christians in
Galatia to live "under the law" (4:21).[6] In an effort to persuade the Galatians to give up this desire, Paul wrote the
letter.[7]

Although the idea of living "under the law" as a whole is
criticized by Paul, the acceptance of circumcision in particular is singled out for special emphasis.[8] This suggests that,
when Paul uses the phrase "works of the law,"[9] he probably has
in mind circumcision and related Jewish rites and customs. It
is well-known that the Jews made no distinction between laws
pertaining to ethics and those regarding rituals, since the
latter were understood as pertaining to ethics. And yet this

distinction helps to explain Paul's positive attitude toward
"good deeds,"[10] and his at least apparent distinction between
ritual and ethics in 5:6 and 6:15. His recognition that, on
the one hand, a *kind* of life and righteousness is possible "in
the law";[11] and his argument that, on the other hand, eschatological life and righteousness do not come from the law of
Moses but from Christ,[12] are explicable in terms of a distinction between "works of the law" in a narrow sense as referring
to the performance of Jewish rites and customs, and in a broad
sense as including doing "good deeds."[13] It seems best, therefore, to assume that, while the Galatians were considering
living "under" the whole law of Moses, it is to the performance
of Jewish rites and customs that Paul directs the letter's defense.[14] This is because circumcision and related Jewish
rituals and customs, such as dietary laws and other purity laws,
make the law of Moses historically and nationally limited,
rather than eternal and universal. Life in Christ, on the
other hand, transcends and even eliminates national and social
divisions among people, divisions which the law of Moses and
other national or civic laws create (3:28). The "law of
Christ," therefore, is neither historically nor nationally
limited, but universal (5:6, 14; 6:2, 15).

    This is why Paul wrote the letter. He considered the
Galatians' desire to live "under the law" foolish and absurd.
He exclaims that he was "astonished" (1:6) and "perplexed"
(4:20),[15] and he calls the Galatians "foolish" (3:1, 3),[16] because what they seek is not "the" gospel but its "perversion"
(1:7). In Paul's view, what they were about to do is the
opposite of the "truth" (5:7),[17] because it is not from God
(5:8).[18] Finally, Paul reminds the Galatians that what they
desire most, namely life, righteousness and freedom, they already had without the law of Moses;[19] and that what they now
seek to do will take all of these away.[20]

Section 2. Why the Galatians Were Considering Accepting
            Circumcision

    The question, therefore, arises: What motivated Christians
in Galatia to consider accepting circumcision? In answer to

this question it should first of all be stated tnat it quite
probably was not the Galatians' intention or goal to be "shut
out" of or "cut off" from Christ and his "benefits" (4:17,
5:2-4); nor is it certain that Paul's opponents intended this
goal. Paul's bias and his use of rhetoric make it impossible
to take everything Paul denies or rejects as accusations by his
opponents, and everything he accuses the Galatians and his opponents of doing and thinking as representative of their goals
and intentions.[21] That is to say, that we cannot assume the
Galatians considered circumcision and faith and life in Christ
as antithetical. Rather, we should assume that the Galatians,
with Paul's opponents in Galatia, probably thought that circumcision, and the obedience to the law of Moses of which it is
symbolic and to which it leads, and faith and life in Christ
were compatible and complementary. This would be confirmed by
3:3, if here Paul has reformulated the opponents' claim,[22]
which the Galatians were prepared to accept: namely, the claim
that circumcision would finish what the Galatians had begun
with the Spirit, that is, it would bring it to perfection.[23]
This would mean that the Galatians had been persuaded their
conversion would be complete only with accepting circumcision.
Paul's letter is a vehement argument to the contrary, of which
Paul's (re-)formulation in 3:3 is representative: Accepting
circumcision as a sign of obedience to the law of Moses would
result in a reversion to a union with the flesh, a union from
which the Galatians had been liberated when they received the
Spirit through the "hearing of faith."[24]

Paul's counter-argument indicates three reasons why the
Galatians might have been persuaded to consider taking up the
law of Moses and especially circumcision: (1) because the Galatians were "religiously scrupulous";[25] (2) because they wanted
to be "genuine Jews";[26] and (3) because of "transgressions."[27]

(1) That several churches in Galatia were founded as a
result of Paul's missionary preaching already shows that the
Galatians took "religion" seriously, for they had given up
their old religion, which presumably no longer met their needs,
in order to take up a new one. They also give evidence of
their religious seriousness in their regard for experiences of

the Spirit, which can be inferred from their self-designation
as οἱ πνευματικοί (6:1), from Paul's questions in 3:1-5, and
from 4:6. Their having been persuaded by new missionaries,
this time from their new religion, only from a different "de-
nomination,"[28] is consistent with this "religious scrupulosity."
Were they so "religiously scrupulous" that they could not resist missionary propaganda? This seems to be Paul's accusation
in 1:6, 3:1 and 4:8-11.[29] Whether the Galatians really were
that scrupulous, they were religiously scrupulous to some de-
gree, as their "double conversion" and their experiences of the
Spirit show.

    (2) If it can be assumed that Paul's arguments in 3:6-14,
3:26-4:7 and 4:21-31 reflect a reason for the Galatians' consideration of circumcision, it is possible that they desired to
be genuine "sons of Abraham," that is, "genuine Jews." This
situation is paralleled in the account of the conversion and
circumcision of King Izates given by Josephus.[30] Through his
mother and Ananias, King Izates converted to Judaism and, since
he thought he had to be circumcized to be "a genuine Jew,"[31] he
was ready to accept the rite. But his mother and Ananias pre-
vailed, convincing him, for the time being, that his subjects
would not tolerate having a king who was a Jew and who submitted
to "strange and foreign rites," that is "unseemly practices,"[32]
and that being a devout Jew[33] "counted more" than circumcision.[34]
But then Eleazar convinced King Izates that being a "genuine
Jew" meant not only reading the law of Moses but doing what it
commands, including being circumcized.[35] Being persuaded by
Eleazar's argument,[36] the king had the rite performed, "since
he had not completely given up his desire."[37]

    In a note,[38] Louis H. Feldman argues that Ananias' liberal
attitude toward the circumcision of the converted King stemmed
not from "religious beliefs on the question" whether converts
to Judaism were required to submit to circumcision, "but from
caution," that is, from Ananias' belief that King Izates' circumcision would involve danger to the lives of the King, his
mother and Ananias. Feldman concludes from this that even for
Ananias converts were required to be circumcized, although under
certain conditions set out by Jewish law circumcision could be

waived. This does not, however, explain Izates' motive for
wishing to undergo the rite of circumcision in order to be a
"genuine Jew."[39] That this is even mentioned is evidence that
the circumcision of converts was an issue at the time of
Josephus. And that this issue lies behind Josephus' account
of the circumcision of King Izates is confirmed by his use of
catchwords from the debate which arose from the "Hellenistic
reform" of Judaism: the "proselyte" is called Ἰουδαῖος,[40] or
βέβαιος Ἰουδαῖος;[41] but the mere "adherent" is identified by
τὸ θεῖον σέβειν.[42] The difference between them is circumcision.[43] Josephus indicates that he thinks *both* are "genuine
Jews" when he describes Eleazar in terms similar to Ananias'
description of a "devout adherent of Judaism": Ἰουδαῖός τις
ἕτερος ἐκ τῆς Γαλιλαίας ἀφικόμενος Ἐλεάζαρος ὄνομα πάνυ περὶ
τὰ πάτρια δοκῶν ἀκριβὴς εἶναι προετρέψατο πρᾶξαι τοὖργον, and
ζηλοῦν τὰ πάτρια τῶν Ἰουδαίων respectively.[44] The "ethics of
caution" almost seems to be secondary to this issue, since
Eleazar takes up only Ananias' second argument, namely, that
circumcision is unnecessary because the converted King could
worship God without being circumcized, if he really had decided
to be a "devoted adherent of Judaism, for it was this that
counted more than circumcision."[45]

Similarly, Paul speaks in Galatians of the effort to make
Gentile Christians in Antioch "live like Jews."[46] The issue
there as in Galatia was circumcision. And from 3:6-14, 3:26-
4:7 and 4:21-31, we can infer that this issue was brought about
by the Galatians' desire to be genuine "sons of Abraham," that
is, in the language of the crisis over the "Hellenistic reform"
of Judaism,[47] their desire to be "genuine Jews," and the nomists'
claim that this is possible only if the Galatians submit to
circumcision. Paul counters the Galatians' willingness to accept circumcision with the argument, similar to Ananias', that
without circumcision or other "works of the law" they already
are "sons" and they already "know and are known by God."[48]
Paul, therefore, undermines one motive for the Galatians'
willingness to accept circumcision, namely, in order to become
"genuine Jews."

(3) The third factor in the Galatians' consideration of accepting circumcision was quite possibly the obedience to a "code of ethics" of which it is a sign.[49] This is the best explanation for the presence of seemingly two fronts in the churches of Galatia, against which Paul directs his letter: on the one side is the Galatians' consideration of circumcision, and on the other is the occurrence of concrete problems with the flesh in their communities. The letter could appear to be divided between these two fronts, 1:6-5:12 dealing with the first, and 5:13-6:16 with the second.[50] But these fronts are not so distinct, and the letter cannot be so neatly divided. The πνευματικοί are precisely the ones who were considering circumcision;[51] and the Galatians' consideration of circumcision is still prominent in Paul's parenesis regarding problems with the flesh.[52] Schmithals concludes that only one front existed in Galatia, consisting of Jewish-Christian gnosticism, in which pneumatic libertinism was combined with a regard for circumcision as a mystery rite.[53]

More persuasive, however, is the view presented in H. D. Betz's commentary.[54] It is similar to Schmithals' view, in that it attributes to the πνευματικοί both "*flagrant* misconduct" and the desire to receive circumcision, but it differs in its assessment of the function of circumcision for the Galatians. According to Betz, the Galatians were having problems with the flesh after the enthusiasm of the initial stage of Christianity in Galatia had waned; they were left without a "code of ethics" to cope with "transgressions" in their midst; life based on a "naive" confidence in the Spirit had become a "dance on a suspended rope"; so they were about to turn to circumcision and obedience to the law of Moses, which they had been persuaded would instruct them concerning right and wrong, and would provide them with rites of atonement and forgiveness for "transgressions."

This view has the virtue of being able to explain the simplicity of Paul's statement of the cause of the letter in 1:6-7 (and repeated in 4:21 and 6:12-13[55]), his defense of the Spirit in 3:1-5 and his parenesis in 5:13-24. After an initial "naive" confidence in the Spirit, the Galatians had experienced

problems with the flesh, which they could not handle on the
basis of the Spirit alone, so they were considering turning to
the law of Moses, which would "perfect" their life in the Spirit
by providing them with a "code of ethics" and rituals of atonement and forgiveness. Paul's letter is an argument, in the
form of a defense of Paul himself, his gospel and the Spirit,
against the Galatians' proposed marriage of the Spirit and the
law of Moses.

And yet this view of the situation in Galatia has problems
too. If the major problem of the Galatians was *flagrant* misconduct,[56] should not Paul have mentioned this problem explicitly somewhere?[57] Betz recognizes that the generality of the
parenesis seems to leave "no room for 'concrete issues'"; but
he finds a "concrete *Sitz im Leben*" for Paul's parenensis in
6:1.[58] And yet even here, as Betz recognizes, the problem is
less the instance, or instances, of "transgression" (6:1a) than
the way of dealing with it (6:1b). Similarly, the problem behind 5:13-24 is less the failure and abuse or exploitation of
freedom (won by Christ and his Spirit) as an "opportunity for
the flesh,"[59] than the possibility that as a result of problems with the flesh the Galatians will turn to the law of
Moses. In other words, Paul criticizes the Galatians less for
having problems with the flesh than for abandoning the Spirit
in favor of the Mosaic law.[60]

If, secondly, the Galatians (and Paul?) initially had a
"naive" confidence in the Spirit, there is no evidence of it in
the letter, nor is there evidence in the letter that the Galatians' initial enthusiasm had waned. In the first place, Paul
expresses astonishment that the Galatians were considering
"another gospel" (1:6-7), not that they had had problems with
the flesh. In the parenetic section of the letter, Paul ac-
knowledges that problems with the flesh were more than a mere
probability even for πνευματικοί as, for example, 5:16 and 5:25
show.[61] If we can assume that 5:21b refers to Paul's parenesis
on the occasion of his missionary visit to Galatia,[62] most
likely the Galatians would have been taught that life in Christ
and his Spirit was no automatic form of life but a process of
constantly renewing one's union with Christ and the Spirit in

order to keep out "the works of the flesh." This is not a
"naive" confidence in the Spirit which, when it bumps up
against the harsh "realities of daily life," becomes cynical
or desperate.

As evidence that "*flagrant* misconduct" actually had occurred in the Galatian churches, Betz refers to Paul's lengthy
discussion of "the corruption of the 'flesh'," and to 6:1.[63]
Paul's parenesis in 5:13-24 does admit the real possibility
that "the works of the flesh" could happen among πνευματικοί.
And 5:13b, 16, 21b could have been occasioned by actual misconduct in the churches of Galatia. But Betz also recognizes
that these are "reminders" to the Galatians of what they had
learned in their baptismal instruction.[64] This means that the
Galatians were not without a "code of ethics," even during the
period of "initial enthusiasm." Nor would the occurrence of
problems with the flesh have been unexpected in the Galatian
communities. Unlike 1 Cor 5:1ff. and 11:30, in Galatians Paul
nowhere expresses surprise, his nor theirs, that these problems
had arisen.

Quite the opposite is 6:1; for here, as Betz says, Paul
"describes a 'case' as it could *and most likely did* happen in
the life of the community."[65] And yet Paul's language is eva-
sive: Does Paul refer to a real or hypothetical case? If the
καί is taken with the προλημφθῇ, Paul could be describing an
especially improbable case or simply one which is unfavorable
to the fulfillment of the apodosis.[66] If the protasis were a
supposition referring to a particular case in the past, εἰ
with a past tense in the indicative would have been required.[67]
Paul's use of ἐὰν καί with the aorist in the subjunctive means
the protasis is a supposition referring to the *future*, the
event being conceived of as being more than a *mere possibility*,
that is, as a *probability not yet actually realized*.[68] The
generality of Paul's description of the case[69] suggests he had
in mind a general class of events, not a particular concrete
case. All this means 6:1 is not obvious evidence that Paul
knew of problems in Galatia with "*flagrant* misconduct" or
"libertinism."

The function of 6:1 is to illustrate a situation in which
the Galatians might become κενόδοξοι, and to recommend a way of
avoiding this danger.[70] So the emphasis is less on the avoidance of "transgressions" than on the avoidance of κενοδοξία in
the handling of "transgressions."[71] The recommendation to "restore" the "transgressor" ἐν πνεύματι πραΰτητος[72] need not have
as its contrast actual conditions in the Galatian churches. For
Paul's recommendation reflects the discussion among contemporary
philosophers about the proper style of the philosopher's task.[73]
Paul, like Musonius Rufus, Dio Chrysostom and Demonax,[74]
stresses the need for gentleness. This recommendation precludes the use of harsh punishment and condemnation, which
could arise out of a false notion of one's own incorruptibility
and one's neighbor's incorrigibility[75]--in short, out of κενοδοξία, which could produce such "works of the flesh" as "enmity,
strife, jealousy, anger, selfishness, dissension, party spirit"
and the like.[76] This does not necessarily mean, however, that
the Galatians actually had taken the course opposed to Paul's
recommendation. Paul need only think that the alternative to
"gentle restoration" was available to the Galatians as a real
possibility. In fact, Paul probably had in mind as the opposite of his own recommendation the conduct of the nomists in
Galatia,[77] the "circumcision party," Peter and the "rest of the
Jews" in Antioch,[78] and the "false brethren" in Jerusalem.[79]

In summary, what these comments demonstrate is that 6:1
reflects Paul's opinion that the Galatians should consider
"transgressors" as corrigible when treated "gently" in accordance with the Spirit in them. This means that Paul did not
think of the Galatians as having problems with "libertinism" or
"*flagrant* misconduct." "Wrongdoing" perhaps; at least Paul
admits the possibility of πνευματικοί "misbehaving" and, in
5:21b, he indicates the Galatians also knew of this real possibility. But "*flagrant* misconduct" would have called for stronger
corrective measures than "gentle restoration," as Paul demonstrates in his Corinthian correspondence.[80] It seems better,
therefore, to assume "transgressions" did happen in the Galatian
churches out of human weakness, error and failure, rather than
out of the *flagrant abuse and exploitation* of their freedom won
by Christ and his Spirit. The function of Paul's parenesis in

5:13-24 would then be to remind the Galatians that he took
ethics as seriously as they did, and that the way to deal with
"transgressions" is to continue to rely on the Spirit, as they
had been doing, and not to turn to the law of Moses, with its
threats of punishment and condemnation as well as its rites of
atonement and forgiveness.[81]

Finally, there is no evidence that the Galatians' "initial
enthusiasm" had waned. In 3:5 Paul speaks of the continued
presence of experiences of the Spirit in the life of the Galatian communities.[82] This means the Galatians' "initial enthusiasm" had *not* worn off. The problem behind 3:1-5 is not that
the Galatians had given up on the Spirit, but that they were
considering circumcision as an addition to the Spirit which
they had received, and were continuing to receive, from the
proclamation of the crucified Christ. Unless the Galatians'
consideration of accepting obedience to the law of Moses was
accompanied by a continued enthusiasm for and of the Spirit,
Paul's questions in 3:1-5 lose their force. The basis of
Paul's "apology" is the assumption that the Galatians do not
want to give up the Spirit even though they want to add the
rites of the law of Moses to it. It is Paul who introduces
the idea that the gift of the Spirit can be destroyed precisely
by adding the law of Moses to it. The Galatians apparently
were unaware that the gift of the Spirit would be destroyed by
obeying and relying on the law of Moses--that the gift of the
Spirit would be subject to destruction at all, except by allow-
ing the flesh an "opportunity."[83] Expressions of the danger of
the fruitlessness of the Galatians' experiences of the Spirit
are Paul's, not the Galatians'.[84]

The Galatians want to enjoy both the Spirit and the law of
Moses. Paul's contention, however, is that the Galatians have
to choose between them--they cannot have both worlds. If they
choose the law of Moses, it will take the place of the proclamation of the crucified Christ as the source of salvation. But
since, for Paul, salvation is from the crucified Christ, not
the law of Moses, as evidenced among the Galatians by the fact
that they received the Spirit from the proclamation of the crucified Christ and not from the law of Moses,[85] they will lose

their salvation won by Christ and his Spirit.[86]   The Galatians,
on the other hand, seem to have thought of their pneumatic experiences as necessary but in need of "perfecting" by means of
the rites of the law of Moses; not, however, because of the
Spirit's failure to preserve their salvation, but because
pneumatic experiences were considered only a "beginning," that
is, the first steps of converts or neophytes. The rites of the
law of Moses were believed to be the means to "perfection" or
maturity.[87] Paul calls this a turning to "another gospel,"
which is really not a gospel at all (1:6-7). This is the occasion of Paul's letter to the Galatians.

Section 3.   The Spirit and the Historical Occasion of the
             Letter

     We can now summarize the relationship between Paul's
statements about the Spirit and the cause of the letter to the
churches of Galatia. Paul uses the term πνεῦμα in the letter
to refer to a primary datum of the Galatians' Christian experience as evidence of the truth of the gospel which he preached,
and they believed, during his missionary visit. That is to
say, that Paul's statements about the Spirit serve to remind
the Galatians that they were "eyewitnesses" that salvation and
freedom came from the crucified Christ and his Spirit; for they
had received the Spirit, the "highest evidence," from Paul's
gospel.[88] The Spirit, therefore, proves Paul's gospel and
Galatian Christianity had no need of the law of Moses, since
they had received the Spirit from Paul's message about the
crucified Christ before they had opportunity to perform any of
the rites of the law of Moses.

     This shows that Paul's use of the term πνεῦμα in the let-
ter to the Galatians is conditioned by two historical factors.
One is the polemic resulting from the introduction of Jewish
rites into Galatian Christianity. But this alone is not sufficient to explain Paul's use of the term πνεῦμα in this letter.
Another factor is needed; namely, the fact that the Spirit was
a primary datum of experience for the Galatians as Christians.
For the term πνεῦμα is not always a key term in the polemic
over Jewish rites, whether in early Christianity or Judaism.

In Paul's letters, πνεῦμα is a key term only in Galatians,
the Corinthian correspondence and Romans. Of these, Jewish-
Christian nomism is a problem only in Galatians and Romans.
The opponents in Corinth according to the second letter to the
Corinthians have been identified as Jewish Christians, but of a
different type from the nomists in Galatia; for they have been
seen to be characterized by a *theios anēr* theology, according
to which they stood with Christ in line with Moses.[89] On the
other hand, 2 Cor 6:14-7:1 seems to be an "anti-Pauline fragment," which reflects the theology of Paul's opponents in
Galatia.[90] Perhaps the source of the fragment had a connection
with opponents in Corinth; but we have no evidence of this.
While 2 Corinthians 3 does compare in some respects with Gal
4:21-31, it is not in the context of a polemic against Jewish
rites required by the law of Moses; rather, it seems to be
directed more against Moses himself, and the tradition which is
traced back to him, and in this sense is related to the Jewish-
Christian "divine men." In the first letter to the Corinthians
the problem is with flagrant misconduct or libertinism. In
both cases, here and the "divine men" of the second letter, the
Spirit either is associated with the cause of the problem, or
is itself the cause of the problem; that is, in the one the
Spirit is at the base of "flagrant misconduct,"[91] and in the
other it is the basis of the "signs" of the "divine man."[92] In
the four main letters, therefore, the Spirit is acknowledged as
a primary datum of Christian experience in Galatia, Corinth and
Rome; but Paul uses the term πνεῦμα in the context of a polemic
against Jewish-Christian nomists only in Galatians and Romans.
Furthermore, only in these two letters is Paul's "defense of
the Spirit" unqualified. In the Corinthian letters Paul does
not reject pneumatic experiences, but he does subject them to a
critique, because pneumatic experiences were more of a problem
than part of the solution to the cause of the letters to
Corinth.[93]

The letter to the Galatians itself gives evidence that
Paul's use of the term πνεῦμα was historically conditioned by
the fact that the Spirit was a primary datum of experience for
the Galatians, and not simply by the polemic against Jewish-

Christian nomists: Paul mentions the problem with Jewish-
Christian nomists in Jerusalem (2:1-10) and Antioch (2:11-14)
without ever mentioning the Spirit.[94]   Although Paul is not
expected to mention all the points of his argument in the
"narration" of the facts pertinent to the "case,"[95] it is re-
markable that Paul does not mention the Spirit before 3:2 even
though the conflicts in Jerusalem and Antioch are in other respects analogous to the Galatian conflict.   Perhaps Gentile
Christians in Antioch did not think of themselves as πνευματικοί as the Galatians, the Romans and, in a different way, the
Corinthians did.   In any case, Paul's theological language
reflects the self-understanding and experience of his audiences.

We could also point to the Thessalonian Christians, for
whom the Spirit was also a datum of Christian experience,[96]
although they did not understand themselves to be πνευματικοί,
nor did they have problems with Jewish-Christian nomists.   Similar are the Philippians, for whom the Spirit was a datum of
Christian experience,[97] but not *the primary* datum: although the
Philippians seem to have had problems with circumcision, and
Paul uses πνεῦμα in the context of this polemic (3:3), it is
not a key term in the letter.

In other words, Paul's letters give evidence that pneumatic experiences were widespread in the Pauline churches, as
well as in other Christian communities, such as in Rome.   But
these experiences had different theological and sociological
consequences in each community.   Paul responds to each differently, both according to their concrete pneumatic experiences
and according to the controversies which were the causes of his
letters.   In particular, in Galatians Paul defends the Spirit,
because they not only experienced the Spirit but also understood
themselves to be πνευματικοί.   The historical occasion of Paul's
statements about the Spirit in Galatians, however, in contrast
to the Corinthian correspondence, was not "flagrant misconduct"
or "libertinism."   Paul's statements about the Spirit in the
letter to the Galatians have their cause in the Galatians' consideration of the Jewish Christian nomists' "gospel," which
included the performance of Jewish rites required by the law of
Moses.

Conclusion

In this chapter we have argued (1) that the "cause" of the
letter to the churches of Galatia is the Galatians' consideration of obedience to the law of Moses, which Paul calls a turning to "another gospel";[98] and (2) that the Galatians were
considering turning to the law of Moses not because of problems
with "*flagrant* misconduct," but because they were (a) religiously and (b) ethically "scrupulous," that is, they sought out and
accepted whatever promoted religion and morality,[99] and (c) they
wanted to be "genuine Jews."[100] We also argued (3) that Paul's
statements about the Spirit in the letter to the Galatians serve
to present the "highest evidence," of which the Galatians were
"eyewitnesses," in defense of the gospel which he preached, and
they believed, on his missionary visit to Galatia.[101]

These theses lead to the conclusion that Paul's statements
about the Spirit are conditioned historically by the facts that
the Spirit was a primary datum of Christian experience and of
theological reflection in the Galatian churches, and that in
Galatia Jewish-Christian nomists had almost persuaded Paul's
converts that the Spirit was good for "beginners," but to be
τέλειοι they had to perform the rites required by the law of
Moses.[102] This challenged not only Paul's apostolic office and
his gospel without circumcision but also the Spirit, which the
Galatians had received from his gospel, and with which they had
begun their Christian existence. We are led to the further
conclusion, therefore, that Paul's statements about the Spirit
in Galatians are "apologetic," as Betz has already demonstrated.[103]

The fact that Paul had to defend the Spirit means that,
although the Spirit was a primary datum of Christian experience
and of theological reflection in the churches of Galatia, the
Spirit was not an unambiguous reality. The conflict in the
Galatian churches did not concern the existence of God's self-
manifestation as the Spirit. The problem, rather, was what it
signified, and what its consequences for Christian existence
were. These questions could not be answered simply by appealing to manifestations of God as the Spirit in the life of the
Galatian churches. The Spirit's status as "indisputable

evidence" was not independent of other theological claims;
rather, it was in part derived from other theological claims.
For the Spirit, a reality admitted to be a real manifestation
of God in the Galatian communities by all parties to the conflict, was not self-evidently proof of *salvation*; otherwise
Paul's letter would not have been needed, or at least a lengthy
argument like the letter to the Galatians, involving other
theological claims, would not have been necessary. At issue
is precisely what kind of evidentiary value the Spirit had in
Galatia. This is, for Paul, a soteriological issue, and he
calls upon various concepts of "law" and anthropology to
settle it (that is, to defend the Spirit as the agent par
excellence of salvation).

The ambiguity of pneumatic phenomena is also indicated by
1 Thess 5:19, whether it indicates someone in the church in
Thessalonica was trying to eliminate Spirit-experiences there,
or whether it simply is a reminder and encouragement not to let
them wane;[104] in either case, the verse is evidence that the
Spirit could be viewed with less than full appreciation. A
different problem arose in Corinth as a result of the ambiguity
surrounding the Spirit. For one thing ecstatic phenomena had
to be "tested" (1 Cor 12:10), in order to distinguish between
what was good and evil,[105] because not every ecstatic experience was a manifestation of the Spirit of God.[106] Furthermore,
if Paul had given the Corinthians the message that the Spirit
had emancipated them from the flesh, it was not immediately
self-evident to them just what the consequences of salvation
by the Spirit were for life in the flesh (or body); for Corinth
was rife with "problems with the flesh." In other words, at
least in Pauline Christianity, the Spirit and life in the
Spirit had continually to be interpreted, defined and qualified
in relation to other theological claims which were part of
early Christianity. These claims were sociological,[107] soteriological,[108] christological[109] and eschatological.[110]

CHAPTER II

[1]Cf. below, pp. 29-30.

[2]Cf. below, pp. 30-39.

[3]Cf. below, pp. 39-41.

[4]I am following H. D. Betz's compositional analysis of Paul's letter to the Galatians based on rhetorical handbooks in antiquity, which first appeared in "The Literary Composition and Function of Paul's Letter to the Galatians" (*NTS* 21 [1975] 353-79) and appears also in his commentary in the Hermeneia series (*Commentary on Paul's Letter*).

[5]Cf. Betz, *Commentary on Paul's Letter*, passim; and Ehrhard Kamlah, *Die Form der katalogischen Paränese im N.T.* (WUNT 7; Tübingen: Mohr/Siebeck, 1964) 17. For a classic representative of the view that the letter has two preoccupations, nomism and libertinism, see Lütgert (*Gesetz und Geist*). Walter Schmithals thinks the single problem in Galatia was caused by Jewish (Christian) gnosticism (cf. *Paul*, 13-64).

[6]Cf. 2:2-5, 11-14, 5:2-4, 10-12, 18, 23b.

[7]The thesis of Betz's commentary and his earlier article is that Paul's letter to the Galatians is an example of the "apologetic letter" genre, and that it is a defense of Paul himself and his gospel without circumcision.

[8]Cf. 2:2-5, 7-9, 11-14, 5:2-12, 6:12-13, 15 (cf. also 3:28, "neither Jew nor Greek").

[9]Cf. 2:16, 3:2, 5, 10. Cf. also 3:11, 12 and 5:4 in which ἐν νόμῳ and ὁ νόμος are shorthand for ἐξ ἔργων νόμου and ἔργα νόμου.

[10]Cf. especially 6:9-10, but also 5:6, 14 and the whole section 5:25-6:10.

[11]Cf. 3:12 and 5:4 (where Paul uses the present tense, ὅιτινες ἐν νόμῳ δικαιοῦσθε). Similarly, Paul describes his Pharisaic past in terms of exceeding "progress" (cf. his use of προκόπτω in 1:14) and of "blamelessness before the law" (cf. Phil 3:6, κατὰ δικαιοσύνην τὴν ἐν νόμῳ γενόμενος ἄμεμπτος).

[12]Cf. especially 3:6-14, 21-22, and 5:2-6. Cf. also 5:25, 6:8, 15.

[13]It is often said that whereas "good deeds" for Paul are consequences of salvation, for Judaism they are the presupposition of salvation. The recent book by E. P. Sanders (*Paul and Palestinian Judaism: A Comparison of Patterns of Religion*

[Philadelphia: Fortress, 1977]) is a devastating critique of
this comparison. In his commentary, however, Betz seems to
accept this comparison (see *Commentary on Paul's Letter*, on
6:9).

[14]Cf. especially 5:3 and 6:13 (cf. also 3:10). In his
commentary, Betz admits we do not know whether the Galatians,
and/or the Christian nomists, sought to distinguish a "special"
law from the whole Mosaic law (cf. ad loc., and on 6:2: "the
law of Christ," which could come from the Galatians or Paul's
"opponents").

[15]Cf. the rhetorical device of the *interrogatio* in 3:1-5
and 4:21 (cf. Betz, "The Literary Composition," 369-70, 376;
and his commentary, ad loc.).

[16]These are not contradictory but two mutually complementary rhetorical devices (cf. Betz, "The Literary Composition," 376).

[17]Cf. 2:5 ("the truth of the gospel").

[18]Cf. 1:6, also 1:1, 4, 11-17, 3:19d, 20, and 4:8-9.

[19]Cf. 4:31, 5:1, 5, 13, 25. The phrase "new creation"
(6:15) includes all of these. "Blessing," "promise," and
"sonship" (cf. 3:6-14, 22, 24, 26-4:7) are synonyms, as 4:21-31
shows.

[20]Cf. 3:4, 4:8-11, 17, and 5:1, 2, 4. This is the point
of 5:13-24 also; namely, that receiving circumcision results
in producing a union with the flesh rather than with the
Spirit, thereby undoing the union with the Spirit which they
had received through faith in the crucified Christ (cf. especially 5:17-18, with which 3:3 should be compared).

[21]Cf. Betz, *Commentary on Paul's Letter*, "Introduction,
Section 2, C. The Anti-Pauline Opposition."

[22]Cf. ibid. (ad loc. n. 58), where he conjectures that
ἐπιτελεῖν may have played a role for the opponents.

[23]Cf. ibid., "Introduction, Section 7. The Theological
Argument in Galatians" (cf. also below, Chapter IV, pp. 103-04).

[24]For a discussion of the phrase ἐξ ἀκοῆς πίστεως in 3:2,
5, see below, Chapter III, pp. 54-57.

[25]Cf. below, pp. 31-32.

[26]Cf. below, pp. 32-33.

[27]Cf. below, pp. 34-39.

[28]Cf. Betz, *Commentary on Paul's Letter* (passim) for the
use of this term.

[29]Cf. 4:3 and 4:8-10 as a *topos* under the heading of "religious scrupulosity" or "superstition" (cf. Betz, *Commentary on Paul's Letter*, ad loc.).

[30]Josephus, *Ant.* 20.34-48 (LCL 9.406-15); cf. Betz, *Commentary on Paul's Letter*, "Appendix A."

[31]Josephus, *Ant.* 20.38 (LCL 9.408), βεβαίως ᾿Ιουδαῖος.

[32]Josephus, *Ant.* 20.39, 41, 47 (LCL 9.408, 412).

[33]Josephus, *Ant.* 20.41 (LCL 9.410). This is a reference to the observance of Temple worship and the study of the Torah (cf. K. G. Kuhn, *TDNT* 6.731).

[34]Josephus, *Ant.* 20.41 (LCL 9.410), κυριώτερον.

[35]Josephus, *Ant.* 20.43-45 (LCL 9.410, 412).

[36]Josephus, *Ant.* 20.46 (LCL 9.412), ταῦτα ἀκούσα. Earlier he had been persuaded by Ananias' arguments (20.43, LCL 9.410), ἐπείσθη μὲν τότε τοῖς λόγοις ὁ βασιλεύς).

[37]Josephus, *Ant.* 20.43 (LCL 9.410), τὴν γὰρ ἐπιθυμίαν οὐκ ἐξεβεβλήκει παντάπασιν.

[38]Josephus, *Ant.* (LCL 9.410-11).

[39]Josephus, *Ant.* 20.38 (LCL 9.408), νομίζων τε μὴ ἂν εἶναι βεβαίως ᾿Ιουδαῖος, εἰ μὴ περιτέμοιτο.

[40]Josephus, *Ant.* 20.39 (LCL 9.408).

[41]Josephus, *Ant.* 20.38 (LCL 9.408).

[42]Josephus, *Ant.* 20.41 (LCL 9.408, 410); cf. also 20.34 (LCL 9.406).

[43]For a discussion of the above, see K. G. Kuhn, *TDNT* 6. 730-42, especially 732).

[44]Josephus, *Ant.* 20.43, 41 (LCL 9.410). Paul uses the same words to describe his own Pharisaic past (cf. Gal 1:14, περισσοτέρως ζηλωτὴς ὑπάρχων τῶν πατρικῶν μου παραδόσεων).

[45]Josephus, *Ant.* 20.41 (LCL 9.408, 410), δυνάμενον δ᾿ αὐτὸν ἔφη καὶ χωρὶς τῆς περιτομῆς τὸ θεῖον σέβειν, εἴγε πάντως κέκρικε ζηλοῦν τὰ πάτρια τῶν ᾿Ιουδαίων·

[46]Cf. 2:14, where ᾿Ιουδαϊκῶς ζῆν refers to Jews by birth and ᾿Ιουδαΐζειν to the circumcision of converts, so that the two terms become synonymous (cf. Betz, *Commentary on Paul's Letter*, ad loc.).

[47]For a discussion of the "Hellenistic reform" of Judaism, see Martin Hengel (*Judaism and Hellenism: Studies in their Encounter in Palestine during the Early Hellenistic Period* (2 vols.; trans. John Bowden; Philadelphia: Fortress, 1974) esp. 1.255-309.

[48]Paul's phrase, γνόντες θεόν, and Josephus', σεβόμενοι θεόν, are synonymous and, in this context, refer to "genuine Jews," as in the "Hellenistic reformers."

[49]For this thesis, see Betz (*Commentary on Paul's Letter*) on 5:13-24 and 6:1 (cf. also on 6:9).

[50]Cf. Lütgert, *Gesetz und Geist*.

[51]Cf. 3:1-5 and 6:1.

[52]Cf. 5:18, 23b.

[53]Cf. Schmithals, *Paul*, 38. Schmithals does not think Paul was very well informed about the situation in Galatia, except when it comes to the parenesis (p. 18). Even if this were true, which is doubtful, 5:18 and 5:23b reflect a different understanding of the situation in Galatia. In any case, Schmithals' documentation of a gnosticism which regarded circumcision as a mystery rite is inadequate (cf. his telling footnote, p. 59 n. 134, which is discussed above [Chapter I, pp. 3-4]).

[54]Cf. Betz, *Commentary on Paul's Letter*, "Introduction, Section 2, C. The Anti-Pauline Opposition," and on 5:13-24 and 6:1; idem, "Spirit, Freedom, and Law," 153-55; and idem, "In Defense of the Spirit," 106-107.

[55]Cf. 3:3 and 4:12, which might also reflect the Galatians' desire. In the first case, the Galatians quite possibly were about to consider obedience to the law of Moses the "perfection" of life in the Spirit (cf. Betz, *Commentary on Paul's Letter*, on 3:3, n. 58). In 4:12, Paul possibly reflects the Galatians' desire to become as "genuine Jews" are, that is, to become circumcized (cf. 3:28, 5:6, 6:15).

[56]Cf. Betz, *Commentary on Paul's Letter*, on 5:13 ("Flagrant misconduct by Christians must have been one, or even the major, problem of the Galatians.").

[57]Something like 1 Cor 1:11, 5:1, 11:17 and 7:1 (and the περὶ δέ construction used throughout chaps. 7-16) seems to be called for.

[58]Cf. Betz, *Commentary on Paul's Letter*, on 5:13 and 6:1 (cf. also on 6:9).

[59]Cf. 5:13 (μόνον μὴ τὴν ἐλευθερίαν εἰς ἀφορμὴν τῇ σαρκί).

[60]Cf. 2:20c. Paul's summary (2:20-21) of his argument in
3:1-4:31 has at its center the problem whether life "in the
flesh" is to be governed by life "in Christ" or life "in the
law of Moses." What troubles Paul is less that they were having problems with life "in the flesh" than that they would have
solved those problems by living "under the law."

[61]Cf. the combination of indicative and imperative in 5:1,
13, 25.

[62]Cf. ἃ προλέγω ὑμῖν καθὼς προεῖπον (Betz [Commentary on
Paul's Letter, ad loc.] suggests a baptismal-catechetical Sitz
im Leben).

[63]Cf. ibid., ad loc. and on 5:13.

[64]Ibid., on 5:21b.

[65]Ibid., ad loc., emphasis added (cf. also his comments
on 6:1 and 5:13, where he expresses "no doubt" that 6:1 refers
to a concrete case or cases of misconduct).

[66]In the first, the clause is conditional and the καί
intensive; and in the second, the clause is concessive. Cf.
Ernest DeWitt Burton, Syntax of the Moods and Tenses in New
Testament Greek (3rd ed.; Edinburgh: T. & T. Clark, 1955;
orig., 1898) secs. 280, 282.

[67]Ibid., sec. 242.

[68]Ibid., secs. 250, 284, 285b; and Nigel Turner, A Grammar
of New Testament Greek, Vol. 3: Syntax (Edinburgh: T. & T.
Clark, 1963) 109.

[69]Cf. the ἄνθρωπος (cf. also 6:7) and the ἔν τινι
παραπτώματι. Betz also notes the lack of specificity in
Paul's description of the case: παράπτωμα denotes "any kind
of immoral act" (ad loc., n. 36), and the recommendation remains general (ad loc., n. 32 notes that the MSS tradition
tries to make the description of the case more specific, and
n. 33 contrasts Gal 6:1 and 1 Cor 5:1ff.).

[70]Cf. Betz, "2 Cor 6:14-7:1," 107 n. 120.

[71]Cf. above, p. 35 (and Betz, Commentary on Paul's Letter,
ad loc.).

[72]The way Paul recommends corresponds to his acknowledg-
ment of the Galatians as πνευματικοί, for πραΰτης is part of
the "fruit of the Spirit" (5:22). Cf. Betz, Commentary on
Paul's Letter, ad loc.

[73]Betz notes that καταρτίζειν denotes the philosopher's
task (Commentary on Paul's Letter, ad loc., n. 43); so also
δοκιμάζειν in 6:4 (ad loc., n. 90). For a treatment of this

discussion in relation to Paul, see Abraham J. Malherbe, "'Gentle as a Nurse'. The Cynic Background to I Thess ii," *NovT* 12 (1970) 203-17.

[74]Ibid., 210 nn. 4-6.

[75]Cf. 6:3-5 and 6:1c.

[76]Cf. 5:20.

[77]Cf. ταράσσων in 1:7 and 5:10, and οἱ ἀναστατοῦντες in 5:12. Did their "persuasion" (cf. ἡ πεισμονή in 5:8) consist of harsh rebukes and reviling (cf. ἀναγκάζουσιν in 6:12)?

[78]Cf. 2:11-14.

[79]Cf. 2:4.

[80]Cf., for example, 1 Cor 5:1-13. Even the "gentler" Cynics did not completely reject the use of harshness, especially when circumstances called for it (cf. Malherbe, "'Gentle as a Nurse'," esp. 210-11).

[81]For the former in connection with the law of Moses, see 5:21b, 23b (cf. also 2:11-14, 15, 17, which imply the doctrine that the uncircumcised are by definition "sinners," and therefore excluded from salvation). For the latter, see especially 5:2-6 and 6:15.

[82]Cf. ἐπιχορηγῶν and ἐνεργῶν, whose present tenses refer to manifestations of the Spirit at the time of Paul's letter and not just at the time of Paul's missionary visit (cf. Betz, *Commentary on Paul's Letter*, ad loc., and n. 77; and below, Chapter III, p. 69 n. 146). The cry of the Spirit, "Abba," in 4:6 is also a reference to a present experience in the churches of Galatia.

[83]Similarly, Schlier (*Der Brief an die Galater*, 124-125) is unaware that the gift of the Spirit is not a permanent possession but could be given up. Cf. Betz's criticism of Schlier (*Commentary on Paul's Letter*, on 3:4, n. 71).

[84]In 3:4, Paul expresses, on the one hand, doubt that the Galatians' pneumatic experiences were impotent; but, on the other hand, he has no doubt that if the Galatians do perform the rites of the law of Moses, their pneumatic experiences would come to nothing (for a discussion of the εἴ γε καί, see Betz, *Commentary on Paul's Letter*, ad loc.; and Joseph B. Lightfoot, *The Epistle of St. Paul to the Galatians* [Grand Rapids, MI: Zondervan; 1957; orig., 1865], 135). Cf. also 4:10, 15.

[85]This is why Spirit opposes flesh rather than "works of the law"; the latter are opposed to the proclamation of the crucified Christ (cf. 3:2, 3, 5).

[86]Cf. 5:2-4 (cf. also 2:21, 3:3-4 and 4:17).

[87]Cf. the contrast between ἐνάρχεσθαι and ἐπιτελεῖσθαι in 3:3, which seems to be a distinction between the ἀρχόμενοι at the initial stages of conversion and the τέλειοι after full initiation into the new religion (cf. below, Chapter IV, p. 135, n. 7). Cf. also Jewett, "Agitators," 207.

[88]For the use of terms from the law-court, such as "eye-witnesses" and "highest evidence," see Betz, "The Literary Composition," esp. 369-70 and 377-78; and idem, "In Defense of the Spirit," esp. 109.

[89]For a discussion of the opponents in 2 Corinthians, see Dieter Georgi, *Die Gegner des Paulus im 2. Korintherbrief. Studien zur religiösen Propaganda in der Spätantike* (WMANT 11; Neukirchen-Vluyn: Neukirchener Verlag, 1964); and H. D. Betz, *Der Apostel Paulus und die sokratische Tradition: Eine exegetische Untersuchung zu seiner "Apologie" 2 Korinther 10-13* (BHT 45; Tübingen: Mohr/Siebeck, 1972).

[90]Cf. Betz, "2 Cor 6:14-7:1," 88-108; and idem, *Commentary on Paul's Letter*, "Appendix 2."

[91]Cf. 1 Cor 14:12, which seems to be the Sitz im Leben of 3:16, and 6:19 (cf. 10:23-24 and 12:7).

[92]Cf. 2 Cor 11:4, 12:12, 18 (cf. also 1:22, 4:13, 5:5 and 6:6).

[93]Cf. 1 Corinthians 12-14. It is this critique of pneumatic experiences which sets the Corinthian letters apart from Galatians and Romans, as well as the different context of "flagrant misconduct" and "divine men" rather than religious and ethical "scrupulosity" centered in the law of Moses. Nevertheless, Paul does appeal to the Spirit as the "highest evidence" in 1 Cor 2:4 (ἀπόδειξις πνεύματος καὶ δυνάμεως); and 2 Cor 1:22; 3:3, 6, 8, 17, 18; 4:13; 5:5; 6:6; 11:4; 12:18. It is also the basis of his parenesis in 1 Cor 3:16, 6:11, 19.

[94]Acts 15:6-11 presents a different picture, quite possibly because it uses traditions which were not even existent in Paul's time, let alone not known by him. They present a picture more like the conflict in Galatia than that of Antioch, at least as Paul tells about it. Peter sounds like Paul in Galatians: both call circumcision a ζυγός (cf. Acts 15:10 and Gal 5:1); both say Jews as well as Gentiles are to be saved διὰ τῆς χάριτος τοῦ κυρίου Ἰησοῦ (cf. Acts 15:11 and Gal 2: 15-16 and 5:2-6); and both appeal to the Gentile Christians' experiences of the Spirit (cf. Acts 15:8 and Gal 3:2-5, 14, 4:6; also see Acts 10:44-47 and 11:15-18). Cf. Ernst Haenchen, *The Acts of the Apostles: A Commentary* (trans. Bernard Noble et al.; Philadelphia: Westminster, 1971) 361.

[95]For a discussion of the function of the "narrative" section of Galatians (1:12-2:14), see Betz, "The Literary Composition," 362-67; and idem, *Commentary on Paul's Letter*, ad loc.

[96]Cf. 1 Thess 1:4-6, 4:8 and 5:19.

[97]Cf. Phil 1:27, 2:1 and 3:3.

[98]Cf. μεταστρέφω and μεθίστημι in 1:6-7 (also 6:12-13).

[99]Cf. 4:8-10.

[100]Cf. 3:6-9, 14, 26-29, 4:1-7, 21-31.

[101]Cf. 3:1-5, 14, 4:6, 15.

[102]Cf. 3:3.

[103]We do not wish to take up but only to note that Galatians, as an "apology" on behalf of the Spirit of God, raises
the perennial question of the relationship between faith and
reason, philosophy and theology (cf. Betz ["The Literary Composition," 378-79; and idem, "In Defense of the Spirit," 99-
103, 108-13] who brings together two issues which usually are
kept separate; namely, that of "apologetics," and that of the
so-called "irrationality" of ecstatic phenomena).

[104]Cf. 1 Thess 1:4-6, 4:8. Cf. also Rom 12:11.

[105]Cf. 1 Thess 5:21-22.

[106]Cf. 1 Cor 12:3 and 2:12.

[107]Cf. below, Chapter III.

[108]Cf. below, Chapter IV.

[109]Cf. below, Chapter V.

[110]Cf. below, Chapter VI.

CHAPTER III

THE ECSTATIC SPIRIT AND SETTINGS
IN THE GALATIAN CHURCHES

Introduction

An understanding of the Spirit, which is Paul's primary interest in the letter to the Galatians, depends not only on an understanding of the concrete historical occasion, or cause, of the letter, but also on knowledge of the specific Sitze im Leben of the Galatian communities in which experiences of the Spirit had occurred. For this tells us about the social, as well as theological, "place" of the Spirit in the churches founded by Paul in Galatia.

In the letter to the churches of Galatia, which is an "apology" on behalf of the Spirit, Paul reminds the Galatians of their concrete experiences of the Spirit in the life of their communities. References to the social settings of experiences of the Spirit in the Galatian churches, however, are limited to Paul's statements about the Spirit in 3:1-5 and 4:6. Our attention focuses, therefore, on the Sitz im Leben behind the concept of τὸ πνεῦμα λαβεῖν ἐξ ἀκοῆς πίστεως in 3:2, 5, and the "Abba-cry" in 4:6, as well as the concept of ἐπιχορηγεῖν τὸ πνεῦμα καὶ ἐνεργεῖν δυνάμεις ἐξ ἀκοῆς πίστεως in 3:5. Apart from these references, Paul's letter to the Galatians contains scanty evidence necessary for a more complete social profile of the Spirit in the Christian communities founded by Paul in Galatia.[1]

The conclusion reached in this chapter is that the setting of experiences of the Spirit in the churches of Galatia was the occasion of proclamation. The proclamation of the crucified Christ produced the Galatians' first experiences of the Spirit (3:2). This was also the setting of the "Abba-cry" (4:6), and other ecstatic phenomena in the ongoing life of the Christian communities founded by Paul (3:5). The majority opinion, however, is that the converts' initial experience of the Spirit is to be traced to baptism.[2]

We begin with an examination of 3:1-5, and the related
texts, 1 Thess 1:4-6 and 1 Cor 2:4-5, which identify the Sitz
im Leben of the reception of the Spirit by those who were converted by Paul's missionary preaching.[3] Next we directly ad-
dress the question of the Spirit and baptism, and examine 1 Cor
12:13, 6:11, 2 Cor 1:15-24, Rom 5:5, and Gal 3:27.[4] Then we
turn to 4:6, which refers to Paul's converts'' experience of the
Spirit during proclamation as an ecstatic experience of the
"Abba-cry."[5] Finally we take up 3:5, which refers to the experience of the Spirit not only at the time of Paul's missionary visit, but also in the ongoing life of the community, for
example in ecstatic phenomena such as glossolalia.[6] It will
then be clear that the initial experience of the Spirit in the
community was at conversion at the time of Paul's missionary
preaching, and that subsequent experiences of the Spirit were
also closely connected with proclamation.

Section 1.   Proclamation as the Sitz im Leben of the Initial
             Possession of the Spirit

Gal 3:1-5. Paul implies that his converts in Galatia
received the Spirit ἐξ ἀκοῆς πίστεως. This cannot mean that
the converts in Galatia *learned about* the Spirit from Paul's
preaching, as if he had preached about the Spirit; for it is
clear from 3:1 that the crucified Christ was the subject of
Paul's proclamation. When Paul refers to the reception of the
Spirit, therefore, he refers not to the *idea* of the Spirit,
but to the experience of the *reality* of the Spirit itself.

Four features of Paul's argument in 3:1-14 point to his
missionary preaching as the Sitz im Leben for the initial experience of the Spirit by his converts in Galatia: (1) προεγράφη in 3:1; (2) ἐλάβετε in 3:2; (3) ἐξ ἀκοῆς πίστεως in 3:2,
5; and (4) the example of Abraham in 3:6-14.[7] Each of these
features alone indicates Paul refers to his missionary preaching in 3:1-5; and together they cluster around the reference to
his converts' experience of the Spirit, indicating that the
occasion for their initial experience of the Spirit was Paul's
missionary preaching, not baptism.

(1) In 3:1, Paul identifies his readers, who are his converts in Galatia, as οἷς κατ' ὀφθαλμοὺς 'Ιησοῦς Χριστὸς προεγράφη ἐσταυρωμένος. The οἷς κατ' ὀφθαλμοὺς...προεγράφη indicates that Paul is referring to his missionary preaching.[8]
This establishes the Sitz im Leben of the experience of the
Spirit to which he refers in the next verse.

(2) In 3:2, τὸ πνεῦμα ἐλάβετε denotes the initial reception of the Spirit.[9] It is significant that this reference to
Paul's converts' initial experience of the Spirit is preceded
and followed by references to his missionary preaching: namely,
προεγράφη in 3:1 and ἐξ ἀκοῆς πίστεως in 3:2, 5. For elsewhere
Paul uses λαμβάνω in phrases which denote the acceptance of
oral tradition handed on by Paul, and the acceptance of his
missionary preaching.[10] Surrounded by references to his missionary preaching, τὸ πνεῦμα ἐλάβετε suggests, therefore, that
Paul is thinking of the acceptance of his preaching evidenced
by his converts' reception of the Spirit.[11]

(3) The phrase ἐξ ἀκοῆς πίστεως also points to Paul's missionary preaching as the Sitz im Leben of his converts' reception of the Spirit. Since it is parallel to ἐξ ἔργων νόμου,
which refers to cultic or ritual acts of the law of Moses,[12]
and since Paul is playing with cultic terms throughout 3:1-5,[13]
ἐξ ἀκοῆς πίστεως, therefore, also refers to a cultic act. This
means that Paul is not opposing the inward act of faith to outward deeds of "good works," nor faith to self-assertion; rather,
he sets two cultic acts, or two cults, against one another:
namely, the cult of the law of Moses typified by circumcision
and that of Christian proclamation culminating in faith.

The phrase ἐξ ἀκοῆς πίστεως has been variously translated,
because of the ambiguity of ἀκοῆς,[14] πίστεως,[15] and the genitive:[16] (a) "Did you receive the Spirit from works of the law
or from *preaching which has faith as its content?*"[17] (b) "Did
you receive the Spirit from works of the law or from *a
believing-hearing?*"[18] (c) "Did you receive the Spirit from
works of the law or from *an act of hearing whose goal is an
act of faith?*"[19] and (d) "Did you receive the Spirit from works
of the law or from *preaching which evokes faith?*"[20] Although
this phrase is ambiguous, preference should be given to that

interpretation which does justice to the double emphasis in
this context on Paul's missionary preaching on the one hand,[21]
and the act of faith on the other.[22]   In other words, Paul refers to his converts' experience of the Spirit, which they received from his missionary preaching, denoted either by ἀκοῆς
or by πίστεως.[23]   In any case, his converts' initial experience
of the Spirit had its Sitz im Leben in Paul's missionary preaching, not baptism, which is not mentioned in this context at
all.[24]

The relationship between the proclamation which evokes
faith and the reception of the Spirit is expressed by the
preposition ἐκ. This phrase would suffer from over-analysis
if we were to argue that ἐκ is *only* temporal,[25] or *only*
causal;[26] and especially if we were to argue that it denoted
the cause, but *only* in the sense of the origin,[27] or *only* the
reason.[28]   In the absence of compelling evidence that Paul intended ἐκ to be understood in only *one* of these senses, we
should not exclude any of them, as long as they do not contra-
dict one another.[29]   Paul's argument against the nomists is
just as much that Christians in the churches of Galatia received the Spirit *as a result of his proclamation*, as it is
that they received the Spirit *after* his missionary preaching
which evoked their faith--that is, *without* "works of the law"
as well as *before* they had performed any "works of the law."
By means of this argument, Paul reminds his converts in Galatia
that it was his missionary preaching, and not any "works of the
law," which produced their faith and their reception of the
Spirit.

(4) The example of Abraham in 3:6-14 confirms the view
that Paul does not trace the reception of the Spirit by his
converts to baptism, but to his missionary preaching, which
they accepted with faith. When Paul says, "Thus Abraham believed God...," he obviously does not have baptism in view.
The common element shared by Paul's converts in Galatia and
Abraham is not baptism, nor the Spirit for that matter, any
more than circumcision, but faith: "So then, those who believe
are blessed with Abraham, who believed" (3:9).

In 3:1-5, Paul's argument appeals to the experience of the
Galatians as evidence of the legitimacy of his gospel which
evoked their faith. But in 3:6-14, Paul presents an argument
from Scripture, in which the key element is not the proclamation which evokes faith, but the act of faith itself.[30] Another
element in this new context is the fact that here Paul speaks
not only of the Galatians, who were Paul's converts, but of
Abraham, Christians in general, and Jewish Christians in particular. In 3:1-5, however, Paul had in view only those who
were his converts in Galatia, whose faith and reception of the
Spirit came from his missionary preaching. The same could not
be said of Christians in general, and certainly not of Abraham.
The point of similarity, however, is that all have received the
Spirit through faith.

In summary, just as Paul preached him who dwelt within
him--namely, the crucified Christ[31]--so converts in the Galatian churches received the Spirit of the same Christ.[32] This
correspondence of proclamation and conversion to faith, that
is, the presence of Christ on both sides of the proclamation-
event--in the bearer of the message, and in believers who heard
the proclamation--is expressed in the phrase τὸ πνεῦμα ἐλάβετε
...ἐξ ἀκοῆς πίστεως.

Elsewhere in Paul's letters, the experience of the Spirit
by his converts is attributed to missionary preaching. Their
experiences are spoken of in different ways because of the
different circumstances surrounding the writing of each letter.
To see how these other references compare and contrast with
Gal 3:1-5, we turn to two texts: 1 Thess 1:4-6 and 1 Cor 2:4-5.[33]

1 Thess 1:4-6. Here Paul's interest is in the evidence
that the Thessalonians had become μιμηταί of the Lord, as well
as of himself, his co-workers, and the churches of Judea, in
that they had endured great suffering from their own compatriots
"with joy inspired by the holy Spirit."[34] In other words, in
the letter to the Thessalonians, what is significant about the
reception of the missionary preaching μετὰ χαρᾶς πνεύματος
ἁγίου is that Paul's converts did so ἐν θλίψει πολλῇ and,
thereby, became μιμηταί of the churches in Judea, of Paul and
his co-workers, and of the Lord. But in the letter to the

Galatians it is the reception of the Spirit per se from Paul's
missionary preaching that is important. Although the "imitation" motif and the suffering of persecution do appear in the
letter to the Galatians,[35] neither is brought into relationship
with the reception of the Spirit. Paul, therefore, does not
refer in 3:1-5 to the Spirit's empowerment of the converts in
Galatia with courage in the face of "great opposition" and
"suffering."[36] Nevertheless, both 1 Thess 1:4-6 and Gal 3:1-5
refer to missionary preaching as the Sitz im Leben of Paul's
converts' reception of the Spirit.

    1 Cor 2:4-5. The situation in Galatia is also different
from that in Corinth, which is reflected in 1 Cor 2:4-5. There
Paul had to contend with an extreme pneumaticism, which prized
oratorical style (among other things). This called for opposing πειθοῖ σοφίας λόγοι and ἀπόδειξις πνεύματος καὶ δυνάμεως.[37]
But in Galatia, Paul opposed nomism, so that in the letter to
the Galatians a different opposition appears; namely, "works of
the law," from which only "flesh" can come (3:3), and proclamation of the crucified Christ which evoked faith, from which the
Spirit had come. This means that in Galatia the efficacy of
Paul's preaching came into question not at the level of oratorical style, but on the theological ground that "works of the
law" must supplement faith evoked by the proclamation of the
crucified Christ. In the letter to the Galatians, therefore,
Paul appeals to the reception of the Spirit, which he attributes
to his missionary preaching, in order to establish the legitimacy of his gospel without the law. Because the nomists were
not concerned about Paul's oratorical style, or his lack of it,
Paul does not draw attention to the manner in which he preached,
but rather to the effects of his preaching on his audiences:
namely, the converts' faith, their reception of the Spirit, and
the δυνάμεις.[38] Although Paul addresses a different community
with a different set of issues, this is precisely what Paul does
in 1 Cor 2:4-5. In response to criticisms of his oratorical
style, Paul defends his missionary preaching by appealing to the
effects of his preaching on his audience, which included the
recipients of this letter to the Corinthians. The πνεῦμα and
δυνάμεις, which accompanied Paul's preaching, and not merely

"persuasive arguments," provide Paul with the highest "empirical evidence"[39] that the power and wisdom of God was in his
missionary preaching. The contrast in 1 Cor 2:4-5 is not between two types of rhetorical arguments;[40] rather, it is between mere *hypotheses*, which are not backed by empirical evidence, and *empirical evidence* itself. For Paul, in 1 Cor 2:
4-5, the empirical evidence is of the highest order, πνεῦμα καὶ
δυνάμεις, to which the readers themselves could attest, since
they were witnesses of the experiences to which πνεῦμα and
δυνάμεις refer. These were their assent, which is attributed
to the Spirit, to Paul's proclamation, and the manifestations
of the Spirit which ensued.[41] In Galatia the πνεῦμα and δυνάμεις also provide Paul with "empirical evidence" of the legitimacy of his gospel without the law. Both Gal 3:1-5 and 1 Cor
2:4-5, therefore, point to Paul's missionary preaching as the
Sitz im Leben of the reception of the Spirit by his converts.

   Conclusion. These passages, 1 Thess 1:4-6 and 1 Cor 2:4-5,
have in common with Gal 3:1-5 the fact that they are all appeals
to Paul's converts' experiences of the Spirit as empirical evidence in Paul's self-defense.[42] And in each case, their experiences of the Spirit have their Sitz im Leben in missionary
preaching, not baptism. Thus, despite the different historical
situations in Paul's churches, in 1 Thess 1:4-6, 1 Cor 2:4-5
and Gal 3:1-5, πνεῦμα is an empirical datum of Paul's converts'
experience, which has its Sitz im Leben in missionary preaching.

Section 2. Baptism and the Gift of the Spirit

   Introduction. In early Christianity the view that baptism
and the initial gift of the Spirit are closely related is
"general and primitive."[43] Setting aside Paul's letters for
the moment, we find it in Jesus' baptism traditions,[44] traditions contrasting John's baptism with Christian baptism,[45] and
early Christian doctrines of regeneration,[46] as well as in
Acts 2:38 and 9:17-18. However, the reception of the Spirit
and Christian baptism were not always necessarily closely related.[47] In Acts 18:25, Apollos is described as ζέων τῷ
πνεύματι though he knew only John's baptism, which, according

to 1:5 and 19:1-7, lacked the bestowal of the Spirit that distinguished Christian baptism from John's. On the other hand, Christian baptism too can be described as if it did not involve the bestowal of the Spirit: In 8:39 the Spirit sweeps Philip away but nothing is said of the Ethiopian who had just been baptized. Similarly, 16:14-15, 33 and 18:8 say nothing of the bestowal of the Spirit on the baptizand. According to 8:14-24 and 19:5-6, the "laying on of hands" imparts the Spirit. But then 6:3-6 shows that the "laying on of hands" can serve some function other than the imparting of the Spirit, since at least Stephen, if not all seven who were "ordained," already possessed the Spirit. The Spirit can even be bestowed *before* baptism of any kind (Acts 10:44-48). Here, as in Gal 3:2, 5 and 4:6, the reception of the Spirit occurs during Christian proclamation. Bultmann's point, that these passages express the view that a baptism without the bestowal of the Spirit is no proper baptism,[48] does not account for the fact that so-called deficient baptisms are made "proper" not by re-baptism, but by the "laying on of hands," which can impart the Spirit just as well as Christian baptism.[49] It is just as true that 10:44-48 expresses the view that a bestowal of the Spirit without Christian baptism is not a "proper" possession of the Spirit; but then Christian baptism does not re-impart the Spirit any more than the "laying on of hands" re-baptizes. Finally, Acts 15:7-8 does not specify any setting for the initial reception of the Spirit.

The discussion, in Section 1 of this chapter, of the historical setting of the initial gift of the Spirit in the Galatian churches focused on the hearing of the proclamation of the crucified Christ which evokes faith. There it was argued that the aorist ἐλάβετε denotes the initial endowment with the Spirit in distinction from its ongoing work, but that it does not refer to baptism.[50] Also it was argued that the ἐκ-phrases in 3:2, 5, and the διά-phrase in 3:14 refer to faith elicited by proclamation. But, because Paul mentions baptism in 3:27, and because elsewhere he associates the reception of the Spirit with baptism,[51] some scholars identify baptism as the occasion in the Galatian churches when the Spirit was initially received.[52] It is, therefore, necessary to take a look at those

passages which explicitly mention baptism or speak explicitly
of the initial gift of the Spirit; namely, 1 Cor 12:13, 6:11,
2 Cor 1:15-24, Rom 5:5 and Gal 3:27.[53]

  1 Cor 12:13. If Paul attributes the initial gift of the
Spirit to baptism, it would be here if anywhere; for this is
the only place where Paul uses the verb βαπτίζω together with a
reference to the possession of the Spirit.[54] The point of this
verse, and the preceding verses (12:4-11), is that precisely
the Spirit, which each member of the Corinthian church possessed,[55] *constitutes*[56] each Christian in Corinth as a member
of one body, "the body of Christ."[57] The same Spirit which
manifests itself in a variety of χαρίσματα, Paul says to the
Corinthians, is the Spirit which constitutes each Christian as
a member of the "body of Christ."[58] This still leaves open the
question whether baptism *itself* imparts the "causative power"
of the Spirit, or whether the Spirit is *already* bestowed on the
candidate for baptism on *another* occasion *prior* to the baptismal rite. Nothing in this verse settles this issue; and neither
does anything in the immediate context, unless the acclamation
ΚΥΡΙΟΣ ΙΗΣΟΥΣ (12:3) is a "baptismal confession," in which case
it would have been uttered by the "holy Spirit" in the candidate
for baptism *before* the administration of the rite. Some scholars, however, doubt it is a "baptismal" confession, and refer
it simply to worship as a response to Christian proclamation.[59]
In any case, excluded is the view that the Spirit was imparted
to the believer on another occasion *after* baptism, since the
event of the many becoming one in the "body of Christ," of which
the Spirit is the constitutive power, is attributed to baptism
rather than some later occasion and rite.[60]
  Even though the verb βαπτίζω comes in only secondarily and
not as the topic of discussion in 1 Corinthians 12, 12:13c cannot be used as evidence that Paul speaks only metaphorically of
baptism. The καί, which introduces this statement, is epexegetical; but it refers back to the ἐν ἑνὶ πνεύματι--not to
ἐβαπτίσθημεν--in order to reiterate that the Spirit is one and,
as such, a principle of unity not disunity. Therefore, ἐπο-
τίσθημεν refers to the "out-pouring" of the Spirit,[61] or, as
Paul says elsewhere, the giving/sending of the Spirit into the

hearts of believers.[62] Then 12:13c refers neither to baptism,[63] nor to the Lord's Supper,[64] but to the initial reception of the Spirit in conversion from Paul's missionary preaching.[65] Elsewhere in the same letter Paul indicates that the Spirit was evident already on the occasion of his preaching during his missionary visit.[66] This indicates that, at least for Paul, regardless of what the *pre*-Pauline understanding of 1 Cor 12:13 might have been, the gift of the Spirit that was operative in baptism was received in response to Christian proclamation prior to baptism.

1 Cor 6:11. This verse is similar to 12:13 in that it mentions the possession of the Spirit together with a verb which later became a virtual synonym for baptism; namely, ἀπολούεσθαι. As in 12:13, the Spirit is the power that effects the ἀπολούεσθαι, ἁγιάζεσθαι, and δικαιοῦσθαι.[67] These three verbs form a three-part synonymous parallelism meaning "to be made pure."[68] But, regardless of what the *pre*-Pauline understanding of this statement might have been,[69] it is doubtful that Paul took it as a reference to baptism; for, from the standpoint of the concept of "being made pure," insofar as Paul speaks of this notion at all elsewhere, he does not attribute it to baptism.[70] Also, from the standpoint of Paul's understanding of baptism, the result of baptism is not expressed in terms of "being made pure," but in terms of "dying and having life anew"[71] in the death and resurrection of Christ.

2 Cor 1:15-24. In 1:22, another alleged reference to baptism is joined with a reference to the giving of the Spirit. While some scholars identify the "sealing" with baptism,[72] others identify it with the giving of the Spirit.[73] Elsewhere in Paul's letters, σφραγίζω and σφραγίς are not used in baptismal contexts.[74] And, although σφραγίς became a synonym for baptism in early Christian literature by the time of 2 Clement and Hermas,[75] this probably was not due to its association with the Spirit and water, but to its identification with the "naming of the name" over the baptizand.[76] For three reasons, however, it is doubtful that 2 Cor 1:21-22 is a genuine baptismal context.

(1) The "naming of the name" is nowhere in view.

(2) The four verbs are not used elsewhere by Paul in baptismal contexts.[77]

(3) The context points not to baptism but to missionary
preaching as the Sitz im Leben of the giving of the Spirit. In
1:17, Paul raises a question about his own reliability, which
arises from his travel plans. Paul defends his intentions concerning his travel plans by appealing to the Corinthians'
firsthand knowledge of his missionary preaching (1:18-20): The
"Amen" uttered by all Christians in Corinth, including Paul and
his co-workers, to Christian proclamation can only mean that
they accepted this "word" as trustworthy precisely because[78] it
is the "word" of God and God's Son.[79] By naming God as the one
who finally attests to his reliability, Paul concludes his
self-defense.[80] The one who made Paul and his co-workers faithful disciples[81] is the same God who had "anointed" them, that
is, "commissioned" them (1:21). This "commissioning" is then
explained in terms of the "seal" and the giving of the Spirit.[82]

The "seal," as a mark of ownership, means that Paul and
his co-workers would be kept under the "protection" of their
"owner," namely, the God who "commissioned" them.[83] In other
words, as their "owner," the God who commissioned them will
keep them faithful. This God does through the Spirit imparted
in their hearts.[84] In the first instance this refers to the
"inspiration" of Paul and his co-workers' preaching.[85] At the
same time, however, the Corinthians would hear in this statement
a reference to the Spirit which they had received from Paul's
preaching when they were converted to Christian faith.[86] The
Corinthians could provide the highest evidence of Paul's reliability, namely, the Spirit, to which they themselves can attest as having been in Paul as well as having been received by
them from his preaching.

There is, therefore, a formal as well as material similarity between 1 Thess 1:4-6, Gal 3:1-5, 4:6, and 1 Cor 2:4-5, on
the one hand, and 2 Cor 1:21-22, on the other: In each case
Paul appeals, at least implicitly, to his converts' initial
experience of the Spirit on the occasion of the proclamation
preached on Paul's missionary visits. This means that

2 Cor 1:21-22 presupposes proclamation, not baptism, as the
setting in which the Spirit was initially received by his
converts.

Rom 5:5. In addition to the passages already discussed,
this verse speaks of the initial gift of the Spirit; and it is
followed by a "discussion of baptism" in Romans 6. Although
some scholars have read into Rom 5:5 a reference to baptism,[87]
there is even less reason than in those other, more problematic,
passages which it resembles; namely, Gal 4:6 and 2 Cor 1:22,[88]
as well as 1 Cor 12:13.[89] It will not do to refer to Romans 6
either, in order to place it in a baptismal context; for,
Romans 6 does not mention the Spirit at all, while baptism is
not mentioned in Romans 5. Furthermore, Paul mentions baptism
in Romans 6 only secondarily.[90] The death to sin which believers have died is not each individual death in baptism, but
the one death of Christ.[91] Through baptism, the believer accepts his or her death, which Christ already has died. Likewise with the "newness, which consists of life":[92] baptism does
not impart something new; rather, in it the believer binds
him/herself to that which has already been given in Christ
through the proclamation which evoked faith, namely, ζωή. This
"life" is imparted not by baptism but the Spirit, as 7:6 and
chapter 8 show.[93] In terms of the later church's language,
baptism does not bring about the life imparted by the Spirit; it
"sets the seal to it."[94] This is confirmed by the fact that
Paul does not mention the Spirit in Romans 6; that baptism is
only secondarily mentioned there; and that baptism is not even
mentioned, let alone identified with the imparting of the
Spirit, in Romans 8.

Paul is not bound to any one interpretation of baptism.[95]
Each time Paul mentions an interpretation of baptism, he
"quotes" earlier tradition; and each time the interpretation is
different. In Gal 3:27, baptism is interpreted as a "putting
on of clothes." 1 Cor 12:13 interprets it in terms of being
incorporated into a unified and unifying "body," which is
Christ's body. And in Rom 6:3-4, baptism is related to "dying
and having life anew with Christ." It is unclear whether Paul
accepts the view of baptism "on behalf of the dead" in 1 Cor

15:29. In any case, Paul makes no effort to bring these di-
verse interpretations of baptism into a systematic view. He
may not be bound, either, to a view that attributes the imparting of the Spirit to believers to a single setting in the community, such as either baptism or hearing the proclamation
which elicits faith. But, while there is evidence that Paul
does attribute the imparting of the Spirit to *proclamation*,[96]
no evidence can be found that he attributes it to baptism.

Gal 3:27. In the last passage to be examined, Paul
"quotes" from earlier tradition[97] an interpretation of baptism
in which βαπτίζεσθαι εἰς Χριστόν is equated with ἐνδύεσθαι
Χριστόν. On the basis of 1 Cor 12:13, it is tempting to interpret ἐνδύεσθαι Χριστόν as if it were synonymous with ποτίζεσθαι
ἐν πνεῦμα; that is, as the reception of the Spirit.[98] But, as
we argued earlier, the "pouring out" of the Spirit is presented
in 1 Cor 12:13 as *preceding* baptism, providing the candidate
for baptism with the constitutive power of incorporation into
the body of Christ.[99] In other words, 1 Cor 12:13 does not
equate the "pouring out" of the Spirit with baptism. If Gal
3:27 has a parallel in 1 Cor 12:13, it is βαπτίζεσθαι εἰς ἓν
σῶμα (= εἰς Χριστόν). That the baptizand participates in the
existence of Christ, and all that that existence implies,[100] is
expressed with various phrases: εἶναι ἐν Χριστῷ (Gal 3:26),[101]
βαπτίζεσθαι εἰς Χριστόν (Gal 3:27 and 1 Cor 12:13), ἐνδύεσθαι
Χριστόν (Gal 3:27), εἶναι Χριστοῦ (Gal 3:29, 5:24, and Rom 8:9),
and μορφοῦσθαι Χριστὸς ἐν ὑμῖν (Gal 4:19).

It is significant, however, that Paul does not refer to
baptism elsewhere in the letter to the Galatians; and that here
he uses, from earlier tradition, the concept of "putting on
Christ," and not the reception of the Spirit. From the εἶναι
ἐν Χριστῷ in Gal 3:26 and the εἶναι Χριστοῦ in 3:29, we may
conclude that it is Paul's intention to relate the sonship of
Christians to the sonship of Christ by interpreting baptism as
a means of "belonging" to Christ. When Paul appeals in 4:6 to
the Abba-cry of the Spirit as proof of the sonship of the Galatian Christians, Paul is not simply *repeating* the proof from
baptism,[102] but introducing *another* proof, to which he had
already referred in 3:1-5, 14.

Conclusion. This examination of the relationship between
the Spirit and baptism confirms what we found in the NT outside
Paul's letters: The imparting of the Spirit is not necessarily
attributed to baptism.[103] For Paul, the Spirit is a power
which makes baptism effective; but it is bestowed on the believer *before* baptism.[104] Its Sitz im Leben is in Paul's missionary preaching.[105]

Section 3. The Spirit and the Abba-Cry

Gal 4:6. The picture this gives of the experience of the
Spirit in the Galatian churches is perhaps similar to that of
Acts 10:44-45--Paul's proclamation was accompanied by ecstatic
experiences among his converts. Paul refers to one such experience of the ecstatic Spirit in the Galatian churches when he
appeals to the Abba-cry as evidence that the Galatians were
"sons" and "heirs" in 4:1-7.[106] This is the same experience
Paul refers to in 3:1-5. In 4:6, however, three things indicate that this experience of the Spirit by the Galatian Christians on the occasion of proclamation was ecstatic or "enthusiastic" in character:[107] (1) ἐξαπέστειλεν ὁ θεὸς τὸ πνεῦμα τοῦ
υἱοῦ εἰς τὰς καρδίας ἡμῶν; (2) τὸ πνεῦμα...κρᾶζον; and (3)
ἀββά.[108]

(1) When the Spirit enters the "heart,"[109] it enters the
seat of the "impulses" or "passions,"[110] and the "will" or
"intentionality."[111] The heart is also associated with νοῦς
and its cognates;[112] and it can stand in place of the personal
pronoun.[113] This means that the Spirit engages the believer at
the center of his or her existence. Those whose center of
existence is in the Spirit are called πνευματικοί (6:1). Similarly, a person's "center" can be so dominated by Christ that
his or her identity is defined by the Christ-genitive: οἱ τοῦ
Χριστοῦ Ἰησοῦ (3:29 and 5:24). Occasionally experiences occur
in which activities formerly attributed to a person's "center"
are attributed to the Spirit.[114] This is the case in the Abba-
cry. The fact that it is the Spirit itself who utters the
"loud cry" makes this evident.

(2) The "ecstatic" character of the Abba-cry is indicated
by the fact that it is the Spirit who is the subject of the

κράζον. There is no involvement of the "ego," except as an "onlooker."[115] This is also indicated by the verb κράζω. Of course this verb can have the sense of κηρύσσω.[116] But it also introduces the cries of demoniacs.[117] More important is the use of κράζω to introduce an "acclamation," a "cry of affirmation, of astonishment and confession" elicited by a "wonder seen with one's eyes."[118] All of these uses of κράζω refer to inspired utterances; but the latter two suggest that κράζω is used in reference to ecstatic cries.[119]

(3) Finally, "ecstasy" is suggested by the fact that the Spirit utters a foreign word, ἀββά.[120] If we set aside for the moment the question about the tradition-history of the Abba-cry, and consider the ecstatic cry phenomenologically, nothing precludes the possibility that the content of the ecstatic utterance might be traditional.[121] It is possible to learn foreign words either by association, observation, or instruction, and still utter them in a moment of ecstasy as long as the utterance is spontaneous.[122] In fact, *hosannah*, *hallelujah*, *amen* and *maranatha* are examples of just such phenomena, which are attested in early Christianity and have survived to this day.[123]

The question is whether the "liturgical" setting and tradition-history of the Abba-cry can be determined. One suggestion is that ἀββά was not an isolated ecstatic cry but rather the beginning of the Lord's Prayer.[124] This suggestion is based on the presupposition that the Lord's Prayer stems from an Aramaic original attributed to Jesus.[125] But this presupposition is yet to be convincingly demonstrated; for everything in the Lord's Prayer can be found in Judaism. At most, one can say that Jesus might be responsible for drawing these petitions together; but at the same time, so could the early church, either from Judaism or from traditions of Jesus' sayings.[126] Although the Lord's Prayer is handed down in two forms and only in Matt 6:9-13, Luke 11:2-4 and *Did.* 8:2, the Lord's Prayer, whatever its origin, had a wide circulation in early Christianity. That Paul does not hand down a version of the Lord's Prayer may prove only that he does not hand on everything he knows. It cannot, therefore, be proved either way, whether by means of ἀββά ὁ πατήρ Paul refers to the Lord's Prayer.

Another setting would be suggested if we assume that when
Paul argues in 4:1-7 that Gentile believers in Galatia were
"sons" and "heirs" already without "works of the law" and appeals to the Spirit's Abba-cry as proof, he does not tell his
readers something *new*, but something they *already know*, of
which they only needed to be *reminded*. The Abba-cry would then
be a spontaneous response to the proclamation of the crucified
Christ, through whom God received believers into sonship.[127]
When Paul reminds his readers of something they already know,
however, he usually introduces his "reminder" with a phrase
like ἃ προλέγω ὑμῖν καθὼς προεῖπον in 5:21, or with a phrase
using οἶδα, which Paul uses only in 2:16 (εἰδότες δέ) and 4:13
(αὐτοὶ γὰρ οἴδατε).[128] So, although the same function might be
served by the sarcastic Ὦ ἀνόητοι Γαλάται (3:1), which perhaps
stands over the whole letter,[129] Paul probably is telling his
readers something *new*, at least in part, in 4:1-7; namely, that
the Abba-cry is proof from the Spirit that they were "sons"
even while they remained Gentile believers.

Apart from the Abba-cry, the reference to God as "Father"
is not associated with expressions of a self-understanding as
"sons." Other instances of the designation of God as "Father"
express an understanding of God as the source of "grace and
peace,"[130] the one who is worthy of being worshipped,[131] the
"Father" of Jesus Christ and the agent of his resurrection.[132]
On the other hand, the sonship of believers is associated only
with the Spirit's Abba-cry,[133] or being "in Christ."[134]

The association of the sonship of believers with the
Spirit's Abba-cry is a secondary development. This association
is the result of Paul's self-defense against nomism in the
letter to the Galatians, which he repeats in his letter to the
Romans. Paul seized upon the Spirit's Abba-cry as the highest
evidence that Gentile believers were "sons" already without
"works of the law." According to an earlier tradition, believers were made "sons of God" by becoming "in Christ."[135]
By drawing on another earlier tradition in 4:1-7, Paul argues
that this was true for both Jewish and Gentile believers.[136]
Gentile believers in Galatia may have heard Paul preach that
they became "sons" when they took up an existence "in Christ,"

but they apparently did not know that the Spirit's Abba-cry
provided them with the greatest proof of their sonship without
"works of the law." Before Paul's letter, the Spirit's Abba-
cry meant something else to them.[137]

What the Abba-cry meant to the Galatians can be learned
from the pre-Pauline formulae in which God is designated as
"Father." For one thing, it meant a renunciation of all "gods"
other than the "father" of the Lord Jesus Christ,[138] just as
faith meant a renunciation of all "lords" other than Jesus
Christ.[139] Perhaps it was an involuntary response to the proclamation of the crucified Christ,[140] as the bearer of the grace
and peace,[141] the mercy and comfort,[142] or, simply, the love of
God.[143] The Abba-cry would then be a spontaneous cry of exultation at the time of conversion from "slavery to beings which
by nature are no gods" to a true "knowledge of God."[144]

Conclusion. Paul's converts experienced the Spirit's
Abba-cry in response to Christian proclamation. The Abba-cry
was not only an experience of the Spirit; as such it was an
ecstatic experience. We might say that in the Abba-cry, Paul's
converts were overwhelmed by the message of the God and "Father"
of the crucified Christ, whom Paul had proclaimed as their only
"Father" and Lord.[145] It was Paul who, in his defense of the
sonship of his converts in Galatia, and in his own defense,
drew the inference from the Abba-cry of the Spirit that the
Spirit attested to the sonship of Gentile believers. Thus,
finally, it is proclamation, not baptism, which was the Sitz im
Leben of the Spirit's Abba-cry. It was in such ecstatic experiences on the occasion of hearing Christian proclamation that
the Spirit manifested itself in concrete settings in the
churches of Galatia.

Section 4. The Spirit and ΔΥΝΑΜΕΙΣ

In Gal 3:5, Paul implicitly expresses his confidence that
Christian proclamation continued to produce an outpouring of
the Spirit after his departure; and that this produced outward
manifestations of the Spirit in the Galatian churches.[146] This
confidence, that ecstatic phenomena were an ongoing part of the

life of the Galatian churches, is striking in light of the
later controversies over such phenomena. On the one hand, Paul
was not in the least troubled by their occurrence, for they had
not destroyed the Galatian communities as they had the community in Corinth; and they have not been turned against Paul's
apostolic mission. On the contrary, Paul effectively uses them
in his self-defense.[147] On the other hand, as he would do
later in the Corinthian correspondence, Paul already establishes
that these ecstatic phenomena were due to acts of God, rather
than meritorious human deeds; but this was not yet at issue.[148]

This verse makes explicit what is implicit elsewhere in
the letter to the Galatians: The inaugural possession of the
Spirit was always accompanied by ecstatic phenomena. This is
expressed in Paul's use of the formula: ὁ οὖν ἐπιχορηγῶν ὑμῖν
τὸ πνεῦμα καὶ ἐνεργῶν δυνάμεις ἐν ὑμῖν. The δυνάμεις comprise
a well-known class of ecstatic phenomena, any number of which
could be assumed to have accompanied the outpouring of the
Spirit. Paul does not specify which ecstatic phenomena were
known in the Galatian churches; he did not need to, because
they were not at issue. We do know of one ecstatic phenomenon
from 4:6, namely, the Abba-cry. Others could have been prophecy and glossolalia, and their "interpretations."

This suggestion comes from first relating the δυνάμεις of
Gal 3:5 with the ἐνεργήματα δυνάμεων of 1 Cor 12:10a, and then
the latter to the προφητεία, διακρίσεις πνευμάτων, γένη γλωσσῶν
and ἑρμενεία γλωσσῶν of 1 Cor 12:10b. Traditionally the list
in 1 Cor 12:8-10 is divided so that ἐνεργήματα δυνάμεων is
placed at the end of the second group consisting of 12:9-10a.
This presupposes three groups as follows: (1) 12:8, (2) 12:9-
10a, and (3) 12:10b.[149] If indeed there are to be any distinc-
tions between groups of "gifts," however, 12:10 should be taken
as a whole to form one group, as a comparison of the structures
of 12:8 and 12:9, on the one hand, and 12:10, on the other,
shows. 1 Cor 12:8 and 12:9 each consists of a two-member
parallelism distinguished from 12:10 in that each member mentions the Spirit; while 12:10 consists of a five-member series
connected by ἄλλῳ (δέ).

(1) 12:8 = ᾧ μὲν γὰρ διὰ τοῦ πνεύματος...ἄλλῳ δὲ...κατὰ
τὸ αὐτὸ πνεῦμα

(2) 12:9 = ἑτέρῳ...ἐν τῷ αὐτῷ πνεύματι, ἄλλῳ δὲ...ἐν τῷ
ἑνὶ πνεύματι

(3) 12:10 = ἄλλῳ δὲ...ἄλλῳ [δὲ]...ἄλλῳ δὲ...ἑτέρῳ...
ἄλλῳ δὲ...

If any significance is to be attached to the ἑτέρῳ in the third
and eighth positions,[150] it is that, in the first set, the
second pair (πίστις / χαρίσματα ἰαμάτων) is distinguished from
the preceding pair (λόγος σοφίας / λόγος γνώσεως); and, in the
second group, the final two (γένη γλωσσῶν / ἑρμενεία γλωσσῶν)
are distinguished from the preceding three (ἐνεργήματα
δυνάμεων / προφητεία / διακρίσεις πνευμάτων). This suggests a
pattern of a, b, c, a', b'; for Paul subordinates in value
those χαρίσματα in the third, fourth, eighth and ninth positions (πίστις / χαρίσματα ἰαμάτων / γένη γλωσσῶν / ἑρμενεία
γλωσσῶν). Therefore, 12:10a seems to introduce the second set
of pairs constructed parallel to each other. Hence we have the
following pattern.

(1)	12:8	a.1.	λόγος σοφίας	(ᾧ μὲν γὰρ)
		2.	λόγος γνώσεως	(ἄλλῳ δὲ)
	12:9	b.1.	πίστις	(ἑτέρῳ)
		2.	χαρίσματα ἰαμάτων	(ἄλλῳ δὲ)
(2)	12:10a	c.	ἐνεργήματα δυνάμεων	(ἄλλῳ δὲ)
	12:10b	a'.1.	προφητεία	(ἄλλῳ [δὲ])
		2.	διακρίσεις πνευμάτων	(ἄλλῳ δὲ)
		b'.1.	γένη γλωσσῶν	(ἑτέρῳ)
		2.	ἑρμενεία γλωσσῶν	(ἄλλῳ δὲ)

As such, 12:10a presents a general class of ecstatic phenomena,
which are distinguished in the following two pairs of χαρίσματα.
It is to these that Gal 3:5 (ἐνεργῶν δυνάμεις) refers.[151] Certainly these were associated with the occasion of worship, which
was the Sitz im Leben for the δυνάμεις, as the ἐξ ἀκοῆς πίστεως
indicates.[152] In other words, ecstatic phenomena continued to
accompany the outpouring of the Spirit on the occasion of proclamation in the churches of Galatia after Paul's departure.

Conclusion

The thesis of this chapter is that the inaugural possession of the Spirit in the Galatian churches was an ecstatic
experience at the time of conversion to Christian faith by
Christian proclamation. In Galatians, Paul does not say that
baptism was the means by which the Spirit was imparted to believers in Galatia, nor even that baptism was the Sitz im Leben
in which it was received; rather, he traces receiving the
Spirit in Galatia to the proclamation of the crucified Christ
as its occasion (or setting), and preaching and faith as its
means. What is more, Paul's references to the Galatians' experiences of the Spirit show that these were ecstatic experiences in the form of the Abba-cry and probably other forms of
ecstatic speech, such as glossolalia and prophecy.

This view of the beginnings of Christianity in Galatia is
more adequate to the texts than that which presupposes a close
connection between baptism and the Spirit existed in the Galatian churches. Dunn, for example, leaps from the statements
that "in the beginning, no Christian was unbaptized," and that
"no Christian was without the Spirit,"[153] to the conclusion
that the believer "reaches out in faith to receive" the Spirit
by means of baptism.[154] In this formulation, Dunn does avoid
two views which he rejects: on the one hand, the usual Protestant view, which makes the gift of the Spirit depend solely on
believing Christian proclamation,[155] and on the other, the
"Pentecostal" view, which makes the gift of the Spirit a distinct event temporally after and even antithetical to so-called
"water-baptism."[156] Actually he succeeds only partially in
avoiding the "Pentecostal" view, just as he only partially
succeeds in avoiding the third view rejected in his book,
namely, "sacramentalism," according to which the gift of the
Spirit is actually imparted by the performance of the rite of
baptism apart from any act of faith on the part of the recipient.[157] For Dunn, the means by which in faith the believer
"reaches out for" the gift of the Spirit is baptism.[158]   In
this way, Dunn maintains a close relationship between baptism
and the gift of the Spirit, which "Pentecostals" deny; but in

so doing he falls into "sacramentalism" with respect to the
gift of the Spirit. On the other hand, he falls into the
"Pentecostal" view insofar as, in order to reject the "sacramentalist's" doctrine of salvation by the performance of the
rite of baptism, he makes the gift of the Spirit "distinct and
even antithetical" to baptism;[159] for the Spirit, which is received by faith in baptism, is the means of salvation.[160]

Unless this view is inherently confused, it depends on a
distinction, on the one hand, between the means of *salvation*,
which is the Spirit, and the means of *receiving the Spirit*,
which is faith expressed in baptism; and the distinction, on
the other hand, between the *occasion* of receiving the Spirit,
which is baptism, and the *means* of receiving the Spirit, which
is faith--at least this seems to be implied in Dunn's view. In
such a manner Dunn could then affirm with "Pentecostals" that
salvation is neither by faith alone (against the usual Protestant view), nor by baptism (against the "sacramentalist" view),
but by the Spirit received in faith expressed in baptism. But,
against the "Pentecostals," he could also affirm a close connection between baptism and receiving the gift of the Spirit.

It is the latter, however, which this chapter challenges.
For in Galatians Paul does not expressly connect the gift of
the Spirit with baptism. The close connection between them,
which Dunn presupposes, is avoided, intentionally or acci-
dentally, by Paul in the letter to the Galatians. While Paul
does not indicate the setting of the Abba-cry in 4:6, he does
refer to the setting of the initial gift of the Spirit and the
ongoing manifestations of the Spirit in 3:1-5; namely, the
proclamation of the crucified Christ, which elicits faith. And
in the only reference to baptism in the letter to the Galatians, 3:27, Paul fails to mention the Spirit. In Galatians,
therefore, no basis exists for maintaining a close connection
between baptism and the gift of the Spirit.

But neither does 3:27 make it possible simply to dismiss
baptism as having no causal efficacy as far as salvation is
concerned. The causal factors in salvation, according to
Galatians, are many and complex: for they include baptism
(3:27), proclamation (3:1-5), and faith (3:2, 5, 14), as well

as God's acts of "sending" Christ and the Spirit (3:5, 4:6, 29).
But the question about the social setting of receiving the
Spirit is another question. The Spirit, as an agent of salvation, is clearly closely connected in Galatians with proclamation, faith and God's act of "sending," but it is not closely
associated with baptism.

This means conversion to Christianity in Galatia is por-
trayed by Paul as an ecstatic experience of the Spirit. This
experience was part of a whole new "social world," of which
baptism was also a part, but a different part. Other aspects
of the new "social world" in which the Spirit was the center
are mentioned in the letter to the Galatians. Unfortunately,
they are mentioned only in the most general terms, rather than
in terms of specific details. Thus, for example, Paul refers
to the Galatians' emancipation from certain divisions of na-
tionalities, religions and social classes.[161] The letter, however, lacks any evidence which would give the slogan in 3:28 a
sense of political reality, since this could refer either to
the accomplished fact in the Galatian churches of the abolish-
ment of the institutional forms of these conventional divisions,
or to the "death" of these divisions as far as the Christians
in Galatia were concerned.[162] Paul also refers to the Galatians' conversion from "superstition" to "enlightened religion";[163] but Paul describes this change in terms of rhetorical *topoi*,[164] from which we cannot draw specific sociological
conclusions. Finally, Paul also refers to acts of love among
the Galatians, which were the basis of their community and
which flowed from the Spirit in them.[165] Love was not merely
a utopian ideal, nor merely an ethical demand, but a reality
in the Galatian communities, which Paul reminds them to continue. Again, evidence of specific social realities is meagre,
with the exception of 6:1, which is a recommendation about
dealing with "transgressions," and 6:6, which indicates some
system of communal support at least for the Galatian "educa-
tors."[166] Even if we do not know the precise details of life
in the Galatian communities, these references do indicate that
the ecstatic experiences of the Spirit, with which Christianity
began in Galatia, were part of a larger "social world" whose
origin and center was the proclamation of the crucified Christ.

NOTES

CHAPTER III

[1]For a discussion of the "social world" of which the
Spirit was a part in the Galatian churches, see below, p. 74.

[2]Typical is Schlier's commentary (*Brief an die Galater*)
and Dunn's *Baptism*. For a discussion of the latter, see below,
pp. 72-73.

[3]For discussions of these texts, see below, Section 1,
pp. 54-59 (3:1-5 = pp. 54-57; 1 Thess 1:4-6 = pp. 57-58; 1 Cor
2:4-5 = pp. 58-59).

[4]Cf. below, Section 2, pp. 59-66 (1 Cor 12:13 = pp. 61-62;
1 Cor 6:11 = p. 62; 2 Cor 1:15-24 = pp. 62-64; Rom 5:5 = pp.
64-65; Gal 3:27 = p. 65).

[5]Cf. below, Section 3, pp. 66-69.

[6]Cf. below, Section 4, pp. 69-71.

[7]Discussions of these points may be found below as follows: (1) = p. 55; (2) = p. 55; (3) = pp. 55-56; and (4) =
pp. 56-57.

[8]In his commentary, Betz points out that δις κατ' ὀφθαλμοὺς κτλ. is a rhetorical *topos*, "a case of self-ironic exag-
geration," which reminds the Galatians of Paul's original proclamation (*Commentary on Paul's Letter*, ad loc, n. 36; cf. also
n. 39 for προγράφω in a rhetorical context). It is similar to
2 Cor 10:7a and 12:6c in that it appeals to Paul's audience as
"eyewitnesses."

[9]Cf. Gal 3:14, and 1 Cor 2:12, 2 Cor 11:4, Rom 8:15.

[10]Cf. 1 Cor 11:23, which refers to the handing on of the
Lord's Supper tradition (cf. παραλαμβάνω used in the same sense
in 2 Thess 3:6 and Mark 7:4). Cf. 1 Thess 4:1, which refers to
parenesis accepted by the Thessalonians; as well as Gal 1:9
and Phil 4:9. The synonym δέχομαι is used in 2 Cor 11:4 and
1 Thess 1:6 and 2:13 (which also has παραλαμβάνω). Cf. also
Acts 8:14, 11:1 and 17:11. The combination λαμβάνω / ἀκούω
occurs in Gal 3:2 and 1 Thess 2:13; Phil 4:9 (cf. also Mark
4:16, 20, pars.; and John 12:47-48). Τὸν λόγον παραλαβεῖν /
δέχεσθαι is a technical phrase for the reception of missionary
preaching (cf. BAG, "παραλαμβάνω," 2, b, γ; BAG, "δέχομαι," 3, b;
Walter Grundmann, *TDNT* 2.52, 54). For a discussion of missionary terminology, see Joachim Jeremias, *The Parables of Jesus*
(2nd rev. ed.; trans. S. H. Hooke; New York: Scribner's, 1972)
77-78. Cf. now also Betz (*Commentary on Paul's Letter*, ad loc.,
n. 50) who also refers to 1 Thess 2:13, Rom 10:16-17, Heb 4:12
and John 12:38.

[11]Cf. 1 Cor 2:4 (ὁ λόγος μου καὶ τὸ κήρυγμα μου...ἐν ἀποδείξει πνεύματος καὶ δυνάμεως) and 2 Cor 11:4 (...ὁ ἐρχόμενος ἄλλον Ἰησοῦν κηρύσσει...ἤ πνεῦμα ἔτερον λαμβάνετε...ἤ εὐαγγέλιον ἔτερον ὃ οὐκ ἐδέξασθε...).

[12]Cf. 2:3, 11-14, 16, 5:2-6, 11, 6:12-13, 15.

[13]Cf. προγράφω in 3:1; ἐνάρχομαι and ἐπιτελέω in 3:3; and μανθάνω / πάσχω in 3:2, 4 (cf. Betz, "Spirit, Freedom, and Law," 147 nn. 6-7; and idem, Commentary on Paul's Letter, ad loc., n. 45). But see below, Chapter IV, p. 135 n. 7.

[14]The act of hearing, or that which is heard.

[15]Fides qua creditur, or fides quae creditur.

[16]It can be either objective or subjective.

[17]The ἀκοῆς here is a synonym for κηρύγματος; πίστεως denotes the content of the proclamation (fides quae creditur); and the genitive is objective, or epexegetical. Although few commentators are sufficiently exact in their language and complete enough in their explanations to know for sure which interpretation they consider correct, the following seem to accept this interpretation: Ernst von Dobschütz, Die Thessalonicher-Briefe (MeyerK 10; 7th ed.; Göttingen: Vandenhoeck & Ruprecht, 1909) 104; Hans Lietzmann, An die Galater (HNT 10; 4th ed.; Tübingen: Mohr/Siebeck, 1971) 18; Albrecht Oepke, Der Brief des Paulus an die Galater (THKNT 9; 2nd ed.; Berlin: Evangelische Verlagsanstalt, 1957) 68; Ernest Best, A Commentary on the First and Second Epistles to the Thessalonians (HNTC; New York: Harper and Row, 1972) 111 (perhaps); Johannes S. Vos, Traditionsgeschichtliche Untersuchungen zur paulinischen Pneumatologie (Assen: Van Gorcum, 1973) 88 (but on p. 86 he suggests that the Spirit comes from either faith as fides qua creditur, or baptism); and now also Betz, Commentary on Paul's Letter, ad loc. Also included are Charles J. Ellicott (A Critical and Grammatical Commentary on St. Paul's Epistle to the Galatians [Andover: Warren F. Draper, 1884] 66) and G. Kittel (TDNT 1.221), whose statements are characteristically vague. Ellicott says: "the preaching which is related to, had as its subject πίστις." And Kittel, "proclamation, which has faith as its content and goal." Finally, note that the NEB, in a footnote, offers the alternative: "the message of faith."

[18]Ex auditu fidei. Here ἀκοῆς denotes the act of hearing; πίστεως denotes the act of faith; and the genitive is subjective (cf. Burton, Syntax, 147; Lightfoot, The Epistle of St. Paul, 135; Marie J. Lagrange, Saint Paul épître aux Galates [Paris: Gabalda, 1950] 59; and the RSV ["hearing with faith"]). Dunn seems to accept this interpretation (cf. Jesus and the Spirit, 417 n. 135, 439 n. 186); but in his earlier book, in support of (d), he said, "the Spirit is received by the exercise of the faith which the message of Christ stirs up" (cf. Baptism, 108; cf. also Jesus and the Spirit, 108). The JB

("believed what was preached") and *NEB* ("believing the gospel message") seem to reflect the judgment that ἀκοὴ πίστεως = πίστις ἀκοῆς. So also Sanders (*Paul*, 482-83), who prefers "believing what was heard," rather than "hearing about faith" (opposed to "doing the law"), or "faithful hearing" (opposed to "legalistic works").

[19]The genitive here is indirectly objective (cf. C. F. D. Moule, *An Idiom Book of New Testament Greek* [Cambridge: The University Press, 1953] 175).

[20]Here ἀκοῆς denotes the act and message of proclamation; πίστεως = *fides qua creditur*; and the genitive is indirectly objective (cf. H. A. W. Meyer, *Critical and Exegetical Hand-Book to the Epistle to the Galatians* [trans. G. H. Venables and Henry E. Jacobs; New York: Funk & Wagnalls, 1884] 104-105; R. A. Lipsius, *Briefe an die Galater, Römer, Philipper* [HKNT; 2nd ed.; Freiburg: Mohr/Siebeck, 1892] 2/2.35; BAG, "ἀκοή," 2, b; Schlier, *Brief an die Galater*, 122 ["aus der Offenbarung, die den Glauben entzündet"]; Pierre Bonnard, *L'Epître de Saint Paul aux Galates* [CNT 9; 2nd ed.; Neuchâtel: Delachaux et Niestle, 1972] 62-63; R. Bultmann, *TDNT* 6.213 ["the preaching which demands...or...opens up the possibility of faith"]; idem, *Theology*, 1.329-30; and Dunn, *Baptism*, 108 [cf. also *Jesus*, 108]).

[21]Cf. 3:1.

[22]Cf. 2:16, 20, 3:6-9, 11-12, 14 (cf. also 3:22-26, 5:5, 6).

[23]The latter is supported by 1:23; for the former, see above, n. 22. This favors (a) and (d) above.

[24]In his commentary, Betz remarks that "it remains unclear how baptism is related to this experience"; and in a note he adds, "perhaps Paul hesitated to say simply that the Spirit is 'mediated' through baptism" because of reservations Paul had regarding baptism (*Commentary on Paul's Letter*, on 3:2, and n. 48).

[25]Cf. Bonnard, *Saint Paul aux Galates*, 62-63.

[26]Cf. Ellicott (*Paul's Epistle to the Galatians*, 68) and Dunn (*Baptism*, 108) who prefer to take ἐκ in an instrumental sense, indicating the "originating or moving cause" (cf. διὰ πίστεως in 3:14).

[27]Cf. Meyer, *Epistle to the Galatians*, 105 ("proceeded from"); and above, n. 26.

[28]Cf. Ernest de Witt Burton, *A Critical and Exegetical Commentary on the Epistle to the Galatians* (ICC 35; Edinburgh: T. & T. Clark, 1921) 147 ("on ground of"); Schlier, *Brief an die Galater*, 122 ("aus dem Grund"); Lagrange, *Epître aux Galates*, 59 ("par suite"); BAG, "ἐκ," 3, f; also "ἀκοή," 2, b ("as the result of"); and Vos, *Traditionsgeschichtliche Untersuchungen*, 88.

[29]Kurt Stalder (*Das Werk des Geistes in der Heiligung bei Paulus* [Zürich: EVZ-Verlag, 1962] 80) argues that neither faith nor proclamation is the means by which the Spirit is received; rather, it is the Spirit itself that creates the condition and presupposition for the knowledge of the Spirit (Stalder appeals to Barth's comments on 1 Cor 12:13 in *Auferstehung der Toten*). Gerhard Delling (*TDNT* 4.7) argues in a similar vein, that Paul's view is that no one can lay the groundwork for the reception of the Spirit. Since no evidence exists in the text that ἐκ is not used in a causal sense, and that the active sense of λαμβάνω is entirely lacking in ἐλάβετε, this argument can only be based on the assumption that divine and nondivine causes are not possible in the same event--and that Paul shares this assumption. No matter how much merit such an assumption *might* have, it should not be attributed to Paul, for this text suggests that Paul *does* consider his proclamation and his converts' faith, together with God (cf. 3:5 and 4:6), as causal factors in their reception of the Spirit.

[30]Nevertheless, see προευηγγελίσατο in 3:8 (cf. below, Chapter V, p. 166 n. 59).

[31]Cf. 2:19-21 and 3:1; also see 4:14 and 6:17.

[32]Cf. 4:6.

[33]Cf. below, pp. 57-58 and 58-59, respectively.

[34]Cf. 1:6 and 2:13-14. Cf. also H. D. Betz, *Nachfolge und Nachahmung Jesu Christi im Neuen Testament* (BHT 37; Tübingen: Mohr/Siebeck, 1967) 143; Robert C. Tannehill, *Dying and Rising with Christ: A Study in Pauline Theology* (BZNW 32; Berlin: A. Töpelmann, 1967) 102-103; and Charles J. Ellicott, *A Critical and Grammatical Commentary on St. Paul's Epistles to the Thessalonians* (2nd ed.; Andover: W. Draper; Boston: W. Halliday; Philadelphia: Smith, English, 1872) 25; Gottlieb Lünemann, *Critical and Exegetical Hand-Book to the Epistles to the Thessalonians* (trans. Paton Gloag; New York: Funk & Wagnalls, 1885) 453; Dobschütz, *Thessalonicher-Briefe*, 73; James E. Frame, *A Critical and Exegetical Commentary on the Epistles to the Thessalonians* (ICC 38; Edinburgh: T. & T. Clark, 1912) 82-83; Martin Dibelius, *An die Thessalonicher I-II, An die Philipper* (HNT 11; 2nd ed.; Tübingen: Mohr/Siebeck, 1925) 5; and Best, *First and Second Epistles to the Thessalonians*, 77.

[35]Cf. 4:12 for "imitation," and 1:13, 23, 2:12, 4:29, 5:11, 6:12 for "persecution and suffering." In Gal 3:4, τοσαῦτα ἐπάθετε εἰκῆ can only refer to the immediately preceding τὸ πνεῦμα ἐλάβετε...ἐξ ἀκοῆς πίστεως and ἐναρξάμενοι πνεύματι, and not to "suffering persecution"; ἐπάθετε, therefore, means "experience" (cf. also Betz, *Commentary on Paul's Letter*, ad loc.).

[36]Cf. 1 Thess 1:5, 2:2, and Acts 4:31, which all, however, refer to preachers rather than to their audiences.

[37]Cf. 1 Thess 1:5.

[38]Cf. the discussion of 3:5 below, pp. 69-71 (cf. also 2 Cor 13:3-9).

[39]For this sense of the contrast between πειθοί σοφίας λόγοι and ἀπόδειξις, see the following quote from Hero of Alexandria's *Pneumatica*, I, 16.16-26 (Teubner 1.16): ...τοῖς οὖν φαμένοις τὸ καθόλου μηδὲν εἶναι κενὸν ἐκποιεῖ πρὸς ταῦτα πολλὰ εὑρίσκειν ἐπιχειρήματα καὶ τάχα φαίνεσθαι τῷ λόγῳ πιθανωτέρους μηδεμιᾶς παρακειμένης αἰσθητικῆς ἀποδείξεως· ἐὰν μέντοι δειχθῇ ἐπὶ τῶν φαινομένων καὶ ὑπὸ τὴν αἴσθησιν πιπτόντων, ὅτι (...), καὶ (...), καὶ ὅτι (...), οὐδεμίαν οὐκέτι παρείσδυσιν ἕξουσιν οἱ τοὺς πιθανοὺς τῶν λόγων περὶ τούτων προφερόμενοι.

> Those then who assert generally that there is no vacuum
> are satisfied with inventing many arguments for this
> and perhaps seeming plausible with their theory in the
> absence of sensible proof. If, however, by referring
> to the appearances and to what is accessible to sensa-
> tion, it is shown that (...) that (...) and that (...)
> then those who put forward plausible arguments on
> these matters will no longer have any loophole.

For the English translation, see G. E. R. Lloyd, *Greek Science After Aristotle* (New York: W. W. Norton, 1973) 17.

[40]Cf. the references cited by Hans Conzelmann, *A Commentary on the First Epistle to the Corinthians* (trans. J. W. Leitch; ed. G. W. MacRae; Philadelphia: Fortress, 1975) 55 n. 26.

[41]Cf. 1 Corinthians 12-14 and Gal 3:5; and below, pp. 69-71.

[42]These texts appear to allude to discussions about the proper effects of preaching on the audience, which Paul uses in apologetic contexts. For example, see Arrian's letter to Lucius Gallus in Epictetus, *Diss.* 5-8 (LCL 1.6); Musonius Rufus, *Fr.* 49 (Cora E. Lutz, *Musonius Rufus. "The Roman Socrates"* [Yale Classical Studies 10; New Haven, CT: Yale University, 1947] 142); and Plutarch, *Mor.*, 776C (LCL 10.30). I have not found, however, any texts which use πνεῦμα in this context.

[43]The phrase is Oepke's (*TDNT* 1.543). Cf. John A. T. Robinson, *The Body. A Study in Pauline Theology* (SBT 5; London: SCM, 1952) 79; Oscar Cullmann, *Baptism in the New Testament* (SBT 1; London: SCM, 1950) 41; Rudolf Bultmann, "The Problem of Ethics in the Writings of Paul," pp. 7-31 in *The Old and New Man in the Letters of Paul* (trans. Keith Crim; Richmond, VA: John Knox, 1967) 21; idem, "Paul," pp. 111-46 and 307 in *Existence and Faith: Shorter Writings of Rudolf Bultmann* (trans. Schubert Ogden; Cleveland; New York: World, 1960) 142, 144; idem, *Theology*, 1.138-39, 157, 311; Schweizer, *TDNT* 6.413-14; Lohse, *TDNT* 9.432 n. 50. Additional scholars who hold this view are cited in Dunn (*Baptism*, 98 n. 17).

[44]Cf. Mark 1:10, pars., and John 1:32.

[45]Cf. Mark 1:8, pars., John 1:33, Acts 1:5, 18:25, and 19:1-7.

[46]Cf. John 3:3-8 and Tit 3:3-5.

[47]Cf. Schweizer, *TDNT* 6.414. Cf. also Haenchen (*Acts of the Apostles*, 184) where he comments on 2:38 that by the time of Luke the Spirit was not bound to any outward sign, "if it ever had been," which explains why not everyone received the ecstatic Spirit at baptism.

[48]Bultmann, *Theology*, 1.139.

[49]Cf. Acts 8:15-17 and 19:5-6.

[50]Cf. Schweizer, *TDNT* 6.426 n. 621. Cf. also Dunn, *Baptism*, 108 n. 14: "There are more aorist actions in conversion-initiation than baptism, and the one which matters for Paul, here at least, is the reception of the Spirit" (cf. p. 115, where he comments on 5:24-25). Cf. the discussion of λαμβάνω above, p. 55. On the other hand, L. S. Thornton's view, that the phrase ἐξ ἀκοῆς πίστεως "must refer to the catechetical instruction which preceded the sacrament and which led up to the baptismal confession of faith," depends on the aorist being a "baptismal aorist" (*Confirmation, Its Place in the Baptismal Mystery* [London: Dacre, A. & C. Black, 1954] 9-10).

[51]Cf., for example, 1 Cor 12:13.

[52]Cf. Schlier, *Brief an die Galater*, 123; Oepke, *Paulus an die Galater*, 67; idem, *TDNT* 1.543 n. 69; Thornton, *Confirmation*, 9-19; Rudolf Schnackenburg, *Baptism in the Thought of St. Paul: A Study in Pauline Theology* (trans. G. R. Beasley-Murray; New York: Herder and Herder, 1964) 163-65; Vos, *Traditionsgeschichtliche Untersuchungen*, 86 (whose thesis is that Paul uses baptismal traditions which speak of the Spirit); and T. M. Taylor, "'Abba, Father,' and Baptism," *SJT* 11 (1958) 62-71. Commenting on the parallel to Gal 4:6 in Rom 8:15, Otto Michel says: "Vielleicht haben wir es hier mit einem Teil des Taufgeschehens zu tun (v. 15: ἐλάβετε πνεῦμα)" (*Der Brief an die Römer* [MeyerK 4; 11th ed.; Göttingen: Vandenhoeck & Ruprecht, 1957] 169). This is a "baptismal context" for G. W. H. Lampe (*The Seal of the Spirit: A Study of the Doctrine of Baptism and Confirmation in the New Testament and the Fathers* [London: Longmans, Green, 1951] 55 n. 8). Gaugler asserts that the Christian receives the Spirit in baptism (*Der Römerbrief*, Part 1: *Kapitel 1-8*. Prophezei: Schweizerisches Bibelwerk für die Gemeinde [Zürich: Zwingli-Verlag, 1958; orig. 1945] 286).

[53]Cf. below, pp. 61-62 (1 Cor 12:13), 62 (1 Cor 6:11), 62-64 (2 Cor 1:15-24), 64-65 (Rom 5:5) and 65 (Gal 3:27).

[54]Cf. Schweizer, *TDNT* 6.418 n. 563.

[55]Cf. the ἐκάστῳ in 12:7, 11.

[56]The ἐν in ἐν ἐνὶ πνεύματι is instrumental, not local
(against A. Robertson and A. Plummer, *A Critical and Exegetical
Commentary on the First Epistle of St. Paul to the Corinthians*
[ICC 33; 2nd ed.; Edinburgh: T. & T. Clark, 1914] 272; and H.
Lietzmann and W. Kümmel, *An die Korinther I-II* [HNT 9; 4th ed.;
Tübingen: Mohr/Siebeck, 1949] 63), since its function is the
same as the phrase ἐν τῷ ὀνόματι, which introduces the power
that makes baptism effective (cf. Charles K. Barrett, *A Commentary on the First Epistle to the Corinthians* [HNTC; New York:
Harper & Row, 1968] 288; Friedrich Büchsel, *Theologie des
Neuen Testaments: Geschichte des Wortes Gottes im Neuen Testament* [2nd ed.; Gütersloh: C. Bertelsmann, 1937] 133; Schnackenburg, *Baptism*, 29, 83-84; and Schweizer, *TDNT* 6.418 n. 565). It
is difficult to see how βαπτίζειν ἐν could refer to a gift
imparted by or in baptism (against H. A. W. Meyer, *Critical and
Exegetical Hand-Book to the Epistles to the Corinthians* [trans.
D. Douglas Bannerman; rev. and ed. William P. Dickson; New
York: Funk & Wagnalls, 1884] 289; J. Weiss, *Der erste Korintherbrief* [MeyerK 5; 10th ed.; Göttingen: Vandenhoeck & Ruprecht,
1925] 303; P. Bachmann, *Der erste Brief des Paulus an die Korin-
ther* [Kommentar zum Neuen Testament 7; 4th ed.; Leipzig: Deichert,
1936] 384; J. Héring, *The First Epistle of Saint Paul to the
Corinthians* [trans. A. Heathcote and P. Allcock; London: Epworth, 1962] 130; H. Wendland, *Die Briefe an die Korinther*
[NTD 7; 10th ed.; Göttingen: Vandenhoeck & Ruprecht, 1964] 96;
O. Kuss, *Der Römerbrief*, 1st fasc.: *Röm. 1,1-6,11* [2nd ed.;
Regensburg: F. Pustet, 1963] 312; Oepke, *TDNT* 1.543 n. 69; and
Bultmann, *Theology*, 1.138, 157). In his commentary ("Analysis"
for Gal 3:26-28), Betz suggests that ἐν ἐνὶ πνεύματι, parallel
to διὰ τῆς πίστεως in Gal 3:26, may be Paul's "interpretative
addition" (cf. 12:4, 8, 9, 11).

[57]Cf. 12:13 and 12:27.

[58]Cf. the γάρ in 12:12, 13, 14, which introduces the
reason for the claim made in 12:11.

[59]Cf. Werner Kramer, *Christ, Lord, Son of God* (SBT 50;
London: SCM, 1966) sec. 15a, p. 65; and Dunn, *Baptism*, 151.
Cf. Phil 2:11, 2 Cor 4:5 and Rom 10:9. For the view that Rom
10:9 refers to a "baptismal" confession, see Bultmann, *Theology*,
1.312; C. Dodd, *The Epistle of Paul to the Romans* (MNTC 6; New
York: Harper, 1932) ad loc.; Michel, *Brief an die Römer*, ad
loc.; C. Barrett, *The Epistle to the Romans* (HNTC; New York:
Harper & Row, 1957) ad loc.; and E. Käsemann, *An die Römer*
(HNT 8a; 2nd ed.; Tübingen: Mohr/Siebeck, 1974) ad loc. But
must all such confessions be "baptismal"? In *The Cultic Setting of Realized Eschatology in Early Christianity* (NovTSup 28;
Leiden: Brill, 1972), David E. Aune remarks that "the restric-
tion of this confession to the rite of baptism is certainly not
correct" (p. 14 n. 2, on Phil 2:10-11 and 1 Cor 12:13).

[60]Cf. the note on the force of the preposition ἐν above, p. 81 n. 56.

[61]Cf. Rom 5:5.

[62]Cf. Gal 4:6 and 2 Cor 1:22.

[63]Against Meyer, *Epistles to the Corinthians*, 289; Robertson-Plummer, *First Epistle of St. Paul to the Corinthians*, 272; J. Weiss, *Der erste Korintherbrief*, 303; James Moffatt, *The First Epistle of Paul to the Corinthians* (MNTC 7; London: Hodder and Stoughton, 1938) 186; Héring, *First Epistle of Saint Paul to the Corinthians*, 130; Barrett, *First Epistle to the Corinthians*, 289; Kuss, *Der Römerbrief*, 312; Lampe, *The Seal of the Spirit*, 56; Schweizer, *TDNT* 6.418 n. 563; and Schnackenburg, *Baptism*, 84-85.

[64]Against Bachmann, *Paulus an die Korinther*, 384; Lietzmann-Kümmel, *An die Korinther*, 63 (but see Kümmel's note on p. 188); E.-B. Allo, *Saint Paul première épître aux Corinthiens* (2nd ed.; Paris: J. Gabalda, 1956) 329; Wendland, *Briefe an die Korinther*, 97; Conzelmann, *First Epistle to the Corinthians*, 212 n. 17; Gaugler, *Der Römerbrief*, 1.158.

[65]In this respect, Dunn (*Baptism*, 130) is correct; but he is wrong in thinking that Paul speaks only metaphorically of "water-baptism" (cf. pp. 127-31).

[66]Cf. on 1 Cor 2:4-5 above, pp. 58-59.

[67]The ἐν is instrumental (cf. Conzelmann, *First Epistle to the Corinthians*, 107 n. 46; Barrett, *First Epistle to the Corinthians*, 143; Oepke, *TDNT* 2.541; Schweizer, *TDNT* 6.418; and Dunn, *Baptism*, 121-22). Meyer states the vague notion that the Spirit begins its work at baptism (*Epistles to the Corinthians*, 134-35). Büchsel (*Theologie*, 133) seems to take the view that the Spirit can be said to be mediated by baptism only in the sense that baptism becomes effective through the Spirit: "Von der Taufe hat Paulus den Geist *nie ausdrücklich* abgeleitet, aber da er die Taufe *durch den Geist wirksam* denkt (1 Kor 6:11; 12:13), muss sie den Geist vermitteln" (emphasis added). Schnackenburg (*Baptism*, 5, 7-8, 164-65) understands the Spirit to be a causative power in baptism as well as a gift imparted by it. For the view that ἐν introduces the Spirit as a gift, see Lietzmann-Kümmel (*An die Korinther*, 27), Wendland (*Briefe an die Korinther*, 45) and Schrenk (*TDNT* 2.206).

[68]Cf. BAG, "δικαιόω," 3, c; and Sanders, *Paul*, 471.

[69]In the only other NT use of ἀπολούω, Acts 22:16, it is a virtual synonym for baptism. In Heb 10:22, λούω refers to ritual washings, perhaps to baptism (cf. BAG, "λούω," 2, b; but then see BAG, "βαπτισμός," on Heb 9:10). Without distinguishing between earlier tradition and Paul, the following find a

reference to baptism in 1 Cor 6:11: Meyer, *Epistles to the Corinthians*, 134-35; Robertson-Plummer, *First Epistle of St. Paul to the Corinthians*, 119; J. Weiss, *Der erste Korintherbrief*, 154; Bachmann, *Paulus an die Korinther*, 234; Moffatt, *First Epistle of Paul to the Corinthians*, 66; Lietzmann-Kümmel, *An die Korinther*, 27; Allo, *Première épître aux Corinthiens*, 138; Wendland, *Briefe an die Korinther*, 45; Conzelmann, *First Epistle to the Corinthians*, 107 n. 46; Barrett, *First Epistle to the Corinthians*, 141; Schnackenburg, *Baptism*, 3-4; Vos, *Traditionsgeschichtliche Untersuchungen*, 32, 77; Dunn, *Baptism*, 121-22; Otto Procksch, *TDNT* 1.112; Schweizer, *TDNT* 6.427 n. 626; Oepke, *TDNT* 4.303-304 and *TDNT* 1.540; Schrenk, *TDNT* 2.206; Leonhard Goppelt, *TDNT* 8.331; and Grundmann, *TDNT* 9.554.

[70]1 Cor 6:11 can say "sanctification" and "justification" are present realities, but 1 Thess 5:23 and Gal 5:5 say they are a future hope. In 1 Thess 5:23, 1 Cor 1:2 and Rom 15:16, the ἁγιάζειν is attributed to God, Christ and the Spirit respectively; but there is no thought of baptism. The verb δικαιοῦσθαι appears in Rom 6:7 in a baptismal context, but it has the sense of "being made free" rather than "being made pure" (cf. also Sanders, *Paul*, 472).

[71]This phrase seems more appropriate than "dying and rising with Christ," since Paul distinguishes between the believer's "resurrection," which is still in the future (cf. Rom 6:5, 8 and Gal 6:8), and "having life anew," which is a present possibility (cf. Rom 6:4, 11 and Gal 3:3, 5:25).

[72]Cf. Adolf Deissmann, *Paul: A Study in Social and Religious History* [2nd ed.; New York: Harper & Row, 1927) 145; C. F. G. Heinrici, *Der zweite Brief an die Korinther* (MeyerK 6; 8th ed.; Göttingen: Vandenhoeck & Ruprecht, 1900) 83; Lietzmann-Kümmel, *An die Korinther*, 104; Wendland, *Briefe an die Korinther*, 148; Alfred Plummer, *A Critical and Exegetical Commentary on the Second Epistle of St. Paul to the Corinthians* (ICC 34; Edinburgh: T. & T. Clark, 1915) 41; Hans Windisch, *Der zweite Korintherbrief* (MeyerK 6; 9th ed.; Göttingen: Vandenhoeck & Ruprecht, 1924) 72-73; and E.-B. Allo, *Saint Paul seconde épître aux Corinthiens* (2nd ed.; Paris: J. Gabalda, 1956) 28-30.

[73]In this case, the second καί would be epexegetical (cf. Meyer, *Epistles to the Corinthians*, 434). Cf. Jean Héring, *The Second Epistle of Saint Paul to the Corinthians* (trans. A. W. Heathcote and P. J. Allcock; London: Epworth, 1967) 12; C. K. Barrett, *A Commentary on the Second Epistle to the Corinthians* (HNTC; New York: Harper and Row, 1973) 80-81; and Gottfried Fitzer, *TDNT* 7:949. Some scholars go on to say that the Spirit was given *in baptism* (cf. Lampe, *The Seal of the Spirit*, 5-6; Schnackenburg, *Baptism*, 83, 87-88, 91, 162-65; and Grundmann, *TDNT* 9.556). W. C. van Unnik thinks the βεβαιοῦν etc. is accomplished through the gift of the Spirit, which is bestowed in baptism ("Reisepläne und Amen-Sagen, Zusammenhang und Gedankenfolge in 2. Korinther i 15-24," pp. 144-59 in *Sparsa Collecta: The Collected Essays of W. C. van Unnik*, Part 1: *Evangelia, Paulina, Acta* [NovTSup 29; Leiden: E. J. Brill, 1973] 154, 157).

[74]Cf. Rom 15:28, 1 Cor 9:2 and Rom 4:11.

[75]Cf. BAG, "σφραγίς," 2, b.

[76]Cf. Wilhelm Bousset, *Kyrios Christos: A History of the Belief in Christ from the Beginnings of Christianity to Irenaeus* (trans. J. E. Steely; Nashville: Abingdon, 1970) 295-98.

[77]For βεβαιόω, see 1 Cor 1:6, 8 and Rom 15:8. Cf. also Phil 1:7 (βεβαίωσις); and 2 Cor 1:7, Rom 4:16 (βέβαιος). Paul uses χρίω only here. For σφραγίζω, see above, nn. 74-75. And for δοῦναι τὸ πνεῦμα, see above, pp. 55, 61-62.

[78]Cf. the διὸ καί in 1:20b.

[79]The γάρ in 1:19 introduces a summary of Paul and his co-workers' missionary preaching as the first reason backing his claim in 1:18: The Son of God whom they preached, is reliable. Then the γάρ in 1:20a introduces a second reason: God's promises are reliable (cf. Rom 4:16 and 15:8, as well as Phil 1:7 and 1 Cor 1:6).

[80]The δέ in 1:21 has a consecutive nuance.

[81]Cf. BAG, "βεβαιόω," 2.

[82]The first καί in 1:22 is explanatory of χρίσας ὑμᾶς θεός. The second καί in 1:22 is not epexegetical (against Meyer, *Epistles to the Corinthians*, 434); rather, it coordinates ὁ σφραγισάμενος ὑμᾶς and δοὺς κτλ., just as the καί in 1:21 coordinates ὁ βεβαιῶν κτλ. and χρίσας κτλ. (cf. Grundmann, *TDNT* 9.556).

[83]Cf. Barrett, *Second Epistle to the Corinthians*, 79; Lampe, *The Seal of the Spirit*, 6; Fitzer, *TDNT* 7.950; and BAG, "σφραγίζω," 2, b.

[84]Cf. van Unnik ("Reisepläne," 157) and Grundmann (*TDNT* 9.556), who identify the Spirit with the power which effects the βεβαιοῦν κτλ.

[85]The first person plurals in 1:21-22 in the first instance refer back to Paul and his co-workers (1:19), since it is their reliability which is at stake.

[86]Cf. on 1 Cor 2:4-5, above, pp. 58-59.

[87]Cf. W. Sanday and A. C. Headlam, *A Critical and Exegetical Commentary on the Epistle to the Romans* (ICC 32; 2nd ed.; New York: Scribner's, 1896) 126; Barrett, *Epistle to the Romans*, 105; Käsemann, *An die Römer*, 126; and Thornton, *Confirmation*, 9.

[88]They have in common the imparting of the Spirit by God "in our hearts."

[89]Here the common element is the notion of the "outpouring" of the Spirit, expressed in 1 Cor 12:13 by the verb ποτίζω, and in Rom 5:5 by ἐκχέω (cf. above, pp. 61-62).

[90]In this, and in what follows, I follow the interpretation of Romans 6 in Erhardt Güttgemanns' *Der leidende Apostel und sein Herr: Studien zur paulinischen Christologie* (FRLANT 90; Göttingen: Vandenhoeck & Ruprecht, 1966) 210-25.

[91]Rom 6:5-11 states the reason (γάρ: 6:5) for 6:2, which begins Paul's rebuttal, in the form of a rhetorical question, to the objection raised in 6:1. Baptism is mentioned in the rebuttal only in 6:3-4.

[92]Cf. 6:4. The genitives, ζωῆς here and πνεύματος in 7:6, are epexegetical (cf. Günther Bornkamm, *Early Christian Experience* [trans. P. L. Hammer; New York: Harper & Row, 1969] 74, 85 n. 9).

[93]Cf. Schnackenburg (*Baptism*, 163-64) who correctly identifies ἐν καινότητι ζωῆς περιπατεῖν and περιπατεῖν κατὰ πνεῦμα (8:4; cf. Gal 5:16, 25), which is explained in 8:12-14 (cf. Gal 5:18). However, he goes beyond the text when he attributes to baptism the impartation of the Spirit (cf. also Bernhard Weiss, *Der Brief an die Römer* [MeyerK 4; 9th ed.; Göttingen: Vandenhoeck & Ruprecht, 1899] 266; and Hans Lietzmann, *An die Römer* [HNT 8; 5th ed.; Tübingen: Mohr/Siebeck, 1971] 66; and Kuss, *Der Römerbrief*, 307-08, 312-13).

[94]Cf. Deissmann, *Paul*, 145.

[95]In his commentary, Betz also notes the variety of interpretations of baptism in Paul's letters (*Commentary on Paul's Letter*, on 3:27).

[96]Cf. 1 Thess 1:4-6, Gal 3:1-5, 1 Cor 2:4-5 and 2 Cor 1:21-22. This view is later represented in Eph 1:13: Those who "heard" (ἀκούσαντες) the gospel and "believed" (πιστεύσαντες) were "sealed" (ἐσφραγίσθητε) "with the promised holy Spirit" (τῷ πνεύματι τῆς ἐπαγγελίας τῷ ἁγίῳ)--cf. τὸ πνεῦμα ἐλάβετε...ἐξ ἀκοῆς πίστεως in Gal 3:2, 5.

[97]Cf. Betz, "Spirit, Freedom, and Law," 148 n. 9; idem, *Commentary on Paul's Letter*, ad loc.; Wayne A. Meeks, "The Image of the Androgyne: Some Uses of a Symbol in Earliest Christianity," *HR* 13 (1973) 180-82; and the statement of Bousset, *Kyrios*, 158: "How curiously this brief allusion stands out in contrast with the surrounding thought-world in the Galatian epistle! Elsewhere the statements of the apostle about sonship and servanthood, about the inheritance of Abraham, about God's free gracious will, his relation to the law, and his acceptance through faith are almost dominated by a sober judicial rigor. Now here suddenly a mystical note sounds: sonship through the miracle of the sacrament, and the sacramental union with Christ! This is indeed a sound from another world."

[98]Cf. Meyer, *Epistle to the Galatians*, 156; Lampe, *Seal of the Spirit*, 61; Lietzmann, *An die Galater*, 23; and Dunn, *Baptism*, 110 (although he thinks βαπτίζεσθαι εἰς Χριστόν is a metaphor, like ἐνδύεσθαι Χριστόν).

[99]Cf. above, pp. 61-62.

[100]Cf. Schlier, *Brief an die Galater*, 173 (although he incorrectly assumes this participation *begins* in baptism). Cf. also Grundmann's phrase "field of force" (*TDNT* 9.551), by means of which he interprets the ἐν Χριστῷ phrase.

[101]Cf. also the concept of "faith" as a participation term in 3:26 (cf. also Sanders, *Paul*, 463-72).

[102]Betz seems to identify the evidence of baptism and the Spirit, despite his critique of Schlier, when he refers to 3:26-28 and 4:6 as evidence that through the gift of the Spirit, by means of which Christ as "son of God" makes sonship available, the Galatians had come to think of themselves as "sons of God" (cf. *Commentary on Paul's Letter*, ad loc., and "Introduction, 7. The Theological Argument of Galatians"). For a discussion of the Spirit and sonship, see below, pp. 68-69 and Chapter IV, pp. 108-109.

[103]Cf. above, pp. 59-61. Schnackenburg (*Baptism*, 91) allows that *in special cases* (e.g. Acts 2:10) the Spirit is given without sacraments. In his commentary, Betz makes the remark, on the one hand, that it is unclear how baptism is related to the experience of receiving the gift of the Spirit (cf. on 3:2, n. 48), and, on the other hand, that "we know that the Spirit...was connected with baptism in some important way" (*Commentary on Paul's Letter*, 3:26-28, "Analysis"). Bousset, however, raises the question whether "the later conviction that baptism and the bestowal of the Spirit belong most closely together...was possible only on the basis of the conviction that every Christian must possess the Spirit"; and whether this "dogmatic assumption...stems first from the Pauline theology" (*Kyrios*, 82 n. 22). Cf. Hans Conzelmann, *Outline of the Theology of the New Testament* (trans. John Bowden; New York: Harper and Row, 1969) 48: "The question is, however, whether the the bestowing of the Spirit was associated with Christian baptism from the beginning."

[104]Cf. 1 Cor 12:13, 6:11, and above, pp. 61-62. Cf. Lampe (*The Seal of the Spirit*, 89) where he grants that Paul "does not *bind* the action of the Spirit to the sacrament of Baptism, realizing as he does that the Spirit may seize, as it were, upon a man *and lead him* to justifying faith *and so* to Baptism" (emphasis added).

[105]Cf. Gal 3:1-5, 1 Thess 1:4-6, 1 Cor 2:4-5 and 2 Cor 1: 15-24; and above, pp. 54-59, 62-64.

[106]Paul mentions υἱοθεσία, υἱοὶ θεοῦ, when he speaks of
Gentile believers only in contexts where he opposes nomism, and
either in connection with baptism (Gal 3:26) or in connection
with the Spirit (Gal 4:6 and Rom 8:14-15, which mention the
Abba-cry). 2 Cor 6:18 is part of an "anti-Pauline fragment"
and, therefore, represents the view of Paul's opponents; in
Rom 9:4 he speaks of Jews; and in Rom 9:26 he "quotes" from
Hos 2:1. The concept of κληρονομία, which appears only in
connection with πνεῦμα and υἱοθεσία, also occurs only in
polemic against nomism (cf. Gal 3:18, 29; 4:1-7, 21-31; 5:21;
and Rom 4:13-14 and 8:17). The traditional formulae that appear in 1 Cor 6:9-10 and 15:50 are exceptions.

[107]Cf. Betz, "Spirit, Freedom, and Law," 146-47; idem,
Commentary on Paul's Letter, ad loc., and on 3:2, n. 45; Robert
Jewett, *Paul's Anthropological Terms: A Study of Their Use in
Conflict Settings* (AGJU 10; Leiden: Brill, 1971) 99; Bultmann,
"The Problem of Ethics," 22; Martin Dibelius, *Paulus und die
Mystik* (München: E. Reinhardt, 1941) 12 (who calls the Abba-
cry an "oratio infusa"); and Hermann Gunkel, *Die Wirkungen des
heiligen Geistes, nach der populären Anschauung der apostolischen Zeit und der Lehre des Apostels Paulus: Eine biblisch-
theologische Studie* (2nd ed.; Göttingen: Vandenhoeck & Ruprecht,
1899) 36.

[108]Cf. below, (1) = p. 66; (2) = pp. 66-67; (3) = pp.
67-69.

[109]Cf. 2 Cor 1:22, Rom 5:5 and 8:26-27. The φῶς in 2 Cor
4:6 performs a function similar to that of πνεῦμα.

[110]According to 2 Esdr 3:21-22, the heart is the origin of
the "impulses," good and bad, and as such is equivalent to
yeṣer (cf. George Foot Moore, *Judaism in the First Centuries
of the Christian Era, the Age of the Tannaim* [2 vols.; New
York: Schocken, 1927, 1971] 1.480-81, 485, 489-92). At least
once Plato attributes feelings to the heart (cf. *Resp.*, vi,
6.492C [LCL 2.36]); so also Aristotle (cf. *Sens.*, 2.439A [LCL
8.228]; *Part. An.*, 2.656A-B, 666A [LCL 12.174-78, 236]). In
Philo (*Spec. Leg.*, 1.56.305 [LCL 7.276]), the heart is the
seat of the passions. In Paul, this view is present in Phil
1:7, 2 Cor 2:4, 7:3 and Rom 1:24, 9:2, 10:1. And in Gal 5:16-
17, 24, the passions are associated with the activity of the
Spirit and belonging to Christ.

[111]The heart as the seat of the will is well-known in the
Old Testament, Judaism and Greek philosophy (cf. Friedrich
Baumgärtel and Johannes Behm, *TDNT* 3.605-13; Jewett, *Terms*,
323, 448; and Bultmann, *Theology*, 1.220-21). For this view in
Paul, see 1 Thess 3:13 and Rom 2:5, 29. That the Spirit rules
the intentionality of the believer is expressed in Gal 5:16-18,
25 and Rom 8:5-7, 13-14. In his commentary, Betz notes that
the heart was considered the appropriate locus of the Spirit,
since that is where the "will" is controlled (*Commentary on
Paul's Letter*, on 4:6).

[112]Cf. Bultmann, *Theology*, 1.220-21. In Phil 4:7, καρδία and νόημα form a hendiadys. 2 Cor 3:14a speaks of the darkening of the νόημα, while parallel statements in 3:15 and Rom 1:21 speak of the darkening of the καρδία. And ὁ θεὸς...ἐτύφλωσεν τὰ νοήματα τῶν ἀπίστων... in 2 Cor 4:4 parallels ὁ θεὸς ...ἔλαμψεν ἐν ταῖς καρδίαις ἡμῶν... in 2 Cor 4:6.

[113]Cf. Bultmann, *Theology*, 1.220-21. In 2 Cor 1:22, Paul speaks of the Spirit as having been given ἐν ταῖς καρδίαις ἡμῶν, while in 5:5 he speaks of it as having been given ἡμῖν. Paul can use the expression ἀναπαύειν τὰ σπλάγχον τινός in Phlm 7 and 20, but in 1 Cor 16:18 and 2 Cor 7:13 he uses ἀναπαύειν τὸ πνεῦμα τινός; and then in Rom 15:32 he uses συναναπαύειν with a personal pronoun. Further, Paul speaks of "blamelessness" at the Parousia with reference to the καρδία in 1 Thess 3:13, the πνεῦμα, ψυχή, and σῶμα in 5:23, and the personal pronoun in Phil 1:10 and 1 Cor 1:8. In this respect, καρδία is virtually synonymous with the human spirit, as the parallel statement about the Abba-cry in Rom 8:15-16 shows: ἐλάβετε πνεῦμα υἱοθεσίας, ἐν ᾧ κράζομεν· ἀββά in 8:15 parallels αὐτὸ τὸ πνεῦμα συμμαρτυρεῖ τῷ πνεύματι ἡμῶν in 8:16, which indicates that the personal pronoun and the human spirit are closely related, if not identical. Finally, see 1 Thess 2:17 and 1 Cor 5:3, where καρδία and πνεῦμα are interchangeable, as are πρόσωπον and σῶμα.

[114]In Gal 2:19-21, Paul describes Christian existence itself in terms of a structure of existence in which the "ego" both is *displaced by* the indwelling Christ (ζῶ δὲ οὐκέτι ἐγώ, ζῇ δὲ ἐν ἐμοὶ Χριστός) and *exists alongside of* the indwelling Christ (θεῷ ζήσω...ὃ δὲ νῦν ζῶ ἐν σαρκί, ἐν πίστει ζῶ). The idea behind this is that of a change of the power which rules a person's "center" or "heart" (cf. Tannehill, *Dying and Rising*, 59; and Jewett, *Terms*, 323). More is said about this below in Chapter IV, pp. 114-15, 116, 118-23.

[115]The assumption that ecstasy always involves a loss of conscious awareness is behind Grundmann's view that the Abba-cry was *not* ecstatic because there was *no loss* of conscious awareness (cf. *TDNT* 3.903). This assumption, however, is not Paul's (cf. 1 Cor 14:14-15). In *The Greeks and the Irrational* (Berkeley/Los Angeles/London: University of California, 1971), E. R. Dodds explains how in antiquity "enthusiasm" and "ecstasy" were distinguished from Shamanistic "inspiration": In "enthusiasm" a god enters a person and, for example, uses his or her vocal organs, as in the case of the Delphic priestess (pp. 70-71; cf. Plato, *Ion*, 543D [LCL 8.422], where he says that with soothsayers, ὁ θεὸς αὐτός ἐστιν ὁ λέγων, διὰ τούτων δὲ φθέγγεται πρὸς ἡμᾶς; and Philo, *Quis rer. div. her.*, 266 [LCL 4. 418], where he says that when the prophet speaks, καταχρῆται δὲ ἕτερος αὐτοῦ τοῖς φωνητηρίοις ὀργάνοις, στόματι καὶ γλώττῃ). Likewise, "ecstasy" involves the entry of a god into a person, which brings about an abrupt change of mood or mind, a "being out of oneself" (pp. 77, 94-95, n. 84). "Enthusiasm" and "ecstasy," furthermore, can take two forms, lucid and "somnambulistic," of which the latter entails the loss of conscious

awareness (p. 72). Shamanistic "inspiration," on the other
hand, involves an out-of-the-body journey of the Shaman's
spirit, rather than the indwelling of an alien spirit or god
(p. 88, n. 43; cf. 2 Cor 12:1-4; and Plutarch, *Mor.*, 563E-568A
[LCL 7.272-99], for an account of a journey of the τὸ φρονοῦν,
in which the τὸ φρονοῦν leaves the rest of the ψυχή in the body
[564C; LCL 7.276] and then returns to the body; and 590B-592E
[LCL 7.460-77] for a Shamanistic journey of the ψυχή).

[116] Paul uses κράζω again only in Rom 9:27, where it introduces a saying (inspired?) of the prophet Isaiah. Cf. the discussion of κράζω in Bultmann (*The Gospel of John* [trans. G. R.
Beasley-Murray et al.; Philadelphia: Westminster, 1971] 75 n. 1)
and in C. H. Dodd (*The Interpretation of the Fourth Gospel*
[Cambridge: Cambridge University, 1970] 382 n. 1). Cf. John
7:28, 37; 12:44 and Acts 23:6, 24:21. Outside the New Testament, κράζω is used to introduce the words of priests and
priestesses in the mysteries (cf. the references in Bultmann,
Gospel of John, loc. cit.; Grundmann, *TDNT* 3.899; and Schlier,
Brief an die Galater, 198 n. 2). For references to the use of
κράζω to introduce the "cry" of philosophers, and expressions
of a kind of prayer, see H. D. Betz (*Lukian von Samosata und
das Neue Testament: Religionsgeschichtliche und paränetische
Parallelen. Ein Beitrag zum Corpus Hellenisticum Novi Testamenti* [TU 76; 5th series; vol. 21; Berlin: Akademie Verlag,
1961] 64 n. 2).

[117] Cf., for example, Mark 3:11, 5:5, 7, 9:26 and Acts
16:16-18.

[118] Cf. now also Betz, *Commentary on Paul's Letter*, ad loc.
Cf. Erik Peterson, ΕΙΣ ΘΕΟΣ. *Epigraphische, formgeschichtliche
und religionsgeschichtliche Untersuchungen* (FRLANT 24 [n.f.];
Göttingen: Vandenhoeck & Ruprecht, 1926) 213, quoted in
Haenchen, *Acts of the Apostles*, 573 n. 5 (cf. Luke 1:42, Acts
19:28, 32, 34). For the "wonder seen with one's eyes," see
Gal 3:1 (οἷς κατ' ὀφθαλμοὺς...προεγράφη).

[119] Cf. Peterson, ΕΙΣ ΘΕΟΣ, 191-92 n. 1; and Meyer, *Epistle
to the Galatians*, 175; Lipsius, *Briefe an die Galater*, 48;
Schlier, *Brief an die Galater*, 199; Oepke, *Paulus an die
Galater*, 97-98; Bonnard, *Saint Paul aux Galates*, 156 (note to
p. 88); Kuss, *Der Römerbrief*, 603; Barrett, *Epistle to the
Romans*, 164; Käsemann, *An die Römer*, 217-18; Gunkel, *Die
Wirkungen*, 36, 60-61; Dunn, *Jesus*, 240 (although he adds, "but
less likely"); and Henning Paulsen, *Überlieferung und Auslegung
in Römer 8* (WMANT 43; Neukirchen-Vluyn: Neukirchener Verlag,
1974) 91, 95. Cf. now also Betz, *Commentary on Paul's Letter*,
ad loc. (κράζω "has the ring of ecstasy").

[120] The double form, ἀββὰ ὁ πατήρ, in Gal 4:6 and Rom 8:15,
as well as in Mark 14:36, is the result of adding the explanatory ὁ πατήρ for the benefit of Greek-speaking readers; or else
it reflects the bilingual character of the early church (cf.
Betz [*Commentary on Paul's Letter*, ad loc.] who adds that "the
reason for the double expression is not clear").

[121]Even among scholars who think these words stem from
Jesus' usage or the Lord's Prayer, some also agree that they
are uttered in an ecstatic cry (cf. Meyer, *Epistle to the Galatians*, 175; Oepke, *Paulus an die Galater*, 98). Schweizer (*TDNT*
8.391 n. 419) does not settle the question whether the Abba-cry
was ecstatic.

[122]The "amen" in Black churches and the "hallelujah" in
Pentecostal worship services are modern analogies.

[123]Cf., for example, the *maranatha* in 1 Cor 16:22, Phil
4:5b, Rev 22:20, and *Did.* 10:6 (which also mentions *hosannah*
and *amen*).

[124]Cf. Lightfoot, *St. Paul to the Galatians*, 169; Ellicott,
Paul's Epistle to the Galatians, 96; Burton, *Epistle to the
Galatians*, 224; Theodor Zahn, *Der Brief des Paulus an die
Römer* (Kommentar zum Neues Testament 6; 1st and 2nd ed.; Leipzig: Deichert, 1910) 395; Kittel, *TDNT* 1.6; Grundmann, *TDNT*
3.903; Werner Bieder, "Gebetswirklichkeit und Gebetsmöglichkeit
bei Paulus. Das Beten des Geistes und das Beten im Geiste," *TZ*
4 (1948) 26; Oscar Cullmann, *Early Christian·Worship* (SBT 10;
trans. A. S. Todd and J. B. Torrance; Chicago: H. Regnery,
1953) 13; idem, *The Christology of the New Testament* (rev. ed.;
trans. S. C. Guthrie and C. A. Hall; Philadelphia: Westminster,
1963) 208-209; Karl Hermann Schelkle, *The Epistle to the
Romans. Theological Meditations* (trans. Brian Thompson; New
York: Herder and Herder, 1964) 143-44 n. 13; Joachim Jeremias,
The Prayers of Jesus (SBT 6; 2nd series; trans. J. Bowden et
al.; London: SCM, 1967) 34, 65 n. 73, 97-99; idem, *New Testament Theology: The Proclamation of Jesus* (trans. J. Bowden;
New York: Scribner's, 1971) 64-65, 197; Norman Perrin, *Rediscovering the Teaching of Jesus* (New York: Harper and Row, 1967)
41; and idem, *The New Testament, An Introduction: Proclamation
and Parenesis, Myth and History* (New York: Harcourt, Brace,
Jovanovich, 1974) 101. This view is rejected by Gunkel, *Die
Wirkungen*, 61; Schlier, *Brief an die Galater*, 199 n. 1; Bonnard, *Saint Paul aux Galates*, 88; Käsemann, "Formeln II.
Liturgische Formeln im N. T.," pp. 993-96 in *RGG*, vol. 2 (3rd
ed.; ed. Kurt Galling; Tübingen: Mohr/Siebeck, 1958) (esp. p.
994); idem, *An die Römer*, 217-18; Vos, *Traditionsgeschichtliche
Untersuchungen*, 99-100; Kuss, *Der Römerbrief*, 602; Paulsen,
Überlieferung, 88-91; Dunn, *Jesus*, 240; and Betz, *Commentary on
Paul's Letter*, ad loc. Dodd's view is that the *word* ἀββά came
into Gentile usage "possibly *through* the. liturgical use of the
Lord's Prayer" (emphasis added); but that it does not *refer*
here to the *saying* of the Lord's Prayer, since it is a "loud
cry" produced by the "stress of strong spiritual excitement or
exaltation" (*Paul to the Romans*, 129). Schrenk (*TDNT* 5.1006)
is similar: It is not to be "*restricted* to the opening of the
words of the Lord's Prayer....It goes *beyond* the use of a particular liturgical formula" (emphasis added).

[125]For an argument for the uniqueness of the prayer and
its attribution to Jesus, see Jeremias (*Prayers*, 82-84 and *N.T.
Theology*, 193-95).

[126]Cf. H. D. Betz, "Eine judenchristliche Kult-Didache in Matthäus 6, 1-18: Überlegungen und Fragen im Blick auf das Problem des historischen Jesus," pp. 445-57 in *Jesus Christus in Historie und Theologie. Neutestamentliche Festschrift für Hans Conzelmann zum 60. Geburtstag* (ed., Georg Strecker; Tübingen: Mohr/Siebeck, 1975).

[127]Cf. Gerhard Delling, *Worship in the New Testament* (trans. Percy Scott; Philadelphia: Westminster, 1962) 70: The Abba-cry was perhaps "uttered involuntarily" in response to "a preaching of the saving deed of God through which He receives men into sonship." Cf. also Dunn, *Jesus*, 240: "The 'Abba' almost certainly refers to a spontaneous expression of this sense of sonship in a cry of exultation and trust." In his commentary, Betz argues that the Galatians "had come to regard themselves as 'sons of God,'" for which he cites 3:7, 26 and 4:6-7 as evidence (*Commentary on Paul's Letter*, "Introduction, 7. The Theological Argument in Galatians"; cf. also above, p. 86 n. 102; and below, Chapter IV, pp. 137-38 n. 45). Cf. the explanations of the Abba-cry by Jeremias (*Prayers*, 62 n. 56): The Abba-cry can only be understood as a mark of sonship and possession of the Spirit if it is an "echo of Jesus' prayer"; Dunn (*Jesus*, 22): The Abba-cry is an "echo and reproduction of Jesus' own experience"; and Kittel (*TDNT* 1.6): The word Abba is "linked with Jesus' term for God and thus denotes an appropriation of the relationship proclaimed and lived out by Him."

[128]Cf., for example, the first letter to the Thessalonians: καθὼς / καθάπερ οἴδατε in 1:5, 2:2, 5, 11, and 3:4; αὐτοὶ γὰρ οἴδατε in 2:1, 3:3, 4:2 and 5:2; and μνημονεύετε in 2:9.

[129]Cf. the θαυμάζω in 1:6, which does stand over the whole letter.

[130]Cf. the formula χάρις ὑμῖν καὶ εἰρήνη ἀπὸ θεοῦ πατρὸς ὑμῶν καὶ κυρίου ᾿Ιησοῦ Χριστοῦ in Gal 1:3 and Rom 1:7, 1 Cor 1:3, 2 Cor 1:2, Phil 1:2, 1 Thess 1:1 (which omits the ἡμῶν), Phlm 3. Cf. also Gal 1:4.

[131]Cf. the doxological formulae in Rom 15:6, Phil 2:11, 4:20, and 1 Thess 3:11, 13; the blessing and thanksgiving formulae in 2 Cor 1:3 and 1 Thess 1:3; the oath formula in 2 Cor 11:31; and the double credal formula in 1 Cor 8:6.

[132]Cf. Gal 1:1 and Rom 6:4, 15:6, 1 Cor 15:24, 2 Cor 1:3, 11:31.

[133]Cf. Gal 4:6 and Rom 8:14-17.

[134]Cf. Gal 3:26 and 4:4-5. In Rom 9:4, where Paul speaks of the sonship of Jews, and 9:26, where in a "quotation" from Hosea he speaks of the sonship of Gentile believers, neither the Spirit, nor Christ, nor the "Fatherhood" of God is mentioned. And in 2 Cor 6:18, which is part of an "anti-Pauline fragment," the concept of sonship (and daughterhood) is bound up with the concept of God as the Father who demands obedience

to his law contained in the Torah--this view corresponds to
that of Paul's opponents in Galatia (cf. Betz, "2 Cor 6:14-
7:1," 88-108; idem, "Galatians, Letter to the," *IDB* Sup. vol.
(ed. Keith Crim et al.; Nashville: Abingdon, 1976) 352; and
idem, *Commentary on Paul's Letter*, "Appendix 2").

[135]Cf. Gal 3:26-29. For discussions of the pre-Pauline
origin, form and content of 3:26-28, see Betz ("Spirit, Freedom, and Law," 147-50) and Meeks ("The Image of the Androgyne,"
180-82).

[136]For the view that 4:4-5 consists of an edited "quotation" from earlier tradition, see Betz, "The Literary Composition," 372; idem, *Commentary on Paul's Letter*, ad loc.; Kramer,
Christ, sec. 25b, 112-13; Ethelbert Stauffer, *TDNT* 3.328 n. 47;
Ferdinand Hahn, *The Titles of Jesus in Christology: Their History in Early Christianity* (trans. H. Knight and G. Ogg; New
York: World, 1969) 247, 269 nn. 50-52; Reginald H. Fuller, *The
Foundations of New Testament Christology* (New York: Scribner's,
1965) 209; Jewett, *Terms*, 322, 329, 333. Schweizer considers
the *concept* of "the sending of the Son" pre-Pauline (cf. *TDNT*
8.374, 383), but not the *formula* as it stands in Gal 4:4-5
(cf. "Zur Herkunft der Präexistenzvorstellung bei Paulus," *EvT*
19 [1959] 68; and idem, "Zum religionsgeschichtlichen Hintergrund der 'Sendungsformel' Gal. 4.4f; Röm. 8.3f; Joh. 3.16f;
1 Joh. 4.9," *ZNW* 57 [1966] 209).

[137]The same, *mutatis mutandis*, could be said about the
understanding of the Abba-cry among the Christians in Rome to
whom Paul wrote.

[138]Cf. Rom 15:6, 2 Cor 1:3a, 11:31 and Rom 6:4, 1 Cor
15:24, Gal 1:1, Phil 2:11 (these latter references imply God
is the "Father" of Jesus Christ).

[139]Cf. 1 Cor 8:6.

[140]Cf. 2 Cor 1:15-24, where Paul presents a summary of his
preaching in Corinth (1:19), followed by a reference to the
"amen-cry" (1:20b) and the giving of the Spirit "in their
hearts" (1:22).

[141]Cf. Gal 1:3-4, Rom 1:7, 1 Cor 1:3, 2 Cor 1:2, Phil 1:2,
1 Thess 1:1, and Phlm 3.

[142]Cf. 2 Cor 1:3.

[143]Cf. Rom 5:5 and 8:39.

[144]Cf. Gal 4:8-9.

[145]The use of the word ἀββά in Greek-speaking communities
could have been introduced through the use of the Lord's
Prayer in worship--if the Lord's Prayer was transmitted in an
Aramaic form (cf. Dodd on Rom 8:15, cited above, n. 124). The

Abba-cry, however, does not survive outside of Paul's letters
to the Galatians and Romans, with the one possible exception of
1 Clem. 8:3, where the cry πάτηρ is associated with repentance
rather than sonship, which corresponds to the Galatians' understanding of the Abba-cry prior to Paul's letter. *1 Clem.* 8:3
is part of a quote from "pseudo-Ezekiel" (cf. the reconstruction of a fragment containing this text in Campbell Bonner [*The
Homily on the Passion by Melito, Bishop of Sandis, and Some
Fragments of the Apocryphal Ezekiel* (SD 12; London: Chris-
tophers; Philadelphia: University of Pennsylvania, 1940) 185-87]
whose reconstruction is based on *1 Clem.* 8:3). This would con-
firm the view that the association of the Abba-cry and sonship
is peculiarly Pauline. This would be confirmed if Bultmann's
view of the redaction-history of Mark 14:32-42 is correct,
namely, that it "could well have originated in an Hellenistic
Christianity of a Pauline sort" (*The History of the Synoptic
Tradition* [rev. ed.; trans. John Marsh; New York: Harper & Row,
1968] 268, 306); for the Abba-cry was not used in any Greek-
speaking milieu after Mark (14:36), except in Eastern (Syriac)
communities, where it was no longer an ecstatic cry (cf.
Jeremias, *Prayers*, 64). In his commentary, Betz remarks that
"the 'Abba' was taken over from the Aramaic-speaking Palestinian church by Greek-speaking Christians" (*Commentary on Paul's
Letter*, ad loc.).

[146]The present participles refer to acts of God among the
Galatians, rather than to deeds of Paul (cf. above, Chapter II,
p. 50 n. 82; and Betz, *Der Apostel Paulus*, 71; Schlier, *Brief
an die Galater*, 125; and Burton, *Epistle to the Galatians*, 151
[who, however, on p. 152, denies that these are now in
progress]).

[147]Paul's appeal to the ecstatic phenomena of the Spirit,
according to Schlier (*Brief an die Galater*, 125-26), is an attempt to exclude his opponents from the Messianic Age. Paul
would then be defending himself in the same way the so-called
"super-apostles" attacked him in Corinth (cf. above, p. 51 n. 89).

[148]In Gal 4:6, the Abba-cry is described as a divine act;
so also are the χαρίσματα in 1 Corinthians 12 and Romans 12.
2 Cor 12:12 is probably to be interpreted in light of 12:9-10
and 13:3-9, so that Paul makes no claims for himself here, but
."boasts only in the Lord" (cf. Rom 15:18-19).

[149]Cf. Conzelmann, *First Epistle to the Corinthians*, 209.

[150]Cf. BDF, sec. 306.2; and BAG, "ἕτερος," 1, b, δ; and
"ἄλλος," 1, c.

[151]On the other hand, exorcisms and healings are included
by Robertson-Plummer, *First Epistle of St. Paul to the Corinthians*, 266; J. Weiss, *Der erste Korintherbrief*, 301; Moffatt,
First Epistle of Paul to the Corinthians, 181; Schlier, *Brief
an die Galater*, 125-26; Deissmann, *Paul*, 239; Vos, *Traditionsgeschichtliche Untersuchungen*, 87; and Dunn, *Jesus*, 163, 210.
But characteristically none discusses possible Sitze im Leben.

[152]Cf. 1 Corinthians 14. The Sitz im Leben is proclamation also in 1 Thess 1:4-6, 1 Cor 2:4-5, 2 Cor 12:12 (cf. 13:
3-9), and Rom 15:18-19. Gal 3:5 is taken as a reference to
the "success" of Paul's missionary preaching by Albert
Schweitzer (*The Mysticism of Paul the Apostle* [trans. William
Montgomery; New York: Seabury, 1931] 169), Georg Bertram (*TDNT*
2.653), Grundmann (*TDNT* 2.311), Gerhard Friedrich (*TDNT* 2.720),
Schmithals (*Paul*, 141 and *Gnosticism in Corinth: An Investigation of the Letters to the Corinthians* [trans. J. E. Steely;
Nashville: Abingdon, 1971] 281; also *The Office of the Apostle in
the Early Church* [trans. J. E. Steely; Nashville: Abingdon,
1969] 34-37, 212), and Gerd Theissen ("Legitimation und Lebensunterhalt: Ein Beitrag zur Soziologie urchristlicher Missionare," *NTS* 21 [1974/75] 215-16).

[153]Dunn, *Baptism*, 228.

[154]Ibid., 227.

[155]Cf. ibid., 224-25.

[156]Cf. ibid., 225-27 (cf. also pp. 1-5).

[157]Cf. ibid., 3 n. 8, and 224 (cf. also p. 172).

[158]Cf. ibid., 118, 172, 227.

[159]Cf. ibid., 227.

[160]Cf. ibid., 119, 120.

[161]Cf. 3:28. For a discussion of the history of this
traditional formula, and problems in its interpretation, see
Meeks ("The Image of the Androgyne," 165-208) and Betz (*Commentary on Paul's Letter*, ad loc., and "Introduction, 2, A.
Galatia and the Galatians," n. 18).

[162]Cf. 5:24 and 6:14 (cf. also 2:19-20). The powers, on
which these divisions depend for their existence, are for the
Christian "dead"; namely, the flesh and the world (and the law
of Moses). In other words, the Christian is emancipated from
these conventions because they are part of the "evil age," from
which the Christian is set free (cf. 1:4). Even though these
powers, and the divisions which they create and sustain, still
exist, they have no power any more, and are no longer recognized as divine (cf. 4:3, 8-9). A similar view is expressed
differently in 1 Cor 7:21-24 (cf. Betz, *Commentary on Paul's
Letter*, on 3:28).

[163]Cf. 4:8-10 (cf. Betz, "Spirit, Freedom and Law," 152).

[164]Cf. Betz, *Commentary on Paul's Letter*, ad loc.

165Cf. 5:6, 13-14, 22a and 6:9-10.

166Betz suggests that this has its Sitz im Leben in an "educational institution" of some kind in the Galatian communities (*Commentary on Paul's Letter*, on 6:6).

PART II

THE HISTORICALITY OF THE SPIRIT

INTRODUCTION

Paul's use of πνεῦμα as a decisive theologoumenon in the letter to the Galatians has its historical occasion in a controversy over Jewish-Christian nomism. In this setting it is a decisive term because the Spirit already was a primary datum of experience in the churches of Galatia. The term πνεῦμα, therefore, denotes a divine reality whose presence and activity is manifest in the churches of Galatia in the form of ecstatic phenomena during worship (3:1-5, 4:6).

But more than that, the ecstatic experiences of Paul's converts in Galatia must be seen in a larger context. They were not isolated experiences. For a historically new structure of human existence itself emerged with the Spirit at its center (5:13-6:10). Furthermore, the presence and activity of the Spirit is understood to be a historically new mode of divine immanence which began after the appearance of Christ; that is, it is the continued presence of Christ in the churches of Galatia (4:4-6). And Paul assures the Galatians that the gift of the Spirit unites them with the future "righteousness" and "eternal life," for which they hope with longing expectation (5:5, 6:8). All these elements of the experience of the Spirit indicate that Paul understands the time of the Spirit as the "last age." They also mean that Paul conceives of the Spirit as a *historical* reality. In the second part of this study, we explain three aspects of the historicality of the Spirit: its soteriological,[1] christological,[2] and eschatological bases.[3] With Part II, therefore, we turn from a description of the polemical occasion, which is the historical context in which Paul's use of the term πνεῦμα is to be placed (Chapter II), and from a profile of the social setting of experiences of the Spirit in the Galatian churches (Chapter III), to a discussion of Paul's theological understanding of the reality of the Spirit itself.

NOTES

PART II. INTRODUCTION

[1]Cf. Chapter IV.

[2]Cf. Chapter V.

[3]Cf. Chapter VI.

CHAPTER IV

THE SOTERIOLOGICAL BASIS OF THE HISTORICALITY
OF THE SPIRIT

Introduction

The wider context into which the ecstatic experiences of
the Christians in Galatia are to be placed is made up not only
of social settings but also of structures that are properly
called "existential." For Paul describes a new structure of
existence which had begun with ecstatic experiences. In this
sense the historicality of the Spirit consists not only of isolated experiences of ecstasy but also of a new epoch which its
sending inaugurated. Paul calls this new epoch a "new creation."[1] For a description of this "new creation," of which the
Spirit was a part, we turn to statements which express the
epochal significance of the sending of the Spirit: 3:3,[2] 4:6,[3]
4:21-31,[4] and 5:1-6:10.[5]

Section 1. Beginning with the Spirit (3:3)

Behind the question, "Having begun with the Spirit do you
now propose to end with the flesh?," is an agreement between
Paul and the Galatians, including the nomists, that Paul's converts had begun Christian existence with ecstatic experiences
on the occasion of his missionary preaching. No one denied
that Paul's converts had had ecstatic experiences as a result
of his preaching of the crucified Christ; nor that these experiences of the Spirit had inaugurated them into Christian
existence--in short, that they were πνευματικοί.[6] What was
disputed was the nomists' claim that, although in the Galatian
communities Christian existence had *begun* with the Spirit in
ecstatic experiences, it must now be *perfected* by "works of the
law."[7] This involves a disagreement about the significance of
the Spirit in Christian existence. For the nomists, the Spirit
seems to have had no function or significance beyond the experience of ecstasy at conversion; for Paul, however, the Spirit
was the decisive factor in the very structure of Christian
existence itself.

Paul's reformulation of the nomists' claim about perfecting Christian existence by means of the law of Moses reveals
the basis of their disagreement about the significance of the
Spirit in Christian existence. Where "works of the law" stood
in the nomists' claim, Paul substitutes σάρξ. This implies
that "works of the law," far from perfecting the new existence
begun with the Spirit, are antithetical to it, because they are
bound to the flesh rather than to the Spirit. The law of
Moses, therefore, is placed on the side of the old aeon, before
the coming of Christ.[8] The old aeon is that of the flesh, to
which "works of the law" are bound.[9] "Works of the law,"
therefore, are obsolete; for with the Spirit a new creation has
been inaugurated.[10]

The law of Moses has its place in a "pattern of religion"
in which election is followed by commandments that require
obedience, and in which ways of dealing with failure are provided in rites of repentance, atonement and forgiveness.[11]
This "pattern of religion" presupposes that there is but one
structure of existence, in which the human predicament is guilt
for transgressions, whose remedy is a pattern of restoration
through acts of repentance, atonement and forgiveness. For
Paul, on the other hand, the "pattern of religion" is entirely
different, because Paul sees human existence itself as pluralistic in its structures;[12] and, secondly, because he sees the
present human condition as requiring more than restoration.[13]
For Paul the period of human bondage to flesh, sin and death,
the "elemental forces of the universe," for which period the
law of Moses was designed, began with the historical emergence
of transgressions; and it came to an end with the sending of
Christ and his Spirit.[14] In short, in Paul's view the only
adequate remedy for the human predicament, which is not defined
merely in terms of guilt but rather primarily in terms of the
absence of freedom, is a "new creation" in which the obstacles
to human freedom--sin, the flesh and death--are deprived of
their power.[15] It is for this reason that the Spirit is not at
the periphery but at the center of a new historical epoch. As
we shall see,[16] the Spirit enables the Christian to be free of
bondage to the flesh in which sin has its opportunity to work.

Section 2. The Spirit and Sonship (4:6)

Paul refers again to the new existence of his converts in
Galatia when he speaks of their "sonship."[17] As we saw
earlier,[18] Paul appeals to the Abba-cry of the Spirit in the
hearts of Christians in Galatia as evidence that they indeed
were "sons." This is the second proof of the "sonship" of
Gentile Christians in Galatia; the first is based on a baptism
tradition, from which Paul "quotes" in 3:26-28. These proofs
show that they had no need for the law of Moses, its initiatory
rites, nor its rites of purity, atonement and forgiveness.
Without them they already were "sons" in the "Israel of God."[19]

When Paul first speaks of the Spirit in 3:1-5, where he
refers to the Galatians' receiving of the initial gift of the
Spirit, he mentions neither baptism nor "sonship." In 3:26-28,
where he does mention baptism and "sonship," he does not mention the Spirit. And in 4:6 he speaks of "sonship" and the
Spirit, but he does not mention baptism.[20] This raises the
question not only of the relation between the Spirit and baptism, but also of the connection between the Spirit and "sonship." What relationship between the Spirit and "sonship" is
presupposed by Paul in 4:6, when he appeals to the Abba-cry of
the Spirit as evidence that the Galatians were "sons"? Discussion of this question has focused on (1) the present tense
ἐστε and the aorist ἐξαπέστειλεν,[21] (2) the ὅτι,[22] and (3) the
concept of the πνεῦμα υἱοθεσίας in Rom 8:15, which parallels
Gal 4:6.[23]

(1) Antoine Duprez tries to argue that the contrast between the present tense ἐστε υἱοί and the aorist ἐξαπέστειλεν ὁ
θεὸς τὸ πνεῦμα proves the priority of receiving the Spirit and,
therefore, that it shows Paul conceives of the Spirit as the
source and agent of the "sonship" of Christians in Galatia.[24]
The weakness of this argument, however, is that the aorist
ἐξαπέστειλεν ὁ θεὸς τὸ πνεῦμα refers to a nondurative event,
which the phrase κρᾶζον· ἀββὰ ὁ πατήρ describes; whereas the
present ἐστε υἱοί refers to a state of being whose effects continue into the present. The Abba-cry of the Spirit was a mo-
mentary ecstatic experience, which was not identical to the

ongoing dwelling of the Spirit in the life of the Christian.
The latter sense can be derived from the aorist ἐξαπέστειλεν ὁ
θεὸς τὸ πνεῦμα only by divorcing it from the phrase κρᾶζον· ἀββά
ὁ πατήρ, which refers to an event of short duration relative to
the long lasting condition of being "sons." Just when the Abba-
cry of the Spirit occurred in relation to the making of "sons"
out of Gentile Christians in Galatia remains unclear. The contrast between the present ἐστε and the aorist ἐξαπέστειλεν,
therefore, does not clarify whether the "sonship" of the Galatians commenced before or after the Spirit's Abba-cry, nor
whether the former was contemporaneous with the latter.

(2) Discussion of this question has also focused on the
ὅτι in 4:6a. Should the ὅτι be regarded as causal ("since"),[25]
or declarative ("that")?[26] If the ὅτι is causal, 4:6 would
make the Spirit's cry of "Abba" a *consequence* of the "sonship"
of Christians in Galatia, rather than vice versa; that is, the
Galatians' "sonship" would be the *reason* "God sent the Spirit
of his son into our hearts crying, 'Abba'," so that the Spirit
could not be the source or agent of their "sonship." A causal
ὅτι, therefore, is in conflict with 4:21-31, which attributes
being "sons" to the causal agency of the Spirit,[27] and with the
concept of the πνεῦμα υἱθεσίας in Rom 8:15.[28]

A declarative ὅτι, on the other hand, does not necessarily
lead to a conflict between 4:6 and 4:21-31, and Rom 8:15. Even
on other grounds it seems preferable to a causal ὅτι; for,
Paul's argument depends on the Spirit's Abba-cry as proof that
(declarative ὅτι) Christians in Galatia were "sons," as the
conclusion to Paul's argument states in 4:7: "You are, therefore, no longer a slave but a son; but if a son, then an heir
through God." In other words, a declarative ὅτι brings out
that the reason Christians in Galatia have proof they were
"sons" is because God sent the Spirit of his "Son" into their
hearts crying, "Abba"; whereas a causal ὅτι turns this argument
around by introducing the "sonship" of Christians in Galatia as
the reason for God's "sending" of the Spirit to cry "Abba."[29]

But as far as the question of the priority of "sonship" or
the Spirit's Abba-cry is concerned, the declarative ὅτι-clause

is inconclusive. A declarative ὅτι would permit the conclusion
that the Spirit made Christians in Galatia "sons";[30] but it
does not require this concept of the Spirit as an agent of
"sonship," since the Spirit could *witness* to the "sonship" of
Christians in Galatia without being the *source* or *agent* of
their "sonship." But the converse is also true; namely, that a
declarative ὅτι allows but does not require interpreting 4:6 as
stating that the Spirit through the Abba-cry witnesses to the
"sonship" of Christians in Galatia without being the source of
their "sonship."

Even if the ὅτι in 4:6, therefore, is declarative, it does
not mean that Paul distinguishes the "objective" reality of
"sonship" from the "subjective" experience of it as knowledge
in the form of a self-understanding as "sons." Although
Schweizer implies this view lies behind Lietzmann's preference
for translating ὅτι in a declarative sense,[31] and Dunn, who
also prefers the declarative ὅτι, interprets 4:6 as a statement
about the "subjective experience" of the "objective fact of
sonship accomplished by the sending of the Son,"[32] this view is
more appropriately attributed to those who take the ὅτι in a
causal sense. Four examples will be sufficient to prove this
point.[33]

Burton understands ἐστε υἱοί to be a reference to "the
first and *objective* stage" of sonship spoken of in 4:5 in distinction from its "full, achieved fact," and the possession of
the Spirit to be a reference to "the *consciousness* of a filial
relation."[34] For Oepke, sonship is the "*Real*grund" of the bestowing of the Spirit; and the latter is the "*Erkenntnis*grund"
of the former.[35] Schlier writes:

Die Sendung des Sohnes hat also als der eschatologische
Akt Gottes die Knechtschaft der Menschen unter das
Gesetz der elementaren Kräfte der Welt beendet und uns
die Annahme an Sohnes Statt gebracht. Mit diesem neuen
Stand als Söhne Gottes ist freilich die Gabe Gottes
nicht erschöpft. Sondern er ist die *Vorbedingung* und
die *Ursache* dafür, dass Gott uns nun auch noch den
Geist ins Herz gibt,....Die Sohnschaft, die mit der
Sendung seines Sohnes *objective Tatsache* wurde, hat
Gott bewogen, uns auch den Geist seines Sohnes in
unsere Herzen zu senden. Gott schenkt uns also nicht
nur den Stand der Söhne, sondern auch die *Art* und das
Wissen der Söhne.[36]

And:

> Hinsichtlich des Seins sind die Menschen der *Möglich-*
> *keit* nach durch das Kommen Christi Söhne Gottes.
> (Der *Wirklichkeit* nach sind sie es durch die Taufe.
> Aber das berücksichtigt Paulus hier nicht ausdrück-
> lich.) Die Gabe des Sohnesgebetes aber lässt dieses
> Sohnsein in seiner Fülle als *Erfahrung* erscheinen.[37]

Finally, although Schweizer does not use the adjective "subjective," and he denies 4:6 refers simply to knowledge of sonship,
he does make a distinction between the "objective" reality of
sonship in the death of Jesus and its becoming effective for
the believer through faith and the gift of the Spirit.[38]

After these statements, Betz's comments are instructive.[39]
He points out, correctly, that "dogmatic-philosophical prin-
ciples," the "categories" used by commentators--objective/
subjective, reality/recognition or knowledge, and legal/
spiritual--not the text itself, create the problem of the
priority of the gift of the Spirit or of sonship. In his view,
the gift of the Spirit, phenomenologically an ecstatic experience, is "objective" evidence, while "sonship" is a "matter of
'subjective' self-understanding."

Each of these statements is an effort to explain not only
the ὅτι in 4:6a but also, and more importantly, Paul's various
statements in Galatians and Romans about "sonship," baptism and
the Spirit. But each also overlooks, or implicitly denies, the
difference between the *initial* gift of the Spirit, to which
Paul refers in 3:1-5, 14,[40] and the experience of the ecstatic
Abba-cry in 4:6. The two are not the same experience; for the
latter could, and most likely did, occur repeatedly after the
believer had received the initial gift of the Spirit.[41] By itself 4:6, therefore, is inconclusive as far as the question
about the priority of the *initial* gift of the Spirit or the
state of being "sons" is concerned.

(3) One way to solve this puzzle is to identify the Spirit
of 4:6 (and 3:2, 3, 5, 14; 4:29) with the πνεῦμα υἱοθεσίας of
Rom 8:15, in which case the issue of priority is eliminated,
since the initial gift of the Spirit and the state of being
"sons" would then be simultaneous.[42] This is consistent with
the declarative ὅτι-clause as well as with the attribution of

causal agency in "sonship" to the Spirit in 4:29. In other
words, becoming "sons" occurs *through* the gift of the Spirit,
rather than before receiving the Spirit.[43]

If this view is correct, in 4:6 Paul would be arguing that
Christians in Galatia were "sons" already--before baptism, let
alone before performing any "works of the law"--as evidenced by
the witness of the ecstatic Abba-cry on the occasion of Christian proclamation.[44] Christians in Galatia seem to have been
unaware of this significance of the Abba-cry. Paul argues from
what they already know--the Abba-cry of the Spirit--to what
they do not know--that they were already "sons" without participating in the covenant of Moses through circumcision.[45]

In conclusion, 4:6 is inconclusive as far as Paul's understanding of the role of the Spirit in establishing the status
of Christians in Galatia as "sons" is concerned. At most it
shows Paul regards the Abba-cry as the Spirit's witness that
they were genuine "sons" without "works of the law." Christians in Galatia had received the initial gift of the Spirit in
the setting of hearing Christian proclamation; subsequently, in
the same setting, ecstatic experiences of the Abba-cry were
common. Paul tells them that these ecstatic experiences are
evidence of their "sonship." But when Paul mentions baptism,
he attributes "sonship" to Christ without mentioning the
Spirit;[46] on the other hand, when he attributes "sonship" to
the agency of the Spirit, he mentions neither baptism nor
Christ.[47] Apparently both Christ's "coming" and the gift of
the Spirit have roles, but Paul does not state explicitly in
Galatians (nor anywhere else) how they are related,[48] unless
this is explained by the identification of the present efficacy
of Christ and the Spirit.[49]

In any case, for Paul the Abba-cry is evidence that Christians in Galatia were "sons." "Sonship" is one of the synonyms
in Galatians for salvation, "freedom" being another,[50] and "a
new creation" another.[51] Paul understands the Galatians' beginnings in this "new creation" as commencing with their receiving the Spirit on the occasion of hearing the Christian
message.[52]

Section 3. The Spirit and Freedom

Introduction. The "new creation" is summarized for Paul
by the term ἐλευθερία.[53] This freedom comes from Christ and
his Spirit.[54] It consists of liberation from "the present evil
age,"[55] which is the same as liberation from the στοιχεῖα τοῦ
κόσμου (4:3), or τὰ ἀσθενῆ καὶ πτωχὰ στοιχεῖα (4:9), which "by
nature are not gods" (4:8), or simply liberation from the
"world" (6:14-15). When Paul defines the "new creation" as
freedom *from*, he defines it as freedom from bondage;[56] specifically, freedom from the law of Moses [57] and from "flesh."[58] In
Galatians Paul does not mention freedom from death (although
he does in Romans), except indirectly in the gnomic saying in
6:8. Liberation from sin is brought up only briefly in 1:4 and
3:19, 22. Perhaps this is because the problem in the churches
of Galatia was not with sin but with the law of Moses.[59] If
the term ἁμαρτία lies behind the language about "flesh" and its
"works," as in Romans 7-8, does Paul avoid the term because it
was associated too closely with a nomistic understanding of
existence? Paul reinterprets παράπτωμα in 6:1 in terms of
"works of the flesh" (5:19-21) instead of in terms of the failure to do "works of the law" (= "sin").[60]

Just as the opposite of freedom can be defined simply as
"slavery,"[61] the "new creation" can be defined simply as "freedom."[62] And yet it too has positive content, which is derived
from its origin in Christ and his Spirit. Freedom *for*, identified as a "walking" by the Spirit,[63] is a consequence of get-
ting life itself from the Spirit;[64] and it is defined by Paul
as the "fruit of the Spirit," or the "law of Christ," which is
summarized by the term "love."[65]

4:21-31. Paul's allegorical interpretation[66] of the story
about Abraham's two sons, Ishmael and Isaac, and their mothers,
Hagar and Sarah,[67] is intended to prove that the Galatians
would become "slaves" again,[68] if they carried out their desire
to be "under" the law of Moses;[69] and that, if they remain as
they already are, they would continue to be free.[70] Paul argues that, while those who are under the law of Moses[71] are
slaves,[72] because they have life (are "born") from a slave,[73]

those who are not under this "covenant," but are "children of
the promise,"[74] are free,[75] because they have life (are "born")
from one who is free.[76]

By his initial question--"You who desire to be under the
law (of Moses), do you hear the Law?" (4:21)[77]--by his identification of the Sinai covenant with Hagar,[78] and by his placement of "the present Jerusalem" in the same series with them,[79]
Paul makes it clear that the "slave-master" is the law of
Moses.[80] For those under the law of Moses are slaves in the
sense that they are bound to a "curse" rather than to a "blessing" or a "promise";[81] to "sin" rather than to "righteousness"
and "life";[82] to the στοιχεῖα τοῦ κόσμου, which are not "gods,"
for they are "weak and beggarly";[83] and, finally, they are
bound to the flesh rather than to the Spirit.[84] The law of
Moses, therefore, produces slaves to itself and, as such, to
these things.

Contrasted with the slavish law of Moses is the "Jerusalem
above," which is free. It is this that is the source of Christian existence, so that, as Paul says, just as nomists have
their existence "from Mt. Sinai" (4:24b), Christians have
theirs from "the Jerusalem above."[85] In other words, Christian
existence has a "supernatural" origin, but nomistic existence
does not. This corresponds to Paul's view that nomists have
life not only from the law of Moses, which is "from Mt. Sinai,"
but also from the flesh;[86] whereas Christians have life from
Christ and the Spirit,[87] which are from "above," that is, from
God.[88]

The contrast between "the present Jerusalem" and "the
Jerusalem above," however, is not only spatial--the one being
merely "of this world," the other being "from God"--but also
temporal.[89] The temporal distinction, however, does not have
to do with a historical sequence such that the "present Jerusalem" would precede the "Jerusalem above"; rather, the contrast between the two realms includes a temporal dimension in
two other senses. The first is that Christ and his Spirit
"came" and were "sent" (3:23-25, 4:4-6). This means that both
were "pre-existent,"[90] and that both are historical entities
which replace or supersede the law of Moses as the center of

so-called "authentic" existence. In other words, to a certain
extent a historical sequence does exist, but only insofar as
the law of Moses and the "sending" of Christ and his Spirit are
concerned. Paul does not say, however, that the ultimate
source of Christian existence, to which "the Jerusalem above"
refers--namely, the divine realm from which God "sent" Christ
and the Spirit[91]--is in sequence with the *source* of nomistic
existence, to which "the present Jerusalem" refers--namely, the
law of Moses, which comes from Mt. Sinai. Paul precludes there
being any sense of *futurity* to the phrase "the Jerusalem above,"
since there is no doubt about the *present* reality of the realm
"above," which is the *present* source of existence for *contemporary* Christians (4:26).[92] And actually, if there is a "historical sequence" in the contrast between the two Jerusalems,
it is that the *temporal* "present Jerusalem" came *after* the
eternal "Jerusalem above," just as the law of Moses came "430
years" after the "promise" (3:17).

It follows that there is no hint that the "Jerusalem above"
will be or is being actualized on earth, since it is not an
effect, such as the "messianic community" or church, but the
source of Christian existence, which is that "realm" from which
God "sent" Christ and his Spirit to establish the "new creation." The "Jerusalem above," therefore, can no more refer to
the church than can the "commonwealth in heaven," from which
Christ is awaited.[93] In other words, one aspect of the temporal dimension implicit in the contrast between the two "Jerusalems" is the temporality of the realities each has wrought in
history; namely, nomism on the one hand, and the new creation
on the other, which are distinguished in time by Moses on the
one end, and the historical "sending" of Christ and his Spirit
on the other.

This immediately suggests the second temporal aspect of
the contrast between the "Jerusalem of this world"[94] and the
"Jerusalem which is not of this world." The Jerusalem which is
dependent upon the law from Sinai is temporally *limited* to a
passing human epoch precisely because the law from Sinai is not
eternal but *limited historically* "at both ends": it is not
"from the beginning," but rather came "430 years" after the

promise was made to Abraham;[95] neither does it stand "for all
times," since God determined to set a time limit over it.[96]
Christian existence, on the other hand, was promised by God from
the beginning (3:6-14); the promise remained valid even during
the period of the law of Moses (3:15-25); and now existence
centered in the Spirit is established as the eschatological
form of life itself.[97] In other words, with respect to the two
sources of distinct forms of existence, nomistic and pneumatic,
one Jerusalem is temporally limited (the present Jerusalem) and
the other is eternal (the Jerusalem above), because the former
is in the present world and the other is ἐν οὐρανοῖς, from
which God "sent" Christ and his Spirit. In addition to "the
Jerusalem above," Paul mentions "the kingdom of God" (5:21b)
and "the Israel of God" (6:16). As in the latter two, "God"
identifies the origin of "kingdom" and "Israel," so in the
first "above" (ἄνω) identifies the origin of the "Christian"
Jerusalem. But with regard to the *forms of existence themselves*, the one which was promised in Abraham, to those who
receive the Spirit through faith in the crucified Christ, became a historical reality only after the death and resurrection
of Christ "when the time had fully come," that is, when God had
brought to an end the period of existence under the law of
Moses.[98]

Paul presents the "new creation" through Christ and the
Spirit as the solution to the problem of slavish existence.
Christians in Galatia had received Paul's message of the crucified Christ, and it had liberated them from slavery to "beings
not by nature gods" and for freedom in Christ and his Spirit.
Paul saw their consideration of following nomists as a step
toward returning to slavish existence.[99] In 4:21-31, Paul
presents this argument by means of proofs from Scripture. In
the final arguments of his letter, Paul contrasts "slavish
existence" under the law with the freedom of the "new creation"
by means of parenesis.

5:1-6:10. In his final defense of Christian existence
based on the Spirit, Paul argues (1) that those who walk or
live in the Spirit, or are led by it, are free from the passions and desires, which are manifest in "works of the flesh";

but those who are seeking righteousness by "works of the law"
remain within the domain of the flesh;[100] (2) that, therefore,
those whose existence centers in the Spirit or Christ are free,
because they no longer need a "master" like the law of Moses;[101]
and (3) that this is proved by the fact that those whom Christ
and his Spirit have set free fulfill "the Law," while those who
are being made righteous by "works of the law" actually do not
fulfill it at all.[102]   Paul thus has interwoven three themes
into a single fabric: freedom from the flesh's domination, the
replacement of the law of Moses as a παιδαγωγός with the ἄγειν
of the Spirit, and ἀγάπη as the "fruit of the Spirit" that
proves that the ἐλεύθερος fulfills "the Law." Each of these
threads must now be unravelled.

  (1) The nomists in Galatia, as we argued above,[103] had a
different understanding of the problem of human existence and
its solution from Paul's. For them righteousness meant freedom
from and atonement for transgressions of the law of Moses.
Freedom was to be obtained and maintained by an existence
"under the law."[104]   For Paul, on the other hand, the human
predicament is more radical than a mere problem with transgressions of the Mosaic law. It is so much more radical that
"righteousness in the law" is actually antithetical to the
solution to the problem of human existence, which is salvation
through Christ. Righteousness is not based on "works of the
law" but on the Spirit which faith receives.[105]

  The predicament of human existence is presupposed in the
terse statement in 5:17. There are only two possibilities for
human existence: to be centered in the flesh or in the Spirit.[106]
The result[107] is that no place exists for the independent assertion of the human "will." The "ego" is active in both
flesh-centered and Spirit-centered existence;[108] but the "will"
is impotent in both cases.[109]   Only the Spirit, therefore, can
overthrow the domination of the flesh.[110]   However the opposition between the flesh and the Spirit is conceived, it excludes
overpowering the flesh by means of an assertion of "will-
power." The interpretation of 5:17 as having to do with a
conflict between "promptings of the conscience" and the "sarkic
will" misses the point.[111]   In other words, if the problem of

human existence is not the failure to perform "works of the
law," but "works of the flesh," which come from the passions
and desires, then Paul's answer is that the "will" cannot
overthrow the flesh which rules it; but that the Spirit, which
"guides" the "will" of the Christian, can and does overthrow
the flesh.[112] Unlike 2:19-20 (and Romans 6), where the believer's unredeemed "ego" or former "self" is the object of
"crucifixion," in 5:17, 24 it is the *power behind* the believer's
unredeemed life, namely, the flesh, which is the object of
"crucifixion."[113] The "benefit" of Christ is that through his
Spirit, which faith receives, the flesh with the passions and
desires is deadened, so that it no longer dominates one's
life.[114] That is to say, that the Spirit "breaks up" one's
old existence centered in the flesh.[115] Paul's view is not
that the Spirit automatically effects the overthrow of the
flesh with the passions and desires. The idea in 5:24,[116] that
those who "belong to Christ" have "crucified the flesh with its
passions and desires," must be understood in light of 5:16, 18
and 6:14-16. The "desires of the flesh" are rendered ineffective by "walking" or "being led" by the Spirit. Likewise, in
6:14-16 the rendering of the world ineffective through the
cross of Christ is accomplished by becoming a "new creation,"
which is maintained by following "this canon":[117] that is, the
"crucifixion" of the flesh (and "world") is something to be
followed. It is as if the crucified Christ functions as a
paradigm to be "imitated."[118]

But those "under the law" lack the power to overcome the
passions and desires of the flesh.[119] Perhaps the nomists'
view was that the law of Moses strengthened the "good impulse"
in the heart.[120] Freedom, however, comes not from "righteousness in the law," Paul argues, but by living in or being led
by the Spirit (5:16, 18, 25). Paul's concern is not only that
the members of the churches in Galatia fulfill the ethical requirements of "the Law,"[121] but also that they enjoy freedom
from the domination of the flesh.[122] His contention, actually,
is that the former is dependent on the latter. Not even "works
of the law" can achieve this freedom. This freedom comes only
from Christ and his Spirit (5:1, 13).

Returning to the anthropology of 5:17: human existence cannot be centered in ἃ ἐὰν θέλητε ποιεῖν;[123] it can only be centered in either the flesh or the Spirit. An existence centered only in "works of the law," therefore, is still centered in the flesh.[124] "Works of the law," far from being able to overcome the dominance of the flesh, actually perpetuate it by leaving the flesh "in position," as it were, because "works of the law" cannot take up residence within the center of a person in order to displace the flesh. The Spirit, on the other hand, being a metaphysical rival of the flesh (5:17b), can actually replace the flesh at the center of a person's existence.[125] In this manner the Spirit, received by faith, brings freedom. But the law of Moses merely perpetuates slavery, creating another slavery of its own.

In an article that describes the development of Pharisaism,[126] Ellis Rivkin says that, for the Pharisees, God is the creator of a *politeuma*, an "internal city," citizenship of which is available to all "who internalized the *Halakah* system" (p. 235). They call the giver of this "constitution" the *Makom*, *Shekhinah*, or the "All Present." Unlike Greco-Roman laws, which are external to the individual, theirs are internal (p. 237). Despite the formal similarities between the Pharisaic "internal city," the concept of the *Shekhinah*, and Paul's πολίτευμα ἐν οὐρανοῖς[127] and the concept of the indwelling Spirit, however, Rivkin argues that Paul violently rejects the Pharisaic system because, should such an internalization fail, it could not be hidden from the *Makom* and there would be no escape from guilt (cf. p. 238). On the contrary, Paul rejects this system not because of the burden of guilt Rivkin alleges this system made Paul feel was inescapable; rather, Paul rejects the internalized *Halakah* system because the human problem is not the failure to do "works of the law," but doing "works of the flesh," which must be avoided. For Paul, those who belong to Christ, the πνευματικοί, are not under the law of Moses because they have put away the flesh with the passions and desires, which are manifest in "works of the flesh."[128] Paul knows nothing of the guilt-burden of which Rivkin speaks.[129] In other words, Paul replaces the Pharisaic "internal constitution" with

another; namely, one based on Christ and the Spirit, rather
than one based on "works of the law." Paul, therefore, alters
the "redemptive media."[130]

(2) The relationship between the law of Moses and those
who are under it is compared with that of the παιδαγωγός and
the "minor," the νήπιος.[131] Since they have no power of their
own to resist evil and to do good, they require a "slave-
master" to restrain them from doing evil and to compel them to
do good. This is the function of the law of Moses, which, to
those whose existence remains centered in the sphere of the
flesh's domination, is their παιδαγωγός. Something like this
double sense seems to lie behind Paul's assertion that the law
of Moses produces slaves (4:21-31); namely, that it leaves un-
changed bondage to the sphere of the flesh, so that the law of
Moses remains their "master." The result is that it can only
restrain and compel, since its charges can do nothing independent of the ruling influence of the flesh (5:17).

Freedom from the law of Moses, which is a παιδαγωγός, is
based on freedom from the control of the flesh. An existence
based on the Spirit no longer has the flesh at its center
(5:17). The need for restraint from a παιδαγωγός, such as the
law of Moses, therefore, no longer exists, since "works of the
flesh" are not produced by one whose life is guided by the
Spirit.

In 5:16, οὐ μὴ τελέσητε should be taken as a promissory
future,[132] as 5:17, 5:18 and 5:24 prove.[133] The πνευματικοί
are not "under the law" because they "belong to Christ," that
is, they have put to death the flesh with the passions and desires, which produce "works of the flesh."[134] The Spirit
leaves no room for the flesh to take an opportunity to exercise its influence and produce its work (and, of course, vice
versa).[135] The Spirit takes away the ἀφορμὴ τῆς σαρκός (5:13)
by pushing the flesh out from the center of a person's existence (5:17). By the same token, the need no longer exists to
be compelled by the law of Moses, which is a παιδαγωγός, to do
good deeds, since those who live in the sphere of the Spirit
produce its "fruit," namely, love, which is the sum of the
"whole Law."[136] The "law of Christ" in 6:2, namely, "to bear

each other's burden," which in 6:9-10 is summarized as "doing
the good," and "doing good to all,"[137] is Paul's definition of
love,[138] just as "being servants to each other through love"
(5:13) is his definition of "the sum of the Law," which he
"quotes" from Scripture: "love your neighbor as yourself"
(5:14).

The irony of the contrast in 3:3 between ἐνάρχεσθαι
πνεύματι and ἐπιτελεῖν σαρκί is that those who *began* with the
Spirit are really no longer mere "beginners," "minors," or
νήπιοι, but are "sons-come-of-age"; that is, the πνευματικοί
are technically τέλειοι.[139] The other side of the irony is
that those who would *end* (ἐπιτελέω) with "works of the law"
are not τέλειοι at all, but rather νήπιοι.[140] For the ἐναρξάμενοι πνεύματι are liberated from the law of Moses, which is a
παιδαγωγός, but the ἐπιτελοῦντες σαρκί become slaves to the
slavish Mosaic law, because it becomes their παιδαγωγός. The
"minor" who is under a παιδαγωγός (3:24), that is, "under the
law," is a δοῦλος (4:1), because he is not "*self*-controlled,"[141]
but ruled by another, namely, the law of Moses.[142]

The anthropology implied in 5:17c is one in which one's
"doing" is no more determined by ἃ ἐὰν θέλητε in the sphere of
the Spirit than in that of the flesh. In the sphere of the
Spirit one's "doing" is governed by the ἐπιθυμεῖν of the Spirit, which is what the epithet πνευματικοί (6:1) means. Elsewhere, however, Paul describes the function of the Spirit not
like that of the law of Moses, as that of a παιδαγωγός who
restrains and compels,[143] but rather as that of a "guide," who
resides, not outside like the παιδαγωγός (the law of Moses),
but within the "heart" of believers (4:6).[144] This seems to
allow for a concept of freedom associated with existence centered in the Spirit; whereas the anthropology implicit in 5:17
seems to conceive of the Spirit as an agent of a new kind of
non-freedom. One way to solve this problem is to attribute
only one of these views to Paul. Betz, for example, concludes
that 5:17 is traditional and, therefore, not Pauline.[145] In
this way, we could exclude from Paul's own view, in distinction
from that of 5:17, the deterministic aspect of the anthropology
implied in 5:17. But this is unsatisfactory, since the

determinism of 5:17 is exactly what Paul relies on to establish
5:16; and it is this part of 5:17 which 5:18 presupposes. Precisely that aspect of the anthropology of 5:17 which conflicts,
at least seemingly, with 5:16, 18, 25 and 6:1, and because of
which 5:17 is attributed to tradition rather than to Paul, cannot therefore be got rid of by the method of tradition-analysis.

Another way this problem can be approached is to find a
way within Paul's theology to reconcile the two views of freedom and the Spirit. We are presented with two possibilities.
Either the "war" between the flesh and the Spirit can be interpreted so that room exists for the individual to decide from
moment to moment which power to follow, and then to interpret
Paul's use of πνεύματι with a verb in a Pelagian manner;[146] or
Paul's statements in 3:3, 5:5, 16, 18, 25 and 6:1 can be taken
to distinguish between the "grammatical subject," which is the
human individual, and the "logical subject," which would be the
Spirit, so that the deeds performed πνεύματι could be understood to be performed *by* the Spirit *in* the individual Christian, rather than by the individual *with the help* of the
Spirit.[147] Given these interpretive alternatives, despite the
best efforts of such scholars as Mussner and Betz, we are left
with a choice between Pelagianism and determinism. According
to these alternatives, Paul's view in Galatians is either that
the Christian actually performs deeds with the help of the
Spirit, or that the Spirit actually performs certain deeds in
the Christian but without the help of the Christian.

The complexity of this difficult problem becomes evident
when we see that the same alternatives exist with respect to
"works of the law" and "works of the flesh." Paul knows no
divine assistance for those who perform "works of the law."[148]
Actually under the law of Moses "flesh" has control of a person's deeds,[149] so that "works of the flesh" are produced. But
how? Is it the human individual who carries out the "desires
of the flesh,"[150] or actually the flesh itself who manipulates
the human subject to perform "works of the flesh"?[151] In Galatians, it is seemingly as impossible to sort out responsibility, blame and guilt with respect to "vice" or sin, as it is to
sort out the problem of free-will and determinism with respect
to "virtue" or doing good.

What is needed is a view that is more drawn out than
Paul's succinct statements about the Spirit and freedom in the
letter to the Galatians. Paul provides such a view in his
letter to the Romans. In Rom 7:23-25, Paul says of unredeemed
humanity, that the human self is actually split into "the law
of sin," whose locus is the flesh, and "the law of the mind,"
whose locus is the "inner man." Paul, therefore, can say both
that it is no longer "I" who does evil but "sin in the
flesh,"[152] and that the "I" actually does evil[153] without contradiction, because the "I" is split. But this view simply
cannot be harmonized with that of Gal 5:13-24. Paul's earlier
view in the latter conceives of the flesh, rather than sin, as
the power behind human evil;[154] and it is not identified with
the human self, nor even with a part of the human "I".[155]

On the other hand, Rom 8:1-17 might come closer to the
concept of the Spirit and freedom in Gal 5:13-24. In Rom 8:4,
Paul contrasts two ways of life: περιπατεῖν κατὰ σάρκα and κατὰ
πνεῦμα, which is synonymous with the contrast between περιπατεῖν πνεύματι and τελεῖν ἐπιθυμίαν σαρκός in Gal 5:16. In Rom
8:5-6, Paul defines κατὰ σάρκα περιπατεῖν (εἶναι) as τὰ τῆς
σαρκὸς φρονεῖν, and κατὰ πνεῦμα περιπατεῖν (εἶναι) as τὰ τοῦ
πνεύματος φρονεῖν. The concept of τὸ φρονεῖν τίνα concerns
not only the intellect or reason, but precisely that exercise
of the "mind" toward an aim or goal, so that it has to do with
the moral disposition of a person toward an object.[156]   In
other words, those who live according to the flesh are morally
disposed toward τὰ τῆς σαρκός, so that they carry out the "desires of the flesh," as Paul says in Gal 5:16. This is expressed in Gal 5:19-21 in terms of the concept of "the works of
the flesh," which define τὰ τῆς σαρκός.[157] Those who live according to the Spirit are likewise morally disposed toward τὰ
τοῦ πνεύματος, so that they carry out its "desires," which are
defined in Gal 5:22-23 in terms of the concept of "the fruit
of the Spirit."[158]

What does this tell us about Paul's concept of freedom?[159]
Paul presupposes that a person first of all must choose which
sphere to belong to, that of the flesh or that of the Spirit.
This is implied by his missionary activity and his concept of

receiving the Spirit by faith in what was preached.[160] Before
one can carry out the intentions of the Spirit (περιπατεῖν /
στοιχεῖν πνεύματι), a person must first give up living in the
sphere of the desires of the flesh, and by faith accept life in
the sphere of the Spirit, from which alone one can perceive the
intentions of the Spirit (τὸ φρονεῖν τὰ τοῦ πνεύματος). This
is expressed in Gal 5:24-25 in terms of "crucifying the flesh
with its passions and desires," and taking up a new life in the
Spirit.[161] For Paul this life is obtained by faith in the crucified Christ; and it is maintained in the same way. As long
as one keeps one's faith in Christ, a person participates in
the sphere of the Spirit, so that one can perceive and carry
out the "desires" of the Spirit. But if one is diverted back
to the flesh, either by turning one's attention to "desires"
of the flesh,[162] or by putting one's faith in "works of the
law,"[163] or any "religion" other than the "religion" which
originated from and is centered in Christ,[164] the new life in
the Spirit can be lost, and then one will not be able to fulfill the intentions of the Spirit.

In other words, a person has the freedom to choose between
two spheres, the flesh and the Spirit, and whether to belong to
one or to the other. Those who belong to the flesh must first
"transfer" by faith to the sphere of the Spirit before they
can fulfill the intentions of the Spirit, an option which until
then would not be open to them. But those who already, by
faith, belong to the Spirit (οἱ πνευματικοί) are as such already free to carry out the intentions of the Spirit. The
choice to live in the sphere of the Spirit, which for Paul is
the decision for faith in Christ, opens up new possibilities
for a person's moral disposition.[165] The Spirit offers the
believer "desires," which could not be carried out before, in a
life in the sphere of the flesh. This constitutes the freedom
of the πνευματικοί. For, those who still live in the sphere
of the flesh only carry out *its* "desires," that is, manifest
only "works of the flesh."

The Spirit and the flesh determine the possibilities of
moral choice for those who live in their "fields of force."
Each person has the freedom to choose to live in one field or

the other. Those who choose to live in the sphere of the flesh
can choose only from the possibilities offered by its "passions
and desires," which Paul calls "works of the flesh."[166] But
those who live in the sphere of the Spirit can choose not only
from these possibilities but also from the possibilities offered by the Spirit, which Paul calls "the fruit of the
Spirit."[167]

Something like this is what Paul could have meant by
statements in the letter to the Galatians about the Spirit as
the norm of human action (πνεύματι with a verb). But then
Pelagianism and determinism are both correct in part. For the
Spirit *determines* Christian "doing," just as the flesh *determines* the action of unredeemed persons, in the sense that it
determines the possibilities, that is, the options and power,
of moral action presented to the free choice of Christians. As
such, it is also true that "the fruit of the Spirit" is manifested as much with *the help of the Spirit* as with *the effort
of the Christian*. For without the effort of the Christian, the
Spirit could not produce its "fruit"; and without the Spirit a
person could only produce "works of the flesh." Paul's concept
of τὸ ἄγεσθαι πνεύματι in Gal 5:18, therefore, means that the
Spirit presents Christians with the power to enact the intentions of the Spirit without coercing them. The choice is finally up to the believer, to enact the desires of the flesh or
those of the Spirit, even though the "guidance" of the Spirit
is weighted in favor of the enactment of the Spirit's "desires."

The determinism of 5:17 is more difficult to explain. For
the human "will" (τὸ θέλειν) is "paralyzed" by both the *flesh*
and the *Spirit*, which seems to imply that human action (ποιεῖν)
is the doing of either the *flesh* or the *Spirit*. But this too
is understandable in terms of the paragraph above: one's *possibilities* of action are determined by the sphere one belongs to,
not by ἃ ἐὰν θέλητε. Moreover, if 5:16 is formulated with the
Galatians' consideration of taking up life "under the law" (cf.
5:18) in mind,[168] then it becomes evident that Paul identifies
the Galatians' consideration of living "under the law" as a
desire to "live as they wish," to borrow a slogan of the Stoics,
which is expressed in 5:17 by the phrase ἃ ἐὰν θέλητε ποιεῖν.[169]

That is to say, that the Galatians may have thought that by
living "under the law" they would "live as they wished," which
was to *not* fulfill the "desires" of the flesh (5:16). Paul
argues, however, that the only way *not* to fulfill the "desires"
of the flesh was for them to continue being led by the Spirit
(5:18), rather than to turn to the law of Moses and as such to
rely only on their will-power to "live as they wished." In
other words, in 5:17 Paul identifies the slogan ἃ ἐὰν θέλητε
ποιεῖν with the Galatians' consideration of living "under the
law," perhaps because the Galatians also identified them;
therefore, 5:17 is formulated polemically precisely to reject
this slogan. The rest of Paul's statements about the Spirit,
however, indicate that Paul does not thereby deny *all* participation of the human "will" in Christian "doing." Rather, he
insists that Christian action takes place within the framework
of the Spirit's guidance, which offers the *power* to enact the
intentions of the Spirit as well as possibilities of moral
choice. Outside this framework, however, the Galatians can
only enact "works of the flesh," even with the law of Moses.
As such their freedom depends on being led by the Spirit, not
on living "as they wished," even if this was identified with
living "under the law."

In summary, Christians in Galatia were considering living
"under the law" (that is, in accordance with the law of Moses)
in order that they would not fulfill the "desires" of the
flesh. Perhaps because the slogan ἃ ἐὰν θέλητε ποιεῖν, or
something similar, was interpreted in the Galatian churches (by
the nomists?) in terms of living in accordance with the law of
Moses, Paul rejects this slogan together with its interpretation. The reason he gives is anthropological and soteriological. Only two possibilities exist: to live in accordance with
the flesh, or to live in accordance with the Spirit. "To live
as one wishes," therefore, even interpreted as living "under
the law," means one can only live in accordance with the
flesh.[170] If Christians in Galatia want to avoid fulfilling
the "desires" of the flesh, Paul argues, they should continue
to live in accordance with the intentions of the Spirit.

(3) This also means that those who live in accordance with
the Spirit, that is, the ἐλεύθεροι, do what "the Law" requires,
while those who live "under the law" do not. The nomists in
Galatia had maintained that "the Law" requires circumcision.[171]
Paul, however, argues that the law *of Moses* requires circumcision, but "the Law" requires "faith working through love,"[172]
that is, a "new creation."[173] The "law of Christ" (6:2) does
not introduce a new law which is different in content from that
of "the Law";[174] rather, it is based on a new possibility of
human existence.[175] This is where the law of Moses and "the
law of Christ" differ. Paul, therefore, argues that contrary
to the law of Moses, the "book of the Law," that is, Scripture,
requires that life be based not on "works of the law" but
faith; that is, that δικαιοσύνη is based not on living ἐν νόμῳ
but on living ἐκ πίστεως.[176] It is, therefore, in a twofold
sense that the ἐλεύθεροι do what "the Law" requires, but those
who live "under the law" do not.[177]

To begin with, the failure of those "under the law" to do
what "the Law" requires. In 3:10-12, Paul distinguishes between
"works of the law" and "the Law" which is contained in, and in
fact is, Scripture. His argument, based on proofs from Scripture, is that those whose lives are based on "works of the law"
are "under a curse," because they do not do what "the Law"
(= Scripture) requires.[178] For the Scriptures state that the
"righteous" live on the basis of faith, proving that no one is
righteous by means of "works of the law."[179] Since "works of
the law" do not originate in faith, therefore, those who do
them live on the basis of them and not on faith.[180] In this
way, "those who live by works of the law" do not do what the
Scriptures require; namely, to base their lives on faith. They
are, therefore, "under a curse."

On the one hand, Paul does not doubt the possibility of
doing all "the Law" requires.[181] For "the whole Law" requires
that one live ἐκ πίστεως.[182] On the other hand, doing all the
"works of the law," which also is not impossible,[183] is not the
same as doing "the whole Law."[184] The "curse," therefore, is
pronounced over οἱ ἐξ ἔργων νόμου, not because of the impossibility of being faithful to *all* that is written in the "book of

the Law" and doing them, but because ἐξ ἔργων νόμου εἶναι is an
existence based on doing "works of the law" rather than on
faith, as the Scriptures require (3:11-12).   .

If Paul does not bring in the idea of the impossibility of
doing all "the Law" requires, he also does not introduce the
idea that doing "works of the law" per se is sin, nor the related idea that obedience to the law of Moses produces "boasting."[185] The issue is not whether doing all that "the Law"
requires is possible, nor whether doing "works of the law" is
sinful or boastful, but whether "the whole Law" is to be defined by and identified with the requirements of the law of
Moses or with "the law of Christ." In Galatians, Paul does
mention "boasting" in connection with the activity and motives
of the nomist missionaries, but not because he thinks performing "works of the law" is inherently boastful; rather, he wants
to portray or expose the nomist missionaries as "charlatans."[186]
And in Gal 3:19, Paul does say that the reason for the law of
Moses was "because of transgressions"; but this statement cannot simply be interpreted in the light of Rom 5:20, even with
the help of Gal 3:22. For, on the one hand, Gal 3:19 simply
says "the law was added because of transgressions," rather than
"law came in to increase the trespass." In the letter to the
Galatians, Paul interprets the purpose of the law of Moses by
means of the image of the παιδαγωγός,[187] whose purpose was not
to *increase* transgressions, but to *prevent* them by restraint
and compulsion.[188] Furthermore, in Gal 3:22, Paul speaks of
"Scripture," not of the law of Moses. Elsewhere, Paul makes
use of the fluctuation of ὁ νόμος to mean "the law of Moses"
and "Scripture"; but in 3:22, by using ἡ γραφή instead of
ὁ νόμος, he makes it clear that "Scripture," that is, the will
of God, "consigned all things to sin." What Paul has in mind
for the function of the law of Moses is made clear by means of
the temporal clause in 3:19, "until the seed to whom the promise was made should come," and the result clause in 3:22, "so
that the promise might be given through faith in Jesus Christ
to those who believe." In other words, Paul's concept of the
law of Moses is that it was a temporary, interim law.[189]

From the perspective of the Gentile, who remained outside
life "under the law," the law of Moses does have the effect of
generating transgressions, since by definition Gentiles would
be "sinners" before the law of Moses (cf. 2:15). Before the
coming of Christ, this was the only status Gentiles could have
vis-à-vis the law of Moses. This presupposes that *failure* to
do "works of the law," not *doing* them, was "sin."

In other words, Paul's argument in 3:10-12 is hermeneutical as well as ethical and soteriological. The Scriptures do
not require living from "works of the law," but rather living
from "faith." For Paul, to receive circumcision is to exist
"under the law" and "from works of the law,"[190] that is, to
seek righteousness in "works of the law."[191] This means that
the θέλειν of the nomists is contrary to that of God.[192] Since
faith is not the basis of an existence "under the law," Christ
will not be of any benefit to those who live "under the law"
(5:2-4), because for Paul living from faith means participating
in the "new creation" originated by and centered in Christ and
his Spirit.[193] That is why those who are seeking righteousness
by "works of the law" are "cut-off from Christ, fallen from
grace."

The functions of each of Paul's statements in 5:2-4 are
not clear, since all but 5:3 are asyndetic. As for their content, 5:2 and 5:4 are parallel, so that ἐν νόμῳ δικαιοῦσθαι
means to receive circumcision. And 5:3 is reminiscent of
3:10.[194] Then 5:5 introduces the reason (γάρ) for the previous
statements (vv. 2-4); that is, δικαιοσύνη comes not ἐν νόμῳ but
"by the Spirit which is received by faith" (πνεύματι ἐκ πίστεως).[195] Further, 5:6 states the reason (γάρ) for 5:5; that
is, that righteousness comes from faith rather than from "works
of the law," because in Christ neither circumcision nor uncir-
cumcision but only πίστις δι' ἀγάπης ἐνεργουμένη is of any
advantage.[196] This means that circumcision does not bring
about participation in Christ and, as such, does not fulfill
"the whole Law," because it is a righteousness based on "works
of the law" rather than on faith, which receives the Spirit.
In this way, 5:2-6 can be seen as a parallel to Paul's argument
in 3:10-12.

When Paul informs the churches of Galatia, therefore, that everyone who receives circumcision must do "the whole Law,"[197] he does not have in mind "works of the law"; rather, he has in mind the requirement that life be based on faith. Not only do the Scriptures require this,[198] but this is the meaning of Christ's coming;[199] and this, in fact, is confirmed by the Galatians' initial experience of the Spirit (3:1-5); namely, that Christian existence is based on faith as a participation in the "new creation" originated by and centered in Christ and his Spirit. In this sense, therefore, the πνευματικοί, that is, those who are set free by Christ and his Spirit, do all that "the Law" requires, while those who exist "under the law" do not.

There is another reason why the ἐλεύθεροι / πνευματικοί, not οἱ ὑπὸ νόμον, keep "the Law." The free, being guided by the Spirit, produce the "fruit of the Spirit," whose primary characteristic is "love" (5:22). According to Paul, this is the center of "the Law."[200] Moreover, it is produced by faith and the Spirit;[201] and it is the meaning of freedom.[202] But those who seek to be righteous by "works of the law"[203] fail to do the "loving" required by "the Law" (5:14), which is identical with the "law of Christ,"[204] because they can only manifest its opposite, "the works of the flesh."[205]

We may infer from Paul's arguments two reasons why only the free are able to love their neighbors. First, because those whose righteousness is based on "works of the law" are under the influence of the flesh,[206] they can manifest only "works of the flesh," which are the exact opposite of love.[207] Love, the primary characteristic of the "fruit of the Spirit," cannot be produced by the Spirit's metaphysical opposite. Only those who are free from the flesh, therefore, love their neighbors.

The second reason only the free love the neighbor as "the Law" requires is that only those who are "self-controlled" are able to be "slaves" to others through love (5:13c). To be free in the Spirit means that one is "self-controlled."[208] "Self-control" means that a person takes charge of one's own life by not giving free reign to the passions and desires, which work

through the flesh to produce "works of the flesh."[209] The
ἐγκρατεῖς are not conceited (5:26a), because they are not de-
luded (6:3). They, therefore, do not provoke or envy others
(5:26b); rather, they treat others gently.[210] That is to say,
that they "bear the burdens of others" as the "law of Christ"
requires (6:2). The ἐγκρατεῖς (πνευματικοί) can have a genuine
care for others precisely because they have an authentic care
for themselves. In other words, ἐλεύθεροι are set free from
anxiety about themselves, and from other unwanted "passions and
desires,"[211] since the Spirit fills them with joy, peace, etc.,
so that they can devote their care to others.[212] Those who
have an *improper* concern for *themselves*, that is, those who,
for example, desire fame and fear persecution,[213] cannot have
a *proper* concern for *others*.[214] Therefore, not only do the
ἐλεύθεροι fulfill "the Law," but *only* they do what "the Law"
requires, namely, to love each other (the neighbor).

The free are not of the flesh, but of the Spirit. A person who lives "under the law," on the other hand, is still
bound to the flesh's control. For this reason, the latter has
need of a παιδαγωγός, but the former does not. The one is a
"child" who must have another who is his or her master; namely,
the law of Moses. The other is "mature," or "of age," through
Christ and his Spirit. The free, therefore, have a "master
within" who, precisely because it is *within*, makes them their
own master (ἐγκρατεῖς).[215] Whereas the law of Moses, as a
παιδαγωγός, exercises restraint and compulsion *over* the deeds
of those *under* it,[216] the Spirit gently guides those *within*
whom it dwells.[217]

This means the πνευματικοί are free. But their freedom is
paradoxical. On the one hand, they are free from powers which
would be their slavish masters, namely, flesh and the law of
Moses; and yet they are their own masters only insofar as they
do the will of the Spirit in them.[218] On the other hand, if
Christians in Galatia take up life "under the law," they will
not be faithful to "the Law"; they can be faithful to "the Law,"
as they wish, not by being *under the law of Moses* (4:21), but
by continuing to live out their faith through love, which comes
from living in and by the Spirit. They are free, therefore,
who live in accordance with the guidance of the Spirit.

Conclusion. We have shown that Paul presents the "new
creation" as a life of freedom. At the origin and center of
this freedom are Christ and the Spirit. The freedom which they
create is contrasted with slavish existence centered in the
flesh. This contrast has its Sitz im Leben in the controversy
in the churches of Galatia over the Galatians' consideration
of taking up "works of the law" as a way of life. The freedom
of the "new creation," therefore, is contrasted with nomistic
existence, which, like life centered in the flesh, is slavish.
Nomistic existence, which is life centered in "works of the
law," is in fact presented as a life centered in "works of the
flesh," at the same time that it is cast as an inferior compe-
titor of Spirit-centered existence as the way to righteousness.

By contrasting the freedom of "Spiritual" existence with
the slavery of nomistic existence, as rival alternatives to
life centered in the flesh, Paul reveals an underlying understanding of the problem of human existence which is more radical than that of the nomists. For the nomists, the problem is
the failure to do "works of the law"; circumcision, then,
symbolizes and effects serious obedience to God's will through
"works of the law." For Paul, on the other hand, the human
predicament is the slavish power of the flesh at the very center of human existence, which is manifest in "works of the
flesh." In Paul's view, "works of the law," epitomized by
circumcision, are only superficial efforts at redemption from
the power of the flesh, in the sense that they are only external. They are not radical enough; for they do not, in Paul's
opinion, go to the root of the problem, which is the flesh's
domination of the center of human existence.

The reason Christ and the Spirit solve the problem of
slavery to the flesh, whereas the "works of the law" do not,
is that Christ and the Spirit are the flesh's metaphysical
opponents, whereas "works of the law" are not.[219] Christ and
the Spirit, therefore, affect the very structure of human existence. They push out the flesh from the center, so that the
passions and desires no longer have any opportunity to produce
"works of the flesh." In contrast, "works of the law" cannot
remove the flesh from its position, because they offer no

alternative power capable of holding a place against the cen-
trality of the flesh. Since the Spirit is the only metaphysical rival of the flesh, and since "works of the law" do not
bring the Spirit (3:1-5), they can only try to strengthen the
"will," which cannot do battle with the flesh (5:17).

This then accounts for the contrast between slavish nomistic existence and the freedom brought by Christ and the Spirit.
Since "works of the law" leave the flesh in position, those who
live "under the law" need the restraint and compulsion of a
παιδαγωγός; therefore, they are δοῦλοι. Christ and the Spirit,
on the other hand, expel the flesh from its central position in
human existence and take its place. The Spirit does not, however, try to strengthen the "will" by restraint and compulsion,
like the "works of the law"; rather, it takes the place of the
flesh as the source of doing and living.[220] In other words,
the ἄγειν of the Spirit replaces the rule of the flesh (which
through the passions and desires produces "works of the flesh")
and, therefore, also the rule of the law of Moses.[221]

This, finally, is the reason why *only* the ἐλεύθερος, who
is πνευματικός and, therefore, also ἐγκρατής, fulfills "the
Law" (of Christ, not of Moses). The free live ἐκ πίστεως, as
"the Law" requires; while the nomist lives ἐξ ἔργων νόμου.
Furthermore, those who live by "works of the law," Paul argues,
can only manifest "works of the flesh." But Christ sets at
liberty those who receive the Spirit with faith in order that,
instead of being slaves to the flesh, they might be servants
to one another through love. Since the sum of "the Law" is
love, and since the "fruit of the Spirit" is love, those who
live in the liberty of the Spirit fulfill "the Law."

The freedom brought by Christ and the Spirit is a "new
creation." It is new because it replaces a former existence
dominated by "works of the flesh." But it is also new because
Spirit-centered existence replaces existence based on "works of
the law" as the only "authentic" alternative to sarkic existence. The freedom brought by Christ and the Spirit, therefore, is *historically*, as well as soteriologically, a "new
creation."

Conclusion

Paul traces the "new creation" to ecstatic experiences,
with which Christians in Galatia had begun Christian existence
(3:3). Using irony, Paul argues that, in contrast to the
nomists, who, in Paul's view, would have the Galatian Christians *end* with the flesh and thus become again νήπιοι and
δοῦλοι, the Galatians who *had begun* with the Spirit actually
were τέλειοι; that is, they were υἱοί and ἐλεύθεροι.

Then Paul identifies this "new creation" brought by Christ
and his Spirit with "sonship" and "freedom." In 4:6, Paul appeals to the ecstatic Abba-cry as evidence that through Christ
the Galatians had been made υἱοί. That they were *free* "sons"
is the thesis of Paul's allegorical interpretation of Abraham,
Hagar and the two sons (4:21-31). By means of a series of
proofs from Scripture, Paul establishes not only that the
Christians in Galatia were ἐλεύθεροι, but that the nomists were
δοῦλοι. Having established in 4:21-31 that, in the words of
5:1, Christ sets at liberty those who, like the Galatians, had
received the Spirit through faith, Paul solves the problem of
how this liberty was to be maintained and expressed. Three
possibilities lay before him: by the righteousness which comes
from "works of the law" (5:4), by giving an opportunity to the
passions and desires to produce "works of the flesh" (5:13-24),
and by living in the Spirit and producing its "fruit" (5:16-
25). Since Paul's solution is to live in the Spirit, he also
shows why righteousness by means of "works of the law" does not
preserve or lead to freedom. At the same time, he demonstrates
that his ethics based on the Spirit will not, and does not,
lead to giving opportunity to "works of the flesh." Paul defends this concept of ethics by appealing to the Galatians'
initial experiences of the Spirit (3:1-5 and 4:6) and to proofs
from Scripture (3:6-4:31), and by parenesis (5:1-6:10).

In the letter to the Galatians, Paul knows of two forms of
so-called "authentic" human existence: one is centered in the
law of Moses, the other in Christ and his Spirit. However,
since he calls one "bondage" and the other "freedom," it is
doubtful Paul considered both genuinely "authentic" forms of

human existence. The problem with the category of "authentic
existence" is that it suggests only two possibilities between
which a person can and must choose. It is clear that for Paul,
whatever he may have thought of Abraham and Isaac's relationship to faith in Christ and his Spirit,[222] nevertheless for the
period between the Abrahamic age and the coming of Christ and
his Spirit, viewed from the perspective of Christian existence,
the only two possibilities of human existence were two forms of
slavish existence, nomistic and sarkic. Of these two, nomistic
existence is more "authentic," but it remains slavish. During
that period, freedom through Christ and his Spirit was not yet
a possibility. As long as that form of existence remained out
of reach, the only form of "authentic" existence was nomism.
According to 3:19-22, the period of the law of Moses was a
period under ἁμαρτία. "Sin" was the state of existence *as such*
prior to the coming of Christ and his Spirit.[223] But after
Christ and his Spirit came, three forms of existence became
possible: sarkic, nomistic, and pneumatic or Christian. A decision not possible before now had to be made: Was the power of
the flesh (exercised through the passions and desires) to be
overthrown through "works of the law" or through Christ and
his Spirit? Paul's answer is that the only way to overthrow
the flesh is to "belong to Christ" and to live in and with his
Spirit. Paul's justification of this "only" is that being
"under the law" does not ultimately overthrow the flesh at the
center of a person's existence, since "works of the law" leave
the flesh "in position" while trying to "fence" it in. Christ
and the Spirit, on the other hand, replace the power of the
flesh by dwelling in its place at the center of a person's
existence.[224] This, finally, is why nomistic existence is
slavish, while Christ and his Spirit bring freedom, as Paul
makes clear in his argument in 5:1-6:10.[225]

     The point we wish to make, in conclusion, is that freedom
is not an original possibility open to men and women always and
everywhere,[226] at least in Paul's view in the letter to the
Galatians. Since Christ and his Spirit are genuinely historical entities, freedom, being dependent on Christ and the Spirit
as its source, is a historically emergent possibility and, in

that sense, a genuinely *new* "creation"; that is, new not only
with respect to a person's own former existence, but also as a
new form of existence in history. But it is historically
emergent, it must be emphasized, not in the sense that its
emergence was dependent on the development of essential features of the structure(s) of human existence; rather, Paul's
view in Galatians is that a "new creation" emerged historically
because of God's action of "sending" Christ and his Spirit into
the world (4:4-6).[227]

The Spirit, therefore, is manifest in a structure of existence that is both soteriologically and historically a *"new*
creation." It consists of "sonship" as well as "self-control"
(ἐγκράτεια), that is, freedom from "works of the flesh" and
from the "yoke of slavery" to "works of the law." The Spirit,
therefore, inaugurates a "new creation" as the solution to the
pervasiveness of "works of the flesh"; that is, as a solution
to the human predicament.

[1]Cf. Gal 6:15 and 2 Cor 5:17.

[2]Cf. below, pp. 103-104.

[3]Cf. below, pp. 105-109.

[4]Cf. below, pp. 110-13.

[5]Cf. below, pp. 113-28.

[6]Cf. 6:1.

[7]Cf. the antithesis, ἐνάρχομαι / ἐπιτελέω in 3:3. Paul seems to refer to a *topos* here (which reappears in 3:24 and 4:1-7 as a contrast of the minor and son-come-of-age; cf. also 1 Cor 2:6-3:4, where the τέλειοι are contrasted with the νήπιοι). For an example of this *topos*, see Crates, *Ep.* 6 (R. Hercher, *Epistolographi Graeci* [Paris: Didot, 1873] 209-209), where the ἄρχεσθαι of Antisthenes is contrasted with the τελεῖν of Diogenes in doing philosophy (cf. above, Chapter II, p. 51 n. 87). The common opinion is that this antithesis uses technical terms from a cultic context (cf. above, Chapter II, p. 51 n. 87; and Chapter III, p. 76 n. 13; cf. also Lightfoot, *St. Paul to the Galatians*, 135; Lagrange, *Epître aux Galates*, 59-60; and Schlier, *Brief an die Galater*, 124).

[8]Cf. 3:6-4:11, 21-31, 5:1-12; especially 5:4 (cf. 2:21).

[9]Cf. 5:13-6:10; especially 5:18, 23b and 25 (cf. 3:3b).

[10]Cf. 3:15-25 and 6:14-15 (cf. 3:3a).

[11]This is half of the thesis of the suggestive article by E. P. Sanders ("Patterns of Religion in Paul and Rabbinic Judaism: A Holistic Method of Comparison," *HTR* 66 [1973] esp. 465) (cf. now also his *Paul* [passim]).

[12]Cf. H. D. Betz, "Paul's Concept of Freedom in the Context of Hellenistic Discussions About Possibilities of Human Freedom," pp. 6, 8 in *Protocol Series of the Colloquies of the Center for Hermeneutical Studies in Hellenistic and Modern Culture*, #26 (ed. W. Wuellner; Berkeley, CA: Graduate Theological Union and University of California, 1977]).

[13]This is the other half of Sanders's thesis ("Patterns of Religion," 469, 476).

[14]Cf. Gal 4:3-7 and 1:4. For the view that the law of Moses is bound to a limited human epoch, see 3:15-25 (especially vv. 19-22); see also Rom 5:12-21.

[15]Cf. Betz, "Paul's Concept," 6, 8, 10. The guilt-forgiveness-repentance language is virtually absent in Paul's letters (cf. Sanders, "Patterns of Religion," 466-76; and Krister Stendahl, *Paul Among Jews and Gentiles and Other Essays* [Philadelphia: Fortress, 1976] 23-40, 78-96).

[16]Cf. below, pp. 110-13, which take up 4:21-31, and pp. 113-28, which take up 5:1-6:10.

[17]Cf. 3:26-29, 4:1-7, 21-31.

[18]Cf. above, Chapter III, pp. 68-69.

[19]Cf. 4:21-31, 6:14-16 (cf. also 2:15-16, 3:6-14).

[20]Cf. 4:21-31, which also speaks of "sonship" and the Spirit without mentioning baptism.

[21]Cf. below, pp. 105-106.

[22]Cf. below, pp. 106-108.

[23]Cf. below, pp. 108-109.

[24]Cf. Antoine Duprez, "Note sur le rôle de l'Esprit-Saint dans la filiation du chrétien, à propos de *Gal.* 4:6," *RSR* 52 (1964) 428 n. 17.

[25]For taking the ὅτι in a causal sense, see Lightfoot, *St. Paul to the Galatians*, 169 (but his explanation treats it as a declarative); Meyer, *Epistle to the Galatians*, 174; Lipsius, *Briefe an die Galater*, 48; Burton, *Epistle to the Galatians*, 221-22; Schlier, *Brief an die Galater*, 197-98; Oepke, *Paulus an die Galater*, 97; Bonnard, *Saint Paul aux Galates*, 87 (but his translation renders it as a declarative; cf. p. 83); Betz, *Commentary on Paul's Letter*, ad loc.; Turner, *A Grammar*, 345; and Schweizer, *TDNT* 6.426 n. 624 (cf. also *KJ* and *RSV*).

[26]The ὅτι in 4:6 could be eliptical for either εἰς ἐκεῖνο ὅτι (BAG, "ὅτι," 1, c; BDF, sec. 480.6; and Dunn, *Baptism*, 113-14), or ὅτι δὲ...δῆλον, ὅτι, a formula used in 3:11 (cf. Ellicott, *Paul's Epistle to the Galatians*, 95; Lagrange, *Epître aux Galates*, 103-104; Lietzmann, *An die Galater*, 27; Moule, *An Idiom Book*, 147; Duprez, "Note sur le rôle," passim; Jeremias, *Prayers*, 65 n. 74; and idem, *New Testament Theology*, 197; cf. also *NEB* and *JB*).

[27]Cf. 4:29 and below, p. 111.

[28]Cf. below, pp. 108-109.

[29]Cf. Duprez, "Note sur le rôle," 429.

[30]Cf. the cautious conclusion in ibid., 421, 431.

[31]Cf. Schweizer, *TDNT* 6.426 n. 624. Lietzmann (*An die Galater*, 27), however, says nothing to support Schweizer's reading of him.

[32]Cf. Dunn, *Baptism*, 114.

[33]Cf. also examples in Meyer, *Epistle to the Galatians*, 174; Lipsius, *Briefe an die Galater*, 48; and Franz Mussner, *Der Galaterbrief* (HTKNT 9; Freiburg/Basel/Wien: Herder & Herder, 1974) 274-75. Cf. below, Chapter V, pp. 154-56.

[34]Cf. Burton, *Epistle to the Galatians*, 221-22 (emphasis added).

[35]Cf. Oepke, *Paulus an die Galater*, 98 (emphasis added).

[36]Cf. Schlier, *Brief an die Galater*, 197 (emphasis added).

[37]Cf. ibid., 199 (emphasis added).

[38]Cf. Schweizer, *TDNT* 6.426 n. 624; and *TDNT* 8.391 n. 418 (where he formulates his view against Schlier's distinction between the *possibility* of sonship made available by the "coming" of Christ and the *reality* of sonship given through the sacrament of baptism). This is similar to Dunn's view (*Baptism*, 114), even though he takes the ὅτι as declarative and Schweizer takes it as causal.

[39]Cf. Betz, *Commentary on Paul's Letter*, on 4:6.

[40]Cf. also 4:29.

[41]It is possible that the ecstatic Abba-cry was uttered only once following baptism (cf. Taylor, "Abba, Father," 62-71), rather than repeatedly after proclamation (as I argue above, Chapter III, pp. 66-69). Even so, the Abba-cry of the Spirit would have been an ecstatic experience *after* the initial gift of the Spirit had been received.

[42]Cf. Lagrange, *Epître aux Galates*, 104; Betz, *Commentary on Paul's Letter*, ad loc., n. 79; and Jeremias, *Prayers*, 65 n. 74.

[43]Against Oepke, *Paulus an die Galater*, 98; Schlier, *Brief an die Galater*, 197; Mussner, *Galaterbrief*, 274-75 (cf. below, p. 111).

[44]Betz suggests that 4:5b refers to baptism (3:26-27), so that "'sonship' appears to be some kind of a link between baptism and the gift of the Spirit, which Paul tends to keep apart here and also in Romans" (*Commentary on Paul's Letter*, on 4:5).

[45]Cf. above, Chapter III, p. 86 n. 102, p. 91 n. 127 and pp. 68-69. Betz argues that Christians in Galatia, who *originally* understood themselves to be "sons of God," have been made to doubt this by the nomists' propaganda (*Commentary on Paul's*

Letter, "Introduction, 7. The Theological Argument of Galatians," and on 4:6).

[46]"Sonship" is also attributed to Christ in 4:5b.

[47]Cf. 4:29.

[48]Cf. Duprez, "Note sur le rôle," 431.

[49]Cf. the concept of "the Spirit of Christ" in 4:6 (cf. below, Chapter V).

[50]Cf. 5:1, 13 (cf. also 1:4 and 4:5a). In Galatians, υἱός and ἐλεύθερος are virtually synonymous (cf. Kurt Niederwimmer, *Der Begriff der Freiheit im Neuen Testament* [Theologische Bibliotek Töpelmann 11; Berlin: Töpelmann, 1966] 195 n. 62).

[51]Cf. 6:15.

[52]Cf. 3:1-5 (and above, pp. 103-04). Cf. also the concept of ζῆν πνεύματι in 5:25a (and below, pp. 110-30).

[53]Cf. 2:4, 4:31, 5:1, 13. For the literature on, and a discussion of, the concept of freedom in Paul and in Greek philosophy, see Betz ("Paul's Concept").

[54]Cf. 2:4 (Christ), 4:31 (Spirit), 5:1 (Christ), 5:13 (God), and 1:4 (Christ), 3:13 (Christ), 4:5 (Christ), 6:14 (Christ). Cf. also 2 Cor 3:17.

[55]Cf. 1:4.

[56]Cf. δουλεία in 4:24, and 5:1; δουλεύω in 4:8, 9, 25 (and 5:13); δοῦλος in 3:28, 4:1, 7; δουλόω in 4:3; and παιδίσκη in 4:22, 23, 30, 31. This soteriological antithesis occurs only in polemic against nomism, and in Paul's letters outside Galatians only in Romans (for bondage, see 6:6, 16-20, 22; 7:6, [25]; 8:15, 21; and for freedom, see 6:18, 20, 22; 7:3; 8:2, 21).

[57]Cf. 3:13, 23-25; 4:1-7, 21-31; 5:1-12, 18, 23b (cf. also 2:19-21).

[58]Cf. 5:13-6:10.

[59]Cf. above, Chapter II.

[60]Cf. 2:15, 17.

[61]Cf. 4:24-25, 5:1 and 4:7.

[62]Cf. 5:1, 13 and 2 Cor 3:17, Rom 8:21. In these passages ἐλευθερία is used without a connecting "from" or "for" clause and, therefore, must be interpreted or defined in terms of its context.

[63]Cf. 5:16 (πνεύματι περιπατεῖν), 5:18 (πνεύματι ἄγεσθαι), 5:25b (πνεύματι στοιχεῖν) and also 6:16 (τῷ κανόνι τούτῳ στοιχεῖν). The opposite is a "walking" by the flesh (cf. 5:13, 16, and 6:8), or by the law of Moses (cf. 4:21, 5:18, 23b, 6:14-16 and 5:6).

[64]Cf. 4:29 (γεννηθῆναι κατὰ πνεῦμα), 5:25a (ζῆν πνεύματι) and also 3:3 (ἐνάρχεσθαι πνεύματι). The opposite is to get life from the law of Moses (cf. 3:12, 21), or from the flesh (cf. 4:23, 29 and 6:8).

[65]Cf. 5:22-23 and 5:6, 14; 6:2, 9-10.

[66]Cf. 4:24a (ἅτινά ἐστιν ἀλληγορούμενα), which begins Paul's interpretation of Scripture ("quoted" in 4:22-23) by stating his interpretative method. In 4:24b (αὗται γὰρ εἰσιν δύο διαθῆκαι) he states his hermeneutical thesis as the reason (γάρ) for adopting the allegorical method.

[67]In 4:22-23 Paul "quotes" from the birth narratives of Abraham's sons, Ishmael and Isaac (cf. 4:22c--γέγραπται γὰρ ὅτι Ἀβραὰμ δύο υἱοὺς ἔσχεν--and 4:22b-23--ἕνα...ἕνα...ἀλλ' ὁ [μὲν] ...ὁ δὲ...); but Paul's interpretation takes up the two mothers (cf. 4:24b--αὗται), the παιδίσκη and the ἐλευθέρα, that is, Hagar and Sarah (cf. 4:24-27). Then, when Paul applies this "text" and his interpretation of it to his readers, he returns to the theme of the two sons (cf. 4:28-31).

[68]Cf. 4:9 (πάλιν...πάλιν); and 5:1 (πάλιν).

[69]Cf. 4:21 (οἱ ὑπὸ νόμον θέλοντες εἶναι). These are not the nomists but Christians in Galatia who are contemplating becoming nomists. Paul addresses *all* Christians in Galatia, not just a faction (cf. also Betz, *Commentary on Paul's Letter*, ad loc.; against Lütgert, *Gesetz und Geist*, 11, 88).

[70]Cf. 4:12 (γίνεσθε ὡς ἐγώ), which can only mean "*remain* as I am," rather than "*become* as I am"; otherwise the ὅτι κἀγὼ ὡς ὑμεῖς would not make sense. For if they had already become nomists, Paul could not say he *is* as they *are*. Paul's meaning is that they are to *remain* free from the law of Moses, just as Paul had been made, like them, free from the law of Moses (cf. 2:18-21, 3:13, 23-25, and 4:5). Cf. also Betz, *Commentary on Paul's Letter*, ad loc.

[71]Cf. 4:24c (which identifies one "covenant" as being ἀπὸ ὄρους Σινά).

[72]That is to say, to the law of Moses (cf. Meyer, *Epistle to the Galatians*, 203; and Burton, *Epistle to the Galatians*, 258), or to the law of Moses, sin and death (cf. Schlier, *Brief an die Galater*, 224; and Mussner, *Galaterbrief*, 321).

[73]Cf. 4:22b, 23a, 25c, 30-31.

[74]Cf. 4:23b, 28.

[75]Cf. 4:26. This conclusion is actually stated in 5:1, 13.

[76]Cf. 4:22b, 23b, 26, 30-31.

[77]In 4:21, Paul vacillates between νόμος as "the law of Moses," and νόμος as "Scripture and tradition, interpreted allegorically" (cf. Betz, *Commentary on Paul's Letter*, ad loc.). Cf. below, p. 124.

[78]Cf. 4:24e, 25a.

[79]Cf. 4:25b. The verb συστοιχέω means "to belong to the same series" (cf. Delling, *TDNT* 7.669; BAG; and the commentaries). The subject of the verb is either Hagar (cf. Meyer, *Epistle to the Galatians*, 204; Lietzmann, *An die Galater*, 31; and Burton, *Epistle to the Galatians*, 259-60) or the Sinai covenant--probably the former (cf. below, n. 80). In either case, all "belong to the same series."

[80]Cf. 3:24--the law of Moses is a παιδαγωγός, i.e., a slave attendant (cf. BAG; and Georg Bertram, *TDNT* 5.599). In 4:25c, Paul states the reason (γάρ) for aligning "the present Jerusalem" with Hagar, who is the παιδίσκη; that is, the point of comparison between them is that both are in slavery, and both produce offspring for slavery (cf. 4:22b, 23a, 30-31 and 4:25c; and Ellicott, *Paul's Epistle to the Galatians*, 112; Lipsius, *Briefe an die Galater*, 55; Lagrange, *Epître aux Galates*, 128). In 4:24d, using the image of giving birth, Paul also speaks of the Sinai covenant as producing slaves as its adherents. Lietzmann (*An die Galater*, 32) correctly notices that 4:25c establishes proof of 4:24d. In some sense, therefore, the Sinai covenant is also a "slave."

[81]Cf. 3:6-14.

[82]Cf. 3:19-22, 5:2-6 and 6:8.

[83]Cf. 4:1-11.

[84]Cf. 3:3 and 4:29.

[85]Cf. 4:26b and Phil 3:20.

[86]Cf. 3:3 and 4:23, 29.

[87]Cf. 4:29 and 5:1. This holds whether γεννηθῆναι τῆς ἐπαγγελίας / κατὰ πηεῦμα refer to miraculous regeneration (cf. J. M. Robinson, "Regeneration," pp. 24-29 in *IDB* 4 [ed. G. A. Buttrick; Nashville: Abingdon, 1962] esp. 28; Herman Ridderbos, *Paul, An Outline of His Theology* [Grand Rapids, MI: Eerdmans, 1975] 226; Egon Brandenburger, *Fleisch und Geist: Paulus und die dualistische Weisheit* [WMANT 29; Neukirchen-Vluyn: Neukirchener Verlag, 1968] 201; Büchsel and Rengstorf, *TDNT* 1.665-67; Gunkel, *Die Wirkungen*, 75; Meyer, *Epistle to the Galatians*, 210; Burton, *Epistle to the Galatians*, 253; Lietzmann, *An die Galater*, 30; Lipsius, *Briefe an die Galater*, 54; Lagrange, *Epître aux*

Galates, 123; Oepke, *Paulus an die Galater*, 110-11; Schlier,
Brief an die Galater, 217-18, 225; Betz, *Commentary on Paul's
Letter*, on 4:23; Bultmann, *Theology*, 1.237; and C. K. Barrett,
"The Allegory of Abraham, Sarah, and Hagar in the Argument of
Galatians," *Rechtfertigung. Festschrift für Ernst Käsemann zum
70. Geburtstag* [ed. J. Friedrich et al.; Tübingen: Mohr/Siebeck;
Göttingen: Vandenhoeck & Ruprecht, 1976] 10 [Ellicot (*Paul's
Epistle to the Galatians*, 114) and Schweizer (*TDNT* 6.429 and
7.131) reject this view]), or to prophecy uttered by the
Spirit (cf. Anthony T. Hanson, *Studies in Paul's Technique
and Theology* [London: SPCK, 1974] 87-91, 98), or simply to
providential care (cf. Bonnard, *Saint Paul aux Galates*, 96).
The birth-image occurs also in 4:19 in connection with the indwelling of Christ (μορφοῦσθαι Χριστὸς ἐν ὑμῖν). Christ is
also the liberator in 1:4, 2:20, 3:13, 23-25, 4:5, 5:24, and
6:14. The Spirit is the origin of Christian existence according to 3:3 and 5:25.

[88]Cf. 4:23 (ὁ ἐκ τῆς ἐλευθέρας διὰ τῆς ἐπαγγελίας) and
3:1-5, 4:4-6, 5:13 (cf. also 1 Thess 1:10 and Phil 3:20). That
the origin of Christian existence is God, while that of nomistic existence is not, is the point of 3:19-20 and 5:8. This
contrast is also reflected in the way Paul speaks of his gospel
as having come through "revelation" rather than from "men" (cf.
1:1, 6-17, 2:2, 8-9). It is also reflected in the contrast
between boasting in the flesh, which Paul attributes to the
nomists, and Paul's boast in the cross of Christ (cf. 6:12-14).

[89]Cf. Ernst Käsemann (*Perspectives on Paul* [Philadelphia:
Fortress, 1971] 98) where he observes that temporal sequence
and spatial contrast are merged, as in typology. On the other
hand, Niederwimmer contends that the contrast is not temporal
but only spatial (cf. *Der Begriff*, 194).

[90]For the notion that "sending" implies "pre-existence,"
see Kramer (*Christ*, 113-14 and 119-21).

[91]Cf. 1 Thess 1:10 and Phil 3:20. The concept of the
"Jerusalem above," therefore, is christological (cf. Mussner,
Der Galaterbrief, 327).

[92]Similarly, Ulrich Luz argues that the two "covenants"
stand side by side in time ("Der alte und der neue Bund bei
Paulus und im Hebräerbrief," *EvT* 27 [1967] 322).

[93]Cf. 1 Thess 1:10 and Phil 3:20. For the contrary view,
see Lipsius, *Briefe an die Galater*, 55; Lagrange, *Epître aux
Galates*, 128; Schlier, *Brief an die Galater*, 223-25; Bonnard,
Saint Paul aux Galates, 98, 161; and Hermann Strathmann, *TDNT*
6.531. The effort to determine whether the "Jerusalem above"
is present or future, or somehow both (cf., for example, Ellicott, *Paul's Epistle to the Galatians*, 96-97) rests on the
assumption that it is somehow to be identified with the Christian community.

[94]The νῦν carries with it the connotation of "this present evil age" (cf. 1:4 and 4:29) and "this world" (cf. 4:3, 6:14). Schlier (*Brief an die Galater*, 224) correctly identifies this Jerusalem as the *world* subjected to law, sin and death, as well as the present earthly city of Jerusalem (see also Betz, *Commentary on Paul's Letter*, on 4:25, 26).

[95]Cf. 3:17.

[96]Cf. 4:2 and the "before," "until," and "no longer" in 3:23-25. Cf. Brandenburger, *Fleisch und Geist*, 201 n. 2; Paul Vielhauer, "Paulus und das Alte Testament," pp. 33-62 in *Studien zur Geschichte und Theologie der Reformation. Festschrift für Ernst Bizer* (ed. L. Abramowski and J. F. G. Goeters; Neukirchen-Vluyn: Neukirchener Verlag, 1969) esp. 45, 48 (where he argues that historical sequence plays no role here, and that the antithesis is soteriological rather than historical); C. F. D. Moule, "2 Cor 3,18b, καθάπερ ἀπὸ κυρίου πνεύματος," pp. 231-37 in *Neues Testament und Geschichte: Historisches Geschehen und Deutung im Neuen Testament. O. Cullmann zum 70. Geburtstag* (ed. H. Baltensweiler and B. Reicke; Tübingen: Mohr/Siebeck; Zürich: Theologischer Verlag, 1972) esp. 233-34; and Stendahl, *Paul*, 19-22.

[97]Cf. 4:4, 5:5, 6:8, and below, Chapter VI.

[98]Cf. 3:6-25 and 4:1-7 (cf. below, pp. 131-32).

[99]Cf. the use of μεθίστημι and μεταστρέφω in 1:6-7; and ἐπιστρέφω in 4:9; and πάλιν in 4:8-9 and 5:1.

[100]Cf. below, pp. 114-17.

[101]Cf. below, pp. 117-23.

[102]Cf. below, pp. 123-28.

[103]Cf. above, p. 104.

[104]Perhaps Paul reflects the views of the nomists in the νόμος-phrases in 2:16, 21b; 3:2, 5, 10, 11, 18, 21, 23; 4:4-5, 21; 5:4, 18.

[105]Cf. 3:1-14, 5:2-7, as well as 2:15-21.

[106]Cf. Tannehill's concept of the two dominions (*Dying and Rising*, 14-20, 70-72, 123ff.; cf. also Sanders, *Paul*, 553-54). Both flesh and Spirit are "übermenschlich," "dem *egō* ursprunglich fremd" (Gunkel, *Die Wirkungen*, 73-74).

[107]The ἵνα in 5:17c introduces the result of the opposition between flesh and Spirit (cf. BAG, "ἵνα," II, 2; BDF, sec. 391.5; the *JB*; Lightfoot, *St. Paul to the Galatians*, 210; and Lagrange, *Epître aux Galates*, 148). Others, however, opt for the purposive ἵνα (cf. the *KJ*, *RSV*, *NEB*; Ellicott, *Paul's Epistle to the Galatians*, 130-31; and Burton, *Epistle to the*

Galatians, 302). Betz translates the ἵνα as "so that," but treats it in his comments as "as a result" (*Commentary on Paul's Letter*, 5:13-24 translation, and ad loc., n. 76).

[108]Cf. 2:19-20 and the use of πνεύματι with a verb in 3:3, 5:5, 16, 18, 25, as well as οἱ τοῦ Χριστοῦ with the active ἐσταύρωσαν in 5:24 (cf. also 4:19).

[109]Cf. the separation of θέλειν and ποιεῖν in 5:17c (cf. also Lagrange, *Epître aux Galates*, 148; and Jewett, *Paul's Anthropological Terms*, 323). A similar, but not identical, view is expressed in Rom 7:15-23, where the antithesis of θέλειν / μίσειν is introduced in the separation between θέλειν and πράσσειν / ποιεῖν. There Paul speaks of a split in the structure of unredeemed human existence caused by the struggle between two νόμοι, namely, that of the νοῦς / ἔσω ἄνθρωπος and that of ἁμαρτία. The vocabulary, and probably the conceptuality, in Gal 5:17 are, therefore, different (cf. also Betz's discussion of the "paralysis" of the human "will" by the flesh and Spirit, in *Commentary on Paul's Letter*, on 5:17).

[110]The γάρ in 5:17a introduces the reason for the assertion in 5:16 (cf. Ellicott, *Paul's Epistle to the Galatians*, 130; and below, pp. 117-18). Ἐπιθυμέω with κατά τινος means "to strive against" (cf. BAG, "ἐπιθυμέω"; and BAG, "κατά," I, 2, b, γ; and the *NEB*).

[111]Cf. Lightfoot, *St. Paul to the Galatians*, 210; Lietzmann, *An die Galater*, 39-40; and Lagrange, *Epître aux Galates*, 148.

[112]Cf. 5:18, 25. Cf. Ellicott, *Paul's Epistle to the Galatians*, 131: "the state of the true believer is conflict, but *with final victory*"; therefore, this applies only to "the *earlier* and *more imperfect* stages of a Christian course." The struggle ceases when the Spirit "becomes truly the leading and guiding principle" (cf. also Schweizer, *TDNT* 6.429). For Betz, 5:17 speaks of Christian existence (in contrast to Rom 7:15ff.); but, because it is in conflict with Paul's statements in which πνεύματι is used with a verb (especially 5:18), and because it is in tension with Paul's "more complex" views expressed in Romans 5-8, Betz regards it as pre-Pauline (cf. *Commentary on Paul's Letter*, on 5:17). He, therefore, does not hold Paul to all the anthropology implicit in 5:17.

[113]But in 6:14 these two concepts are combined (cf. Tannehill, *Dying and Rising*, 61).

[114]Cf. also Betz (*Commentary on Paul's Letter*, on 5:24): this is accomplished by the gift of the Spirit, which is the "overwhelming presence of Christ."

[115]Cf. 5:16, 24, 6:14-16, as well as 2:19-20 (cf. also Betz, "Paul's Concept," 9-10).

[116]While some scholars refer 5:24 to baptism as the Sitz
im Leben of becoming "Christ's," basing this view on the aorist
(cf. Kamlah, *Die Form*, 16; Schweitzer, *Mysticism*, 119, 121;
Ellicott, *Paul's Epistle to the Galatians*, 18; Meyer, *Epistle
to the Galatians*, 241; Lipsius, *Briefe an die Galater*, 63;
Lagrange, *Epître aux Galates*, 153; Oepke, *Paulus an die
Galater*, 143; and Schlier, *Brief an die Galater*, 263-64),
others attribute it simply to an act of faith, either at an
indefinite time (cf. Lightfoot, *St. Paul to the Galatians*,
213; Burton, *Epistle to the Galatians*, 319-20; and Tannehill,
Dying and Rising, 61 n. 2), or prior to baptism, which "seals"
it (cf. Bonnard, *Saint Paul aux Galates*, 115-16; and Mussner,
Der Galaterbrief, 390-91). Cf. Betz, *Commentary on Paul's
Letter*, ad loc., n. 172; and above, n. 114).

[117]Cf. 5:25 and 6:16.

[118]Is this idea of "imitation" also behind 2:19-21? For a
contrary view, see Tannehill (*Dying and Rising*, 70-71) whose
view is that the death and resurrection of Christ is not a mere
type or symbol of what one should do (cf. Burton, *Epistle to
the Galatians*, 319-20), but rather is an event which has the
power to include Christians in it, because it draws them into
a "corporate person" (cf. also *Dying and Rising*, 123-24).

[119]Cf. Mussner (*Der Galaterbrief*, 377-78), who, however,
does not identify the unredeemed as "those under the law." Cf.
also Max Pohlenz, *Freedom in Greek Life and Thought: The History of an Idea* (trans. C. Lofmark; Dordrecht-Holland: D.
Reidel, 1966) 171: God "could present [freedom] to man because
with the coming of Christ a new age began for mankind, a 'new
creation', in which the *pneuma* offers to the faithful quite a
different kind of strength for the battle with sin and the
snares of the flesh than was the case under the old law."

[120]For this view in Rabbinic Judaism, see Moore (*Judaism*,
1.485, 489-92).

[121]Cf. 5:6, 13-14, 23b; 6:2, 9-10 (and also below, pp.
124-28).

[122]Cf. Niederwimmer, *Der Begriff*, 189: "Freiheit von der
Sünde liegt also auf einer anderen Ebene als auf der moral-
ischen. Freiheit von der Sünde ist nicht moralische Tadel-
losigkeit, die aus dem entschlossenen und ausdauernden Befolgen
einer Norm folgt. Freiheit von der Sünde ist Freiheit von sich
selbst, eine Freiheit, die durch den Gehorsam einer Norm gegen-
über grundsätzlich nicht erreicht werden kann." Cf. also Franz
Mussner (*Theologie der Freiheit nach Paulus* [Quaestiones Dis-
putatae 75; Freiburg/Basel/Wien: Herder, 1976] 24, 31), where
he cites Niederwimmer with approval. This view is essentially
correct, except that it makes an identification of the flesh
with "sich selbst," an identification which Paul does not make
in 5:17, and which is unnecessary to make Niederwimmer's point
(cf. above, p. 142 n. 106; and below, p. 147 n. 155 and p. 151
n. 218).

[123]The similarity between this phrase, the phrase πάντα μοι ἔξεστιν in 1 Cor 6:12, 10:23, and the slogan ζῆν ὡς βούλεται τις in Greek philosophy is intriguing (for the connection between the last two, see Betz, "Paul's Concept," 2 n. 7, 4 n. 30). Is this evidence that in Gal 5:17 Paul rejects one of the philosophical options of his day (cf. below, pp. 122-23)?

[124]Cf. 3:3, where σάρξ refers to "works of the law" (cf. also Betz, Commentary on Paul's Letter, ad loc.).

[125]In 4:6, Paul says God sent the Spirit into the believer's "heart"; and 2:20 implies that Christ and the "ego" co-reside at the center of a Christian's existence (cf. Niederwimmer, Der Begriff, 186 n. 50).

[126]Ellis Rivkin, "The Internal City: Judaism and Urbanization," JSSR 5 (1966) 225-40.

[127]Phil 3:20 (cf. also the ἄνω 'Ιερουσαλήμ in Gal 4:26).

[128]Cf. Lipsius, Briefe an die Galater, 63; and Mussner, Der Galaterbrief, 390-91 on 5:24.

[129]Cf. above, p. 136 n. 15.

[130]This phrase is borrowed from Sheldon R. Isenberg, "Power Through Temple and Torah in Greco-Roman Palestine," pp. 24-52 in Christianity, Judaism and Other Greco-Roman Cults: Studies for Morton Smith at Sixty, Part 2: Early Christianity (SJLA 12; ed. Jacob Neusner; Leiden: Brill, 1975); and idem, "Millenarism," 21, 31, 34-35.

[131]Cf. 3:19-25 and 4:1-7.

[132]Cf. Lightfoot, St. Paul to the Galatians, 209; Meyer, Epistle to the Galatians, 235; Ellicott, Paul's Epistle to the Galatians, 130; Lipsius, Briefe an die Galater, 62; Burton, Epistle to the Galatians, 297-99; Lagrange, Epître aux Galates, 147; Oepke, Paulus an die Galater, 135; Schlier, Brief an die Galater, 248 n. 1; and Schmithals, Paul, 48. For οὐ μή with the aorist subjunctive as a form of emphatic denial, see the grammars. Cf. also Burton (Epistle to the Galatians, 297, 299) who takes the present imperative as an exhortation to continue as they were already doing (cf. also Betz, Commentary on Paul's Letter, ad loc.). Betz translates 5:16b as a promissory future ("Spirit, Freedom, and Law," 158; and Commentary on Paul's Letter, ad loc.), but he also translates it as a hortatory subjunctive ("In Defense of the Spirit," 105; cf. also Lietzmann, An die Galater, 39; Bonnard, Saint Paul aux Galates, 113; and Burton, Syntax, secs. 167, 488).

[133]Cf. also Rom 13:14.

[134]Cf. also Mussner, Theologie der Freiheit, 38. Tannehill is correct when he writes, "the Christian cannot lead a life of sin while under grace just because the new master, like

the old, has a complete claim to his service and holds him in
his power" (*Dying and Rising*, 17). Then he understands "dying
with Christ" to be a repetitive act, because the Christian
still lives in the old aeon (cf. *Dying and Rising*, 127, and his
PART II). Conzelmann expresses a typical interpretation of
Paul when he says, "The imperative 'Thou shalt' does not apply
in spite of the indicative of the promise of salvation; it
springs from it and is its particularization. How can that be?
It is because we are endowed with the Spirit, *but have experienced no habitual change as a result of it*" (*Outline*, 284;
the first emphasis is his, the second is mine). The last sen-
tence, however, is not Pauline theology.

[135]Cf. Betz's notion that the "fruit of the Spirit" so
completely "fills" the Christian's life that "works of the
flesh" are "pushed out, or their manifestation will be prevented" ("Spirit, Freedom, and Law," 158; and *Commentary on
Paul's Letter*, on 5:16). Although the "fruit of the Spirit" is
produced in the center of the Christian's existence, or in the
believer's "soul" (cf. Burton, *Epistle to the Galatians*, 290),
or rather precisely because it is, it is also manifest publicly
in the life of the community (cf. 5:26-6:6, 9-10, as well as
5:6 and 5:13-14).

[136]Cf. 5:22 and 5:6, 13-14.

[137]The last phrase, μάλιστα...πίστεως, is an "epistolary
cliche" (cf. Betz, "The Literary Composition," 377 n. 1; and
Commentary on Paul's Letter, ad loc., n. 197).

[138]Cf. 5:22 and 6:1.

[139]Cf. 3:19-4:7. Instead of the term τέλειοι in Galatians,
Paul uses υἱοί (cf. 1 Cor 2:6-3:4). See, however, the suggestion by Meyer (*Epistle to the Galatians*, 106) that ἐπιτελεῖσθε
in 3:3 means τέλειοι ποιεῖσθε.

[140]Cf. 4:1 (and 1 Cor 3:1). In 5:16, ἐπιθυμίαν σαρκὸς οὐ
μὴ τελέσητε recalls the ἐπιτελεῖσθε σαρκί in 3:3. This indicates that 5:16, like 3:3 and 5:18, was formulated by Paul
against the nomists' view (cf. also Betz, *Commentary on Paul's
Letter*, on 5:16, n. 58).

[141]Cf. ἐγκράτεια as part of the "fruit of the Spirit"
(5:23).

[142]Cf. Niederwimmer, *Der Begriff*, 195.

[143]Cf. ἀναγκάζεσθαι in 2:3 and ἀναγκάζειν in 6:12; as well
as the φρουρεῖν of the παιδαγωγός, to which the συγκλεῖσθαι of
those under the law of Moses corresponds (3:21, 23; cf. the use
of ἐκκλείω in 4:17). The notion of the restraint and compulsion of those "under" the law of Moses is also expressed by the
ὑπό-phrases: ὑπὸ νόμον (3:23; 4:4, 5, 21; 5:18), ὑπὸ κατάραν
(3:10), ὑπὸ ἁμαρτίαν (3:22), ὑπὸ παιδαγωγόν (3:25), ὑπὸ ἐπιτρό-
πους καὶ οἰκονόμους (4:2), ὑπὸ τὰ στοιχεῖα τοῦ κόσμου (4:3).

Furthermore, the nomists "hinder" (ἐνέκοψεν) the Galatians
(5:7); while Paul himself had "progressed" (προέκοπτον--1:14).

[144]Cf. the ἄγειν of the Spirit in 5:18 and the use of
πνεύματι with a verb in 3:3 (ἐνάρχεσθαι πνεύματι), 5:5 (πνεύματι ἀπεκδέχεσθαι), 5:16 (πνεύματι περιπατεῖν), 5:25 (πνεύματι
ζῆν / στοιχεῖν), and 6:1 (καταρτίζειν τι ἐν πνεύματι πραΰτητος).

[145]Cf. Betz, *Commentary on Paul's Letter*, ad loc.

[146]This seems to be Mussner's position (cf. *Der Galaterbrief*, 377-78). Cf. Betz's criticism (*Commentary on Paul's
Letter*, on 5:17, n. 83).

[147]This seems to be Betz's position despite his best efforts to avoid determinism (cf. *Commentary on Paul's Letter*,
on 5:3, 6, 14, 21b, 22-23; 5:25-6:10; also see his comment on
5:16 with regard to the "fulfilling of the desires of the
flesh," and his criticism of Mussner, on 5:17).

[148]Cf. 3:10, 12, and 5:2-4.

[149]Cf. 3:3.

[150]Cf. 5:16 (ἐπιθυμίαν σαρκὸς οὐ μὴ τελέσητε).

[151]The latter view is Betz's (*Commentary on Paul's Letter*,
on 5:16).

[152]Cf. 7:17, 20.

[153]Cf. 7:15-16, 19.

[154]Cf. Betz (*Commentary on Paul's Letter*, on 5:17), where
he says that in Rom 6:12 and 7:7-23 the flesh looks more like
the passive victim and tool of sin; but in Gal 5:13-24, sin is
not part of the picture at all.

[155]Cf. Betz (ibid.), where he says that in Rom 8:15-23 the
human "I" is split between two "wills"; but in Gal 5:13-24
there are three "wills," namely, the human "I," flesh and
Spirit (the last two "paralyze" the "willing" of the human "I"),
but neither the flesh nor the Spirit is identical with the
human "I". Niederwimmer and Mussner incorrectly identify the
flesh with "sich selbst" (cf. above, p. 144, n. 122). For the
interpretation of σάρξ as "the weakness of man," "his own
strength," or "his own will," see Bultmann, *Theology*, 1.232-46;
and Schweizer, *TDNT* 6.428-30.

[156]Cf. Käsemann, *An die Römer*, 209. For Plato's concept
of τὸ φρονεῖν as the knowledge of good and evil, "the purpose
and epitome of human education and culture" (παιδεία), see
Werner Jaeger (*Paideia: The Ideals of Greek Culture*, Vol. 3:
The Conflict of Cultural Ideals in the Age of Plato [trans.
G. Highet; New York: Oxford University, 1944] 149). That Paul
formulated Romans 7 with a criticism of the Greek ideal of
παιδεία in view has been argued by Hildebrecht Hommel ("Das

7. Kapitel des Römerbriefes im Licht antiker Überlieferung,"
pp. 90-116 in *Theologia Viatorum* 8 [Jahrbuch der kirchlichen
Hochschule Berlin, 1961/62; ed. Fritz Maass; Berlin: Walter
de Gruyter, 1962]). Betz suggests Gal 5:13-6:10 might also
contain a similar critique (cf. *Commentary on Paul's Letter*,
on 5:11 and 5:25-6:10 "Analysis"). This suggestion needs to
be worked out more fully, but came too late to be included
here.

[157]Cf. Kuss, *Der Römerbrief*, 499.

[158]Ibid.

[159]Cf. Rom 8:2 (ἠλευθέρωσεν).

[160]Cf. Gal 3:1-5.

[161]In 3:3, this is implied by ἐνάρχεσθαι πνεύματι (cf.
also 2:19-20 and 6:14-15). Cf. Rom 6:4, 7:6 and 8:12-13.

[162]Cf. Gal 5:13.

[163]Cf. 3:3 (cf. also 2:16, 21, 3:10-12, 4:21 and 5:2-4).

[164]Cf. 4:8-11 and 5:1-6 (cf. also 1:6-7).

[165]τὸ φρονεῖν.

[166]Cf. Gal 5:19-21 and 5:24.

[167]Cf. 5:22-23.

[168]Cf. Betz, *Commentary on Paul's Letter*, on 5:16.

[169]Cf. above, p. 145 n. 123.

[170]The human "will" is "paralyzed" by the sphere in which
it lives, but it is not identical with that sphere, whether
the sphere is the flesh or the Spirit.

[171]Cf. 2:4, 5:2-12, 6:12-13. This requirement is also
implied in the Antioch episode in 2:11-14.

[172]Cf. 5:6, 13-14; 6:2, 9-10.

[173]Cf. 6:14-16.

[174]For Paul's fluctuating use of ὁ νόμος, see above, p.
140 n. 77.

[175]Cf. Wolfhart Pannenberg, *Jesus--God and Man* (trans.
Lewis Wilkins and Duane Priebe; Philadelphia: Westminster,
1968) 177: Being "led by the Spirit" does not involve a new
ethical standard to which the individual must conform; rather
it means being in a new "sphere of power," in which one's
"behavior is no longer subject to his own decision" (he cites

Ernst Käsemann, "Geist," 1272-79 in *RGG*, vol. 2 [3rd ed.; ed.
Kurt Galling; Tübingen: Mohr/Siebeck, 1958] esp. 1275), which
is nevertheless "experienced as freedom, not compulsion." "The
personal center of Christian action is the Holy Spirit." Cf.
Niederwimmer, quoted above in n. 122; and Bultmann, *TDNT* 6.220.

[176]This is Paul's argument in the whole letter, but especially 2:15-16, 3:6-25 and 5:2-12.

[177]Cf. 5:23b on the one hand, and 6:13 on the other (cf.
below, pp. 124-28).

[178]The γάρ in 3:10a introduces the reason for the previous
statement, that the blessing is on οἱ ἐκ πίστεως; namely, because οἱ ἐξ ἔργων νόμου are ὑπὸ κατάραν. Then in 3:10b, the
γάρ introduces the reason why οἱ ἐξ ἔργων νόμου are under a
curse: they are not faithful to what is written in "the book
of the Law," and they do not do them (cf. 5:3 and 6:13a; and
below, pp. 126-27).

[179]3:11 continues (δέ) the statement of the reason begun
in 3:10b. The ὅτι in 3:11b introduces a second quotation from
Scripture which states that part of the "book of the Law" to
which οἱ ἐξ ἔργων νόμου are unfaithful precisely because they
do not do it, as 3:12b makes clear. The conjunction of ἐν νόμῳ
and δικαιοῦσθαι in 3:11a is repeated in 5:4 (cf. 2:15-16, 21
and 3:21).

[180]The δέ in 3:12a is adversative, introducing a contrast
to the quotation from Scripture in 3:11b. In 3:10, Paul
equates ὁ ἐξ ἔργων νόμου and ὁ ἐπικατάρατος. This is contrasted in 3:11b, by means of a quotation from Scripture:
ὁ δίκαιος ἐκ πίστεως ζήσεται. Paul's argument, therefore, is
that those who live from "works of the law" are under a curse
because they do not live from faith (ἐκ πίστεως ζῆν) as "the
book of the Law" requires; rather, they live ἐξ ἔργων νόμου.
This is Paul's point in quoting Scripture again in 3:12b;
namely, that those who *do* "works of the law" *live* by them. In
3:10a, ἐξ ἔργων νόμου εἶναι parallels ζῆν ἐν αὐτοῖς in 3:12b,
and both are contrasted with ἐκ πίστεως ζῆν in 3:11b (cf. οἱ
ἐκ πίστεως in 3:9 and ἐκ πίστεως in 3:12a). This means ἐκ
πίστεως is to be taken with ζήσεται, not ὁ δίκαιος (cf. Ellicott, *Paul's Epistle to the Galatians*, 73). For ὁ δίκαιος
parallels ὁ ἐπικατάρατος in 3:10b.

[181]Cf. Schlier, *Brief an die Galater*, 132-35; Lagrange,
Epître aux Galates, 68-69; and Bonnard, *Saint Paul aux Galates*,
67, 149. For the contrary view, see Lightfoot, *St. Paul to the
Galatians*, 137; Ellicott, *Paul's Epistle to the Galatians*, 71;
Meyer, *Epistle to the Galatians*, 112; Lipsius, *Briefe an die
Galater*, 37-38; Burton, *Epistle to the Galatians*, 164; Lietz-
mann, *An die Galater*, 19; Oepke, *Paulus an die Galater*, 72;
Mussner, *Der Galaterbrief*, 225-26; Hans Joachim Schoeps, *Paul.
The Theology of the Apostle in the Light of Jewish Religious
History* (trans. H. Knight; Philadelphia: Westminster, 1961),
176-77; and Friedrich Hauck, *TDNT* 4.577. Neither group, how-
ever, distinguishes between Paul's two uses of ὁ νόμος to refer
to the law of Moses and "the Law" (see above, pp. 124, 140 n. 77).

[182]Cf. 3:11b and 5:5-6 (cf. below, pp. 126-27).

[183]Before Paul's "conversion" he "excelled" (προέκοπτον) in them (cf. Gal 1:14 and Phil 3:6b).

[184]Cf. 3:10-12, 5:2-6, 14 (also 6:14-15).

[185]Cf. Sanders, Paul, 482-84.

[186]Terms like εὐπροσωπῆσαι and καυχήσωνται in 6:12-13 (and ζηλοῦσιν ὑμᾶς in 4:17?), as well as οἱ ταράσσοντες ὑμᾶς in 1:7 (cf. 5:10) and οἱ ἀναστατοῦντες ὑμᾶς in 5:12 (and τίς ὑμᾶς ἐνέκοψεν in 5:7?), seem to be topoi in the exposure of "charlatans."

[187]Cf. 3:24-25 (cf. also the image of the ἐπίτροπος and οἰκονόμος in 4:2).

[188]This sense of the image of the παιδαγωγός is, therefore, in tension with Betz's interpretation of 3:19, which seems to be based more on Rom 5:20 (cf. Commentary on Paul's Letter, ad loc.).

[189]Cf. also 3:23-25 and 4:1-5.

[190]Cf. 2:4, 4:21, 6:12, and, implicitly, 2:11-14.

[191]Cf. 3:11 and 5:4.

[192]Cf. 1:4; and Betz, "Spirit, Freedom, and Law," 153.

[193]Cf. 5:5-6, 16, 18, 24-25; 6:14-16; as well as 2:15-21; 3:1-5, 14, 26-28; and 4:6.

[194]Ὀφειλέτης ἐστίν parallels ἐμμένει; and ὅλον τὸν νόμον ποιῆσαι parallels πᾶσιν τοῖς γεγραμμένοις ἐν τῷ βιβλίῳ τοῦ νόμου τοῦ ποιῆσαι αὐτά--unless 5:3 (μαρτύρομαι πάλιν) is a repetition of 5:2 in different terms (cf. νόμον φυλάσσουσιν in 6:13).

[195]Cf. 3:2, 5, 14.

[196]In 5:2, ὠφελήσει parallels ἰσχύει in 5:6.

[197]Cf. ποιῆσαι in 5:3 and 3:10, 12; and πᾶς / ὅλος νόμος in 3:10 and 5:3, 14.

[198]Cf. 3:6-14.

[199]Cf. 3:15-25.

[200]Cf. 5:6, 14 (cf. also 6:2).

[201]Cf. 5:6, 22.

[202] In 5:13a, ὑμεῖς γὰρ ἐπ' ἐλευθερίᾳ ἐκλήθητε covers both v. 13b and v. 13c, so that "being slaves to one another through love" is the definition of freedom that Paul defends in contrast to giving an opportunity to the flesh (cf. μόνον μὴ τὴν ἐλευθερίαν...ἀλλά...).

[203] It is clear from 5:2-4 that ἐν νόμῳ refers to circumcision as the epitome of "works of the law."

[204] Cf. 5:6, 6:2, 9-10.

[205] Cf. above, pp. 113-23.

[206] Cf. 3:3, 6:8, 12-13.

[207] Cf. 5:19-23.

[208] Cf. 5:23a. The πνευματικός manifests ἐγκράτεια, which is virtually synonymous with ἐλευθερία.

[209] In most of the commentaries, ἐγκράτεια is interpreted in light of the "works of the flesh" having to do with over-indulgence in eating and drinking, and with sexual immorality (cf. Meyer, *Epistle to the Galatians*, 241; Lipsius, *Briefe an die Galater*, 63; Burton, *Epistle to the Galatians*, 314, 318; Lagrange, *Epître aux Galates*, 153; and Oepke, *Paulus an die Galater*, 142).

[210] Cf. 5:22-23a and 6:1.

[211] Cf. 5:16-21, 24 and 5:26.

[212] Cf. 5:13-14, 22-23, 25 and 6:1-2, 9-10.

[213] Cf. 2:12, 4:17, 6:8, 12-13 (cf. the mention of ὑπόκρισις in 2:13).

[214] Cf. the duality of *oneself* and *others* in 5:13-15 and 5:26-6:10.

[215] The law of Moses remains external, because it is *over* those who live by it (cf. the ὑπό phrases cited above, n. 143). Cf. also Niederwimmer (*Der Begriff*), where he expresses the view that with the law of Moses, one experiences from the *outside* what one must do; but with the Spirit at one's personal center, it comes from *within* (cf. the discussion of Rivkin above, pp. 116-17).

[216] Cf. 3:23 and 2:3, 6:12.

[217] Cf. 5:23a (πραΰτης) and 6:1 (ἐν πνεύματι πραΰτητος).

[218] Cf. the Spirit as the dative of manner or norm in 3:3, 5:16, 25 and 6:1; the concept of the ἄγειν of the Spirit in 5:18; and the concept of the ἐπιθυμεῖν of the Spirit in 5:17. Cf. also Niederwimmer, *Der Begriff*, 183: "Im Geist steht der

Mensch ganz unter der Verfügung Gottes und doch zugleich--nicht
als Einschränkung dieser Verfügung, sondern als die paradoxe
andere Seite dieses Verhältnisses--in der Selbstverfügung. Im
Geist verfügt Gott über den Menschen und ebendarin der Mensch
über sich selbst. Denn im Geist ist der Mensch in der Einheit
mit Gott." This comes to expression in the concept of the
Spirit which dwells in the human spirit, "unser innerstes
Wesen" (p. 184), where it governs in place of the flesh. At
the same time, the Spirit is from God and Christ, so that it
remains alien to the "ego." The identity and difference in
the relationship between Spirit and "ego," for Niederwimmer,
is christologically based; that is, in Christ the human and
divine "will" were united (pp. 184-85). Therefore, he writes,
"Im Geist ist unser Wille und unser Wirken mit dem Willen und
Wirken Gottes so einig geworden, dass in unserem Wirken Gott
wirkt" (p. 184). Although Niederwimmer identifies the flesh
with "sich selbst" (cf. also above, n. 122), the paradox of
Christian freedom remains essentially correct in his description of it here; for, the latter is not dependent upon the
former (cf. also above, pp. 118-23).

[219]Cf. 4:8. The implication is that the law of Moses,
like the στοιχεῖα, is not by nature divine, while Christ and
the Spirit are (cf. 3:17-20, 4:4-6 and 21-31).

[220]Cf. πνεύματι περιπατεῖν (ποιεῖν, ζῆν, στοιχεῖν) in
5:16, 17, 25.

[221]Cf. 5:18, for which 5:16-17 is an introduction and
5:19-24 is a proof.

[222]Cf. 3:6-9 and 4:28-29 (cf. below, Chapter V).

[223]Cf. τὰ πάντα and the ἵνα-clause in 3:22.

[224]Cf. the "heart" as the locus of the Spirit in 4:6.

[225]Cf. above, pp. 113-28.

[226]This is the view of Schubert M. Ogden in *Christ Without
Myth*.

[227]Cf. above, pp. 111-13. Cf. Betz, "Paul's Concept,"
6-8. Cf. also John B. Cobb, Jr. (*The Structure*), for whom the
life of Jesus in history made possible a new structure of human
existence, which he calls "spiritual existence," and whose
essential feature is "self-transcending selfhood."

CHAPTER V

THE CHRISTOLOGICAL BASIS OF THE
HISTORICALITY OF THE SPIRIT

Introduction

The Spirit is a historical entity in the sense that it
participates in historical events in the life of the Christian
community, such as in expressions of ecstasy (Chapter III), and
in the sense that it inaugurates a "new creation," which establishes a new human epoch (Chapter IV). In other words, in
Paul's letter to the Galatians the Spirit is a mode of the
presence of God in history; for the Spirit is a divine entity
"supplied" and "sent" by God (3:5 and 4:6). We might say,
therefore, that for Paul the concept of the Spirit enables him
to conceive of God as being both remote from the events of the
world, and at the same time active and ingredient in history.

There is another sense in which the Spirit is a genuinely
historical mode of divine participation in and influence upon
the world. In Galatians the activity of the Spirit is connected with a particular historical period. The Spirit, promised in the time of Abraham to those who believe (3:6-25), was
"sent" in the "last age," as a special act of God in history
after the "sending" of God's "Son" (4:4-6); and it is the basis
of hope in the righteousness and eternal life to come (5:5 and
6:8).

This aspect of the historicality of the Spirit is expressed
in Galatians in christological and eschatological terms. In
this chapter our attention is on the christological basis of the
historicality of the Spirit. Chapter VI takes up the eschatological basis. In the following, therefore, we look at the concept of "the Spirit as the promise" in 3:6-25;[1] "the Spirit and
God's Son" in 4:4-6;[2] and, finally, the question of "the Spirit
before Christ" in 4:21-31.[3]

Section 1. The Spirit as the Promise (3:6-25)

In 3:14, Paul identifies the Spirit as the "promise."[4] On
one end, this "promise" is related to the "blessing of Abraham";

153

on the other, it follows the death of Christ.[5] This marks out
the period of the Spirit; for the interim is the period of the
law of Moses.[6] Paul's assumption, apparently, is that those
who believe in Christ have the Spirit because the Spirit is the
present, living reality of Christ himself.[7] Such an assumption
is supported, on the one hand, by 3:1-5, which establishes that
the Spirit is received by faith in the crucified Christ of
Christian preaching and, on the other, by 3:15-25, which identifies Christ as the "offspring" to whom, together with Abraham,
the "promise" was made.[8] The Spirit, therefore, is given only
to those who believe in Christ;[9] as such it had to await the
historical coming of Christ to be given to those who believe.
In this sense, the historicality of the Spirit has a christological basis. This basis is made even more explicit in 4:4-6.

Section 2. The Spirit and God's Son (4:4-6)

In the letter to the Galatians, Paul identifies the Spirit
explicitly only once, in 4:6, where he calls it the Spirit of
God's "Son." Elsewhere, Paul speaks simply of "the Spirit."[10]
Nevertheless, the same Spirit is meant throughout.

According to 4:4-6, the "sending" of the Spirit of God's
"Son" is separate and distinct from the "sending" of God's
"Son." From this it can be inferred that the Spirit, as the
mode of the continued presence and activity of God's "Son,"[11]
is a *particular* mode of divine presence in the world. This
relationship is also expressed in Galatians by the fact that the
faith which "receives the Spirit" is faith "in Christ."[12] In
other words, having faith in Christ is virtually synonymous with
receiving his Spirit ἐκ πίστεως.[13]

Giving further support to this relationship between Christ
and the Spirit is the fact that both have the same function and
do the same "work" in establishing the "new creation."[14] The
"new creation" is signified by "sonship" and "freedom." In both
instances Christ and his Spirit are designated as agents of this
"new creation." Those who believe in Christ are made "sons"
both by Christ,[15] and by his Spirit.[16] Freedom also is attributed to the work of the Spirit,[17] as well as to Christ;[18] for the

Spirit pushes out the "works of the flesh,"[19] and replaces the
"works of the law,"[20] just like Christ.[21]

Further, the manner in which both Christ and the Spirit
bring freedom is the same. One is no more "objective" or "external" than the other; likewise, neither is more "subjective"
or "internal" than the other.[22] The conception of the Spirit
as the cosmic opponent of the flesh[23] makes it as "objective"
and "external" as Christ, who opposes the flesh and the
"world."[24] The concept of "sending," which Paul uses with the
Spirit (4:6) as well as with God's "Son" (4:4), also expresses
the "objectivity" and "externality" of both the Spirit and
Christ. And the Spirit is as much alien to "human nature" as
Christ; thus in this sense too it is as "objective" and "external" as Christ. In other words, the Spirit is no less "transcendent" when it is fully "immanent." By the same token, such
phrases as ἐν ἐμοὶ Χριστός (2:20), Χριστὸν ἐνδύεσθαι (3:27),
μορφοῦσθαι Χριστὸς ἐν ὑμῖν (4:19), and οἱ τοῦ Χριστοῦ (3:29 and
5:24),[25] express the same manner of "internality" and "subjec-
tivity" attributed to the Spirit by means of the dative[26] and
the concept of receiving the Spirit.[27]

Fundamentally, however, the very contrasts, "internal/
external" and "subjective/objective," are problematic. For, in
Paul's use of the terms Χριστός and πνεῦμα in his letter to the
Galatians, both denote data of experience, *data* being "objective" by definition, and *experience* "subjective" by definition.
As such, they are both causal factors in human experience--in
some experiences they denote the dominant factor, as, for
example, in ecstasy and in freedom from the flesh and from the
law of Moses. But neither Christ nor the Spirit is simply identical with the experience of which it is ingredient. The Spirit
is no mere cipher for freedom; rather, the Spirit *brings* freedom. In other words, when the Spirit is the dominant causal
factor in human experience, the effect is ecstasy, freedom, or
both. The same can be said about Christ. Paul, therefore,
does not separate Christ and the Spirit as if one were "objective" and the other "subjective."

Nevertheless, a difference between Christ and his Spirit
exists within their identity. God's "Son" is described as a

historical person, that is, as subject to the conditions of
existence in the world.[28] But the Spirit, although it is a
historical entity, is not described as being subject to the
conditions of existence in the world. For, the Spirit is not
said to have been "born" at all, nor was it ever "under" anything, least of all the law of Moses.[29] Finally, only Christ
is said to have "given himself for our sins" (1:4); that is,
only Christ is the "crucified one" (3:1).

        In the letter to the Galatians, Paul does not describe the
circumstances surrounding the "sending" of the Spirit except to
say that it followed the "sending" of God's "Son." At most,
that God sent the Spirit of Christ after the *death and resurrection* of Jesus can be inferred from 3:13 and 4:4-6.[30] But
this is precisely an *inference*. The resurrection of Jesus is
mentioned in the letter only once, in a traditional formula in
1:1, so that Paul does not bring the two together in Galatians.[31]
If in 4:4-6, on the other hand, "humiliation" is expressed in
4:4,[32] then "exaltation" might be implied in 4:6. Nevertheless,
4:4-5 does not mention the death of Jesus;[33] and 4:6 does not
mention his resurrection. In any case, excluded is the view
that the Spirit is the gift of the risen Lord himself.[34] For,
while Paul explicitly attributes to God the "sending" of the
Spirit,[35] nowhere does he even imply that the Spirit was "sent"
by God's "Son."

        If Paul had not tied the Spirit so closely with "freedom,"
the "new creation" and "eternal life," this silence would be
explicable under the assumption that Paul was sensitive to the
dangers of "realized eschatology" because of the crisis in the
Galatian churches.[36] Silence is not Paul's method of dealing
with problems, however; besides, statements like 3:3, 5:1, 6:8,
and 6:14 would only have exacerbated such a problem. Paul does
not always tell everything he knows, especially if something
was well-known in the Galatian churches. For rhetorical reasons, he would avoid making the Galatians feel more stupid than
was necessary to persuade them not to pursue the nomist course.
This would be consistent with the omission of details in the
allegorical interpretation of the Abraham/Hagar story in 4:21-31
(the names of Sarah and Ishmael, and the identification of Christ

with tne "other covenant"). It is also consistent with calling
the Galatians "fools" in 3:1, 3; then, at the same time, expressing the desire to learn from them in 3:2 and 4:21; and
confessing perplexity in 4:20.[37] We must suppose, therefore,
that the association of the Spirit with the risen Christ was
immaterial to the *causa* of the letter to the Galatians.

Both Christ and the Spirit, finally, seem to denote spheres
in which events are affected; that is, they bring about certain
effects in the lives of individuals who participate in them
through faith. To a large extent these "fields of force" over-
lap; for there is no "benefit" of Christ that is not attributed
to the Spirit, as we argued above.[38] "Christ" and "the Spirit"
denote the "fields of force" from which come liberation from
"the present evil age," with its "world," "flesh," and "law."
And, although ecstatic phenomena in the community are identified in Galatians as manifestations only of the Spirit,[39] it
is significant that the only place in Galatians where Paul
names the Spirit as the Spirit of God's "Son" is a reference to
the *ecstatic* Abba-cry.

Apparently in the churches of Galatia converts to Christian faith, on the occasion of hearing the proclamation of the
crucified Christ, experienced both a short and a long-term
transformation of their personal existence. The former was
manifest in ecstatic experiences; the latter in freedom from
the "passions and desires" of the flesh, and consequently the
absence of "works of the flesh"; and, on the positive side, a
sense of personal well-being, as well as loving relationships
among members of the community of faith--in other words, "the
fruit of the Spirit." In the letter to the Galatians, Paul
attributes both the long and the short transformations[40] to the
"field of force" alternately called "Christ" and "the Spirit."

Section 3. The Spirit Before Christ? (4:21-31)

So far we have maintained that Paul, in the letter to the
Galatians, speaks of the Spirit as a mode of the continued
presence and activity of Christ; and that, therefore, he conceives of the Spirit as beginning with the historical epoch inaugurated by the coming of Christ. But in the Abraham and Hagar

allegory, Paul attributes the presence and activity of the
Spirit to the age of the Patriarchs of Israel. For, when he
says in 4:29 that ὁ κατὰ σάρκα γεννηθεὶς ἐδίωκεν τὸν κατὰ
πνεῦμα, which is an allusion to Scripture and/or tradition, he
describes Isaac as having his life from the Spirit.[41] The comparison between then and Paul's own day, therefore, includes
not only "persecution" but also "being born from the Spirit."
In 4:29, ὥσπερ τότε...οὕτως καὶ νῦν covers the whole verse:
those who are now "persecuting" Christians in Galatia are the
nomist missionaries,[42] and they are οἱ κατὰ σάρκα γεννηθέντες;[43]
but the Galatians are οἱ κατὰ πνεῦμα, or πνευματικοί.[44] Again
referring to Scripture, Paul describes the birth of Isaac as
being ἐκ τῆς ἐλευθέρας διὰ τῆς ἐπαγγελίας.[45] This parallels
Paul's description of Christian existence with respect to the
"promise,"[46] and "freedom."[47] In other words, in 4:21-31, by
means of "quotations" of Scripture and tradition, Paul not only
attributes to the period of Abraham the presence and activity
of the Spirit, but he also attributes to Isaac the same structure of existence originating from the Spirit that he attributes
to Christians in Galatia.

The traditional view that the Spirit dwelt among the Patriarchs and spoke through the prophets of Israel, after which
period the Spirit withdrew from Israel to return only in the
last age, could be behind 4:29. The problem is that Paul nowhere in Galatians mentions the Spirit in connection with the
prophets, and only here in connection with the Patriarchs. The
idea of the disappearance of the Spirit after the last prophet
of Israel is also missing, as is its corollary, the idea of the
return of the Spirit to Israel in the last age.[48]

The view expressed in 4:29 is also different from the idea
of the "pre-existence" of the Spirit. The latter, which is expressed by means of the "sending-formula" in 4:6,[49] implies a
historical limitation of the immanence of God in the mode of
the Spirit. That is to say, that the "pre-existence" of the
Spirit implies that the Spirit has an eternal aspect, but that
it is present in the world only for a particular historical
epoch, before which it was not, strictly speaking, existent *in
the world*. The Spirit, according to the "sending-formula" in

4:6, therefore, has a transcendent aspect as well as an immanent one.[50] In its immanent aspect, the Spirit is a *historically new* mode of God-in-the-world. The context of 4:4-6 makes
it clear that this new mode of divine immanence, which Paul
calls the Spirit, commenced after the sending of God's "Son"
precisely as a mode of Christ's continued presence and activity.[51] Therefore, 4:4-6 and 4:29 seemingly present a contradiction, which cannot be resolved by means of the implicit idea
of the eternal aspect of the Spirit; for in being eternal, that
is, "pre-existent," it was not, however, present and active in
the world until its "time," which was not until the coming of
God's "Son."[52]

It could also be said that κατὰ πνεῦμα in 4:29 should be
attributed to a pre-Pauline tradition containing an allegory of
Abraham and Hagar,[53] instead of to Paul himself.[54] Then it
could be said that Paul's attention was not on being systemati-
cally consistent with 4:4-6 but merely in marshalling arguments
from whatever source to persuade the Galatians not to pursue
the nomistic course; κατὰ πνεῦμα, it could be argued, was not
material to that purpose, so Paul saw no problem with it. The
difficulty is that κατὰ πνεῦμα *is* material to the *causa* of the
letter as a whole, and to 4:21-31 in particular. For it is
Paul's position that precisely the κατὰ πνεῦμα γεννηθείς (4:29),
the ἐναρξάμενος πνεύματι (3:3), or simply πνευματικός (6:1), is
the "son of Abraham" and "heir,"[55] because he receives the
Spirit ἐξ ἀκοῆς πίστεως,[56] and so lives ἐκ πίστεως.[57] So, whatever the source of κατὰ πνεῦμα is, whether Paul or tradition,
Paul attaches significance to that phrase precisely because it
is material to his argument.

In 3:6-14, which parallels 4:21-31 in arguing from Scripture that those who live by faith, rather than those who live
"under the law," are "sons of Abraham," Paul creates a problem
with regard to Christ that is similar to that regarding the
Spirit in 4:21-31. By means of a quotation from Scripture,
Paul attributes faith to Abraham *before Christ came*.[58] But
there the contradiction is only apparent, since, on the one
hand, Paul's argument hangs on the prophecy regarding Abraham's
"offspring" (singular), which is fulfilled in Christ. On the

other hand, Paul does not regard the story of Abraham's faith
as *historical*; rather, for Paul the Abraham story is "Scripture," that is, *prophecy*, whose reference is not to the past
but to the future, which is being actualized in the present.[59]

In 4:21-31, therefore, the Abraham story might also be,
for Paul, *prophecy* rather than *history*. Certainly the quotations of Isa 54:1 in 4:27 and Gen 21:10-12 in 4:30 are regarded
as prophecy, being actualized in the Christian communities in
Galatia. When, in 4:28, Paul compares the Galatians with Isaac
as their "type,"[60] the ὥσπερ τότε...οὕτως καὶ νῦν in 4:29 takes
on the character of "typological" exegesis.[61] In other words,
for Paul the story about Abraham's sons does not witness to a
Spirit *before Christ*; rather, as prophecy, it "foretells" in
the figure of Isaac the coming of the Spirit *in the Galatians'
own time*, and an existence brought by the Spirit *among the
Galatians*.[62]

Conclusion

In Galatians, Paul does not conceive of the Spirit as the
eternal divine presence in the world identical with the primordial act of God creating and sustaining the universe. Rather, he identifies the Spirit as a special act of God with a
soteriological purpose for a particular period of history.[63]
If Paul's concept of the Spirit in the letter to the Galatians
includes a cosmological function, it is as the metaphysical
opponent of the flesh. The flesh is not merely a psychological
or an anthropological entity for Paul, although it certainly
has psychological and anthropological relevance, insofar as its
locus of activity is in human affairs and through the "passions
and desires" (5:24). Because it is paired against the divine
Spirit (5:16-17), the flesh is conceived of as a cosmic power,
parallel or corresponding to the "world" (6:14). This is why
Paul does not speak merely of a new *humanity* created by the
overthrow of the flesh and the "world" by Christ and the Spirit;
rather, he speaks of a "new *creation*" (6:15).

Nevertheless, the Spirit is not presented in Galatians as
active in the original creation of the world, nor in its main-
tenance; nor is Paul concerned about the effect of the

activity of the Spirit in and on the nonhuman world.[64]   In this
respect, Paul differs from the Old Testament and from the
Stoics.[65]   The Spirit, according to Galatians, can be conceived
of as an expression of God's one intention always to create
life, and to sustain and redeem the world, but only if it is
emphasized that for Paul this intention takes different forms.
The Spirit is the *particular and historical* expression of God's
will for and work in the world that began with the coming of
Christ.

If I am correct about 4:21-31, Paul consistently portrays
the Spirit in the letter to the Galatians as a mode of the continued presence and activity of Christ. In other words, in
Galatians "the Spirit" denotes a special mode of divine immanence whose historical basis is christological. And, just as
the Spirit itself is a novelty in history, so are its effects.
Before Christ and the Spirit came, Paul says, there was no freedom but only slavery in the form of "works of the flesh" and
"works of the law." But now that Christ and his Spirit have
come, there is the possibility of freedom, because Christ and
the Spirit bring a "new creation." In Galatians, therefore,
Paul could have said, "the past is over and gone, the future is
breaking in";[66] for Christ and his Spirit effect manifestations
of the future in the present.[67]

[1]Cf. below, pp. 153-54.

[2]Cf. below, pp. 154-57.

[3]Cf. below, pp. 157-60.

[4]The genitive, τοῦ πνεύματος, is epexegetical.

[5]Cf. 3:6-14.

[6]Cf. 3:15-25.

[7]For the view that the Spirit is the Spirit that was *in Jesus*, see Alfred Wikenhauser (*Pauline Mysticism: Christ in the Mystical Teaching of St. Paul* [trans. J. Cunningham; New York: Herder and Herder, 1960] 86-88, 91).

[8]In 3:23-25, πρὸ τοῦ δὲ ἐλθεῖν τὴν πίστιν (v. 23), εἰς Χριστόν (v. 24), and ἐλθούσης δὲ τῆς πίστεως (v. 25) recall ἄχρις ἂν ἔλθῃ τὸ σπέρμα ᾧ ἐπήγγελται in 3:19, so that the latter refers to Christ as the recipient of the "promise" (cf. 3:16). And 3:14 identifies ἡ ἐπαγγελία ἐκ πίστεως Ἰησοῦ Χριστοῦ (3:22) as the Spirit.

[9]Cf. 3:2, 5, 14, 22.

[10]Paul uses the anarthrous πνεῦμα when it appears as a dative of means, norm or manner (cf. 3:3, 5:16, 18, 25, and 6:1), and with the κατά of the reason (cf. 4:29). Otherwise, Paul uses πνεῦμα with the article (cf. 3:2, 5, 14; 4:6; 5:17, 22; and 6:8). In 6:18, μετὰ τοῦ πνεύματος ὑμῶν refers to the human spirit rather than the divine Spirit.

[11]Cf. Meyer, *Epistle to the Galatians*, 175; Lipsius, *Briefe an die Galater*, 48; Schlier, *Brief an die Galater*, 198; Betz, *Commentary on Paul's Letter*, on 4:6 and 5:24; Reginald H. Fuller, *The Formation of the Resurrection Narratives* (New York: Macmillan, 1971) 174; and Grundmann, *TDNT* 2.311-12.

[12]For the relationship of faith to Christ, see 2:16, 20, 3:22, 26; and for the relationship of faith to the Spirit, see 3:2, 5, 14 and 5:5.

[13]Cf. Burton, *Epistle to the Galatians*, 222, 298; and Tannehill, *Dying and Rising*, 60.

[14]Cf. above, Chapter IV. Wikenhauser distinguishes between "in Christ" and "in the Spirit" as between salvation *as such* and the *nature* of the new "sphere of life" (*Pauline Mysticism*, 54-55).

[15]Cf. 3:26 and 4:5b.

[16]Cf. 4:6, 29.

[17]Cf. 4:1-11, 21-31.

[18]Cf. 5:1, 13.

[19]Cf. 5:16-23.

[20]Cf. 5:18, 23b.

[21]For the work of Christ against the flesh, see 5:24, and against the law of Moses, see 2:19-21, 3:15-25, 4:5a, 19, 5:2-6, and 6:15. Cf. also Deissmann, *Paul*, 138-39; and idem, *The Religion of Jesus and the Faith of Paul* (2nd ed.; trans. William E. Wilson; New York: Doran, 1926) 175.

[22]Here I am taking issue with Peter C. Hodgson (*New Birth of Freedom: A Theology of Bondage and Liberation* [Philadelphia: Fortress, 1976] 324-32), who correctly attributes freedom, in Paul's view, to Christ and the Spirit, but distinguishes between them by identifying the Spirit with an "interior" and "subjective" aspect, and Christ with the "external" and "objective." Cf. above, Chapter IV, pp. 107-108.

[23]Cf. 5:17.

[24]Cf. 1:4, 5:24 and 6:14.

[25]For its opposite, see 5:4 (καταργεῖσθαι ἀπὸ Χριστοῦ).

[26]Cf. 3:3, 5:16, 18, 25, and 6:1.

[27]Cf. 3:2, 5, 14.

[28]Cf. 4:4 ("born of a woman, born under the law").

[29]Cf. 5:18, 23b.

[30]Cf. Betz, "In Defense of the Spirit," 110; and Vos, *Traditionsgeschichtliche Untersuchungen*, 101. Cf. also Pannenberg, *Jesus*, 116-21, 171-72, 174, 177-78; and idem, *Apostles' Creed*, 129, 137, 138. In *The Religion of Jesus* (pp. 171, 174-75), Deissmann identifies Christ in the phrase ἐν Χριστῷ with "the exalted Christ," who is the Spirit, according to 2 Cor 3:17 (cf. also Wikenhauser, *Pauline Mysticism*, 71, 91). Schweitzer attributes possession of the Spirit to dying and rising with Christ, referring to 3:26-27 (*Mysticism of Paul*, 120 and 163-65). Tannehill finds the theme of "dying and rising with Christ" expressed in 2:20, 5:24-25 and 6:14-15 (cf. *Dying and Rising*, 55-65).

[31]On the other hand, see Rom 1:3-4 and 8:11.

[32]Cf. James M. Robinson, *A New Quest of the Historical Jesus* (SBT 25; London: SCM, 1959) 52-53.

[33] Cf. Betz, *Commentary on Paul's Letter*, on 4:5.

[34] For the contrary view, see Gunkel, *Die Wirkungen*, 27; Schnackenberg, *Baptism*, 166 n. 59 and pp. 83, 162-63 (where he refers to the connection between the Spirit and baptism); and Fuller, *The Formation*, 214 n. 13.

[35] Cf. 3:5 and 4:6.

[36] Or, as Lightfoot suggests (on 6:1 and p. 54), Paul may have had the crisis in Corinth in mind. It seems more likely, however, that Paul's position in Galatians might have led to the Corinthian problem than vice versa.

[37] Cf. above, Chapter II, p. 46 nn. 15, 16.

[38] Cf. above, pp. 154-55.

[39] Cf. 3:5 and 4:6.

[40] The transformation manifest in ecstasy is the same as that of "freedom." The distinction is just over the matter of duration and the mode of participation on the part of the "ego," or perhaps even consciousness. Structurally, both entail a change in the dominant power at the center of a person's existence. Cf. above, pp. 88-89 n. 115.

[41] The τότε in this verse refers to the Abraham narrative.

[42] Paul describes the "persecution" that Christians in Galatia are suffering at the hands of the nomist missionaries in 1:7 (τινές εἰσιν οἱ ταράσσοντες ὑμᾶς--cf. 5:10), 3:1 (τίς ὑμᾶς ἐβάσκανεν), 4:17 (ἐκκλεῖσαι ὑμᾶς θέλουσιν), 5:7 (τίς ὑμᾶς ἐνέκοψεν), 5:12 (οἱ ἀναστατοῦντες ὑμᾶς), and 6:12 (ἀναγκάζουσιν ὑμᾶς περιτέμνεσθαι--cf. 2:3-5 and 2:11-14).

[43] Cf. 3:3 and 6:12-13.

[44] Cf. 6:1 and 3:3, 5:18, 25.

[45] Cf. 4:22, 23, 30.

[46] Cf. 3:14, 29.

[47] Cf. 4:31, 5:1, 13.

[48] The Spirit is associated, of course, with the "last age" and with the eschatological "Israel" (cf. 6:8, 16; see also below, Chapter VI); but there is no evidence that Paul regarded the "sending" of the Spirit as the *return* of the Spirit to Israel in the last age.

[49] Cf. Kramer, *Christ*, 113-14, 119-21; and Karl H. Rengstorf, *TDNT* 1.406. It is also implicit in the association of the Spirit and the "Jerusalem above," which is "eternal" (cf. above, Chapter IV, p. 141 n. 90).

[50]Cf. Cobb, *Christ*, 261-62.

[51]It seems that, for Paul in Galatians, "Spirit," as well as "Christ," denotes the immanent aspect of God's "Son." Likewise, both terms refer to manifestations of the future in the present (cf. 5:5, 6:8, 14-16, and below, Chapter VI; cf. also Cobb, *Christ*, 261-62).

[52]Cf. 4:4 (and below, Chapter VI, pp. 169-71).

[53]Barrett, for example, argues that the nomists presented an interpretation of Abraham's sons, against which Paul reacts with his own interpretation (cf. "The Allegory," 6).

[54]Luz ("Der alte," 321) argues that πνεῦμα, rather than ἐπαγγελία (4:23), is pre-Pauline; that is, that Paul has inserted a σάρξ/ἐπαγγελία antithesis where σάρξ/πνεῦμα originally stood, in order to contrast the "visible" with the "invisible." (Luz assumes the Spirit was too "visible" a part of the Christian communities in Galatia to contrast with the "visibility" of the flesh.) For the view that κατὰ πνεῦμα is Paul's phrase, see Betz (*Commentary on Paul's Letter*, ad loc.). For a similar use of πνεῦμα, see 1 Cor 10:1-5.

[55]Cf. 3:6-9, 4:6-7.

[56]Cf. 3:2, 5, 14.

[57]Cf. 3:11.

[58]Cf. 3:6-25 and 4:4-5. For a discussion of this problem, see Hendrikus Boers (*Theology Out of the Ghetto: A New Testament Exegetical Study Concerning Religious Exclusiveness* [Leiden: Brill, 1971] 78-82).

[59]Cf. 3:8 (προϊδοῦσα δὲ ἡ γραφή...προευηγγελίσατο). The πρό of 3:23 recalls the πρό- of 3:8. The reception of the Spirit ἐκ πίστεως, therefore, also fulfills the prophecy of the Abraham story (cf. 3:2, 5, 14 and 4:4-6).

[60]Cf. κατὰ 'Ισαάκ in this verse.

[61]Cf. ἅτινά ἐστιν ἀλληγορούμενα in 4:24e, which includes "typology" (cf. Lietzmann, *An die Galater*, 30; Oepke, *Paulus an die Galater*, 110-11; Bonnard, *Saint Paul aux Galates*, 99; Mussner, *Der Galaterbrief*, 320 n. 20; Bultmann, "Ursprung und Sinn der Typologie als Hermeneutischer Methode," pp. 369-80 in *Exegetica, Aufsätze zur Erforschung des Neuen Testaments* [Tübingen: Mohr/Siebeck, 1967] 377; Goppelt, *TDNT* 8.251-52; Vielhauer, "Paulus," 37; Luz, "Der alte," 322; Käsemann, *Perspectives*, 98; Hanson, *Studies*, 91-94; Betz, "The Literary Composition," 373 n. 3; and idem, *Commentary on Paul's Letter*, 4:21-31, "Analysis," and on 4:29).

[62]In 4:29, Paul offers proof from Scripture that the Galatians were of the same "type" as Isaac, because the prophecy to

which he refers was being fulfilled in their midst by the
"persecuting" activity of the nomists in Galatia.

[63]Cf. above, Chapter IV.

[64]Rom 8:18-23 presents a different picture of the relationship between the Spirit and the world inclusive of so-
called "nature."

[65]For the view that the "biblical" concept of the Spirit,
as the origin of all life, is the basis for "the" New Testament
concept of the Spirit, see Pannenberg (*Jesus*, 171; "The Working
of the Spirit," 13-31; "The Doctrine of the Spirit," 8-21;
Apostles' Creed, 128-43; and *Faith and Reality*, 20-38). In
addition to the problem of speaking of "the biblical" or "the"
New Testament concept of the Spirit, it should be noted that
this concept of the Spirit, as the origin of all life, and as
divine activity and presence in all creation inclusive of "nature," is as much "Stoic" as it is "biblical."

[66]Cf. 2 Cor 5:17.

[67]Cf. below, Chapter VI.

CHAPTER VI

THE ESCHATOLOGICAL BASIS OF THE
HISTORICALITY OF THE SPIRIT

Introduction

The presence and activity of the Spirit were experienced
by Christians in Galatia as evidence of the coming of the "last
age."[1] This is already expressed by Paul in the identification
of existence centered in the Spirit as a "new creation." Other
phrases identifying the epoch of which the Spirit is a part are
"the Jerusalem above" (4:26), "the kingdom of God" (5:21b), and
"the Israel of God" (6:16). In addition, Paul identifies the
"time" of the Spirit as the πλήρωμα τοῦ χρόνου (4:4). Finally,
he associates with the Spirit two things traditionally identified with the "last age," namely, "righteousness" (5:5) and
"eternal life" (6:8). We turn now to examine these elements of
the "last age," which establish the eschatological basis of the
Spirit's historicality: (1) the "time" of the Spirit,[2] (2) the
Spirit and the hope of "righteousness,"[3] and (3) the Spirit and
"eternal life."[4]

Section 1. The Time of the Spirit (4:4-6)

The "time" of the Spirit, like that of Christ, is identified as τὸ πλήρωμα τοῦ χρόνου. That this is the time of the
"last age" is indicated by the phrase itself and by the aorist
ἦλθεν. The verb ἔρχομαι is used by Paul to denote the arrival
of what is foretold in Scripture; namely, the "offspring to
whom the promise had been made," which is Christ,[5] and "faith."[6]
The aorist ἦλθεν, therefore, identifies the time of the sending
of the Spirit as the time of the fulfillment of God's "promises"
(3:16); as such, it is the "last age."[7]

That the "last age" had come when God sent the Spirit is
conveyed by the phrase τὸ πλήρωμα τοῦ χρόνου itself, which is
practically synonymous with ἔσχατος ὁ χρόνος in 1 Pet 1:20.
First of all, it recalls ἡ προθεσμία τοῦ πατρός, which is its
counterpart in the analogy about minors becoming heirs (4:2).[8]
In other words, the sending of the Spirit came at a time

determined by God and no one else.[9] The context also shows,
however, that for Paul the sending of the Spirit happened not
only at a time according to God's plan but also at the end of
the former age and the beginning of the "last age." For, the
time of the Spirit is contrasted with that of the στοιχεῖα τοῦ
κόσμου: the one age is filled with freedom and sonship,[10] while
the other consists of slavery and minority.[11] The former age,
in other words, dominated by evil and evil deeds,[12] or flesh
and "works of the flesh,"[13] is replaced by the time of Christ
and the Spirit, in which love and good deeds prevail.[14] As
such, the time of the Spirit is the "last age."

The reason why the "last age" is the time of Christ and
the Spirit is not stated except to say that it is the time
appointed by God.[15] The phrase τὸ πλήρωμα τοῦ χρόνου may be
pregnant with meaning;[16] but some notions can be extracted from
it only by doing violence to it. For example, the notion of
evolutionary development, or progress under the alleged "education" of the law of Moses,[17] assumes that εἰς Χριστόν in 3:24
identifies the *goal* toward which the παιδαγωγός works. The
same error is behind the view that evil had reached such a
pitch that God sent Christ and the Spirit to put a stop to it;
in other words, τὸ πλήρωμα τοῦ χρόνου is the climax of a pro-
gression of evil, as opposed to good, whose goal is a state
from which only divine intervention could effect redemption,
so that again εἰς Χριστόν states *the goal of the law of Moses*.[18]
But εἰς Χριστόν identifies the limit of one age and the beginning of another.[19] In other words, εἰς Χριστόν is a *temporal*
clause,[20] which like τὸ πλήρωμα τοῦ χρόνου refers to the start
of the "last age" in accordance with the will of God. The
sending of Christ and the Spirit, therefore, is not the result
of the wickedness of humanity; nor is it God's response to the
attainment of "maturity" among Jewish and Gentile peoples.
Rather, the sending of Christ and the Spirit is the primary
impetus from God in the process by which humanity "advances."

By this formulation, I intend to overcome the antithesis
of history (*Historie*) and metahistory (*Geschichte* or *Heils-
geschichte*) by uniting rather than separating them. Using
other terms, this means the process of "advance" is both

"natural" and "supernatural." I would, however, avoid the notion of *inevitable* "advance" by maintaining that, whatever
impetus to "advancement" God offers, they remain *offers* of
genuinely *contingent* "advance," in the sense that, although
such offers are inevitably made by God, since that is what it
means for God to be God, they need not have been in the form of
Christ and the Spirit, and in the sense that they are *lures*,
which are subject to neglect or even rejection. God offers
such epochal lures, however, in a way that provides for a better chance of their acceptance than of their rejection or neglect. I would also avoid the notion of inevitable *progress*,
since I mean by "advance" increased complexity and integration,
with which comes the potentiality for "worse evil" as well as
"better good."[21] In this last respect, however, my perspective
differs from Paul's; for Paul could see, at least in Galatians,
only the increased possibility for good coming from the "advance" inaugurated by Christ and his Spirit.

Section 2. The Spirit and the Hope of Righteousness (5:5)

The eschatological character of the presence and activity
of the Spirit comes to expression in a statement about the
basis of confidence with regard to δικαιοσύνη. In 5:5, ἀπεκδέχεσθαι is used to denote eschatological expectation,[22] as its
object, ἐλπίδα δικαιοσύνης,[23] proves. By using these terms,
Paul expresses not only that the Spirit brings[24] certainty and
assurance of righteousness, but also that righteous somehow
still lies in the future.[25]

Elsewhere in the letter to the Galatians, Paul refers to
righteousness as a present reality.[26] This has led to the view
that hope is based on the Spirit and faith, by which one is
made "righteous" in a *moral* sense, so that, on the one hand,
the object of the expectation is seen to be hope of "eternal
life" as a gift to those who are *morally* "righteous";[27] or, on
the other hand, hope is seen to have its object in a qualitative *moral development*, as the goal toward which the Spirit and
faith work.[28] These interpretations cannot be summarily dis-
missed, since they are made plausible by statements in the

letter that the goal toward which the Spirit works is "eternal
life" (6:8),[29] and *moral* "righteousness."[30]

Nevertheless, "eternal life" and *moral* "righteousness" are
not the whole picture of the future, of which the Spirit gives
assurance and with which it unites the believer; for δικαιοσύνη
also has a "forensic" sense.[31] The context of 5:2-6 brings in
this sense as well as the moral, and perhaps even emphasizes
God's judgment in the last days. For, in 5:4, "Christ" is
parallel to χάρις, which is God's final act of "acquital" or
"absolution" from sin, that is, "justification."[32] It is this
"juridical act" that Paul (in 2:16, 21, 3:6, 8 and 11) declares
a present reality, in which one's standing is maintained by
"walking" in the Spirit (5:13-6:10).[33]

In other words, both Christ and the Spirit refer to the
immanence of God's righteousness. Assurance of this righteousness, and unity with it, is the "fruit of the Spirit," of which
Paul speaks in 5:22; namely, "love, joy, peace," etc.[34] For
this reason the "forensic" righteousness of God cannot be
separated from the "moral."[35] The Spirit, in Paul's view, not
only bears witness to God's "juridical act," it makes God's act
effective in the believer in such a way that the person is not
only "justified" but made morally "righteous." For the Spirit
prevents the "works of the flesh," so that the Christian is no
longer "shut out" from God's grace, that is, from God's
righteousness.[36]

Perhaps the nomists in Galatia had thought of circumcision
as the eschatological sign assuring them of the protection, in
the "last age," of the χάρις and δικαιοσύνη of God. Paul
argues, to the contrary, that circumcision, as one of the
"works of the law,"[37] does the very opposite.[38] The basis of
confidence in righteousness, and unity with it, is the Spirit
received by faith, not "works of the law."[39] For "faith working through love" is guided by the Spirit.[40] This fulfills
"the Law" (5:13-14), and makes present the "new creation"
(6:15). Paul, therefore, identifies the Spirit as the eschatological sign assuring them of the protection of the grace and
righteousness of God in the "last age."[41] This relationship
between the Spirit and the future is also expressed in 6:8.

Section 3. The Spirit and Eternal Life (6:8)

The terms Paul uses in 6:7-10 identify these verses as an eschatological warning:[42] the theme of the harvest,[43] the future θερίσει,[44] φθορά and ζωὴ αἰώνιος, which contrasts destruction and life given as divine recompense in the "last days,"[45] and καιρῷ ἰδίῳ and ὡς καιρὸν ἔχομεν, which, like 4:4, establish the identity of the time of the Spirit as the "last age."[46] At the base of this warning is a contrast between two "ways" of life and their final ends; that is, the antithesis between ζῆν σαρκί / φθορά and ζῆν πνεύματι / ζωὴ αἰώνιος. The way of σπείρειν εἰς τὴν σάρκα ἑαυτοῦ is not only that of "fulfilling the desires of the flesh" (5:16), which produces the "works of the flesh" (5:19-21), but also that of being circumcised, as the context makes clear.[47] The flesh, the sphere which determines this way of life,[48] is a cosmic power alongside of the Spirit,[49] which like the Spirit stands in relation to the future verdict of God in the "last days." Just as in the present life the flesh has power in and over only those who strive after things in the sphere of the flesh, namely, the "passions and desires" (5:24), and as such give the flesh its "opportunity" (5:13), so that its "works" are produced (5:19-21), so also in the "last days" these people remain in the sphere of the flesh, whose end is φθορά, from which they are not "raised."[50] Since life and salvation for those who live by "works of the law," in Paul's view, remain in the sphere of the flesh, their end too is φθορά.[51]

Contrasted with the way of the flesh and its end, φθορά, is that of the Spirit and its end, ζωὴ αἰώνιος. The image of σπείρειν εἰς τὸ πνεῦμα refers to the way of life described earlier as "walking by the Spirit," etc.,[52] and in the following verses as "doing the good."[53] Therefore, the Spirit is the sphere which determines this way of life, in contrast to the flesh and its way of life, so that the Spirit produces its "fruit"[54] in the *present* life of the πνευματικός, just as it is the source of "eternal life" in the *future*. In other words, "eternal life," like "righteousness," is both present and future.[55] Only the *future* life is αἰώνιος, beyond death, and

in this sense "ceaseless" or "endless,"[56] and "indestructable";
that is, it is the "resurrection life."[57]

Behind these ideas is the sense of the distance of the
future from the present at the same time that there is assurance of it and unity with it. For the indestructable life of
the future is not identical with the present life in the Spirit; it comes *from* (ἐκ) it. That Paul, however, does not stress
this distance is evidence that the churches of Galatia were not
experiencing problems with the deaths of some members of their
communities,[58] nor were they having problems with "enthusiasm."[59]
Rather, the problem in the Galatian churches is that nomists had
almost persuaded them that circumcision was the eschatological
sign which gave assurance of righteousness and eternal life in
the "last age." Paul offers instead the assurance that their
life in the Spirit had already united them with these gifts of
the future.

Paul does not, however, at least in Galatians, identify
any specific manner or circumstance of the giving of eternal
life. He mentions neither the idea of the "resurrection of the
dead,"[60] nor that of the "Parousia."[61] Neither is there any
indication of how near or far off the "last days" were.[62] It
is simply stated that the goal toward which life in the Spirit
leads is eternal life, which is a gift of the same Spirit, a
gift of which they already had assurance and with which they
were already united through the present life in the Spirit.
For, since they had already been given "life,"[63] the future
"eternal life" is the consummation of that which had already
begun in Christ and his Spirit.[64]

Conclusion

All elements of the sending of the Spirit identify its
time as that of the "last age." It happened according to God's
plan at a time of God's own choosing; it is the Liberator himself who bears the Spirit that believers receive; and it effects, together with the sending of God's "Son," a shift from
an evil age filled with slavery, idolatry, superstition and
other "works of the flesh," to an age of freedom, faith, love,

and the "fruit of the Spirit." Paul does not, however, support
this presentation of the "outpouring of the Spirit in the 'last
age'" by quoting Scripture or tradition to the effect that now
the Spirit has "returned" to Israel in the "last age." For, in
Galatians at least, as far as the Spirit is concerned, Paul
absolutely contrasts the past and the present, in which the
future is being made manifest, so that there is no continuity,
qualitative or quantitative, between the past and the present
activity of the Spirit. For, before the πλήρωμα τοῦ χρόνου,
there was no activity of the Spirit *in the world*.[65]

Those who heard the message of the crucified Christ, and
believed that it told of God's liberation from the present evil
age, were so filled with exhilaration that some broke into ecstasy. All who believed, Paul implies, were freed from the
compulsion of the "passions and desires," so that they produced
the "fruit of the Spirit" instead of "works of the flesh." In
this way Christians in Galatia experienced the proclamation of
the crucified Christ as the beginning of the "last age," that
is, the manifestation of the future in the form of the presence
and activity of the Spirit. The "fruit of the Spirit," which
Paul summarizes as freedom, can be understood, therefore, as
the influence of the future on the present.[66]

Other evidence that Paul identified the time of the Spirit
as the "last age" is the association of the Spirit with the
kingdom of God. Paul explicitly connects the Spirit with righteousness and eternal life;[67] but the association of the Spirit
with the Kingdom[68] must be inferred in the letter to the Galatians from the relationship between the Spirit and the "Jerusalem above" (4:26), the "Israel of God" (6:16), and the statement in 5:21b about the "kingdom of God." Participation in the
"Jerusalem above" is identified as κατὰ πνεῦμα γεννηθῆναι (4:29).
The "Israel of God," similarly, consists of those whose lives
are in accordance with the Spirit,[69] for only the πνευματικοί[70]
follow Paul's "canon" of living within the "new creation."[71]
From 5:21b it can be inferred that those who do not do "works
of the flesh" would not be barred from the kingdom of God;
therefore, those who manifest the "fruit of the Spirit" participate in the Kingdom. The form in which the kingdom of God is
manifest in the present, therefore, is the Spirit.[72]

In Galatians, two aspects of the Kingdom are righteousness
and eternal life. Since righteousness is the "blessing" promised to those who believe, the future righteousness is the
consummation of what has already begun in the Spirit, which
faith received. So it is with eternal life. This means that
faith, which receives the Spirit, not circumcision, nor any of
the other "works of the law," is the sign of participation in
the kingdom of God.

But, just as between Christ and the Spirit there is a
difference as well as identity, so with the Spirit and the
kingdom of God, or righteousness and eternal life. Between the
Kingdom present as the Spirit and as still in the future a
qualitative and quantitative difference exists. The present
activity of the Spirit manifests the Kingdom *imperfectly and
partially*. For, as Paul says, "through the Spirit, which we
receive by faith, we *wait* for the *hope* of righteousness" (5:5);
he also says that "eternal life" is *yet to come* from the Spirit
(6:8).[73] Although the *language* which expresses the qualitative
and quantitative difference between the present manifestation
of the "last age" in the Spirit and the future is missing in
Galatians,[74] the *concept* is not, as 5:5 and 6:8 prove. Evi-
dently the concept did not need to be emphasized in the letter
to the churches of Galatia because, unlike the church in
Corinth, their problems had not arisen out of an intensely
"enthusiastic" sense of the full and perfect arrival of the
"last age" in their communities.[75] Rather, they were considering following nomists, who had promised participation in the
"last age," in the form of the "heavenly Jerusalem," the "kingdom of God," or the "Israel of God," on the condition that they
receive circumcision. To make them secure in their faith, by
which they had received the Spirit from his missionary preaching, Paul tries to persuade them that the full disclosure of
the kingdom of God is in Christ and the Spirit, not in "works
of the law"; and that assurance of the full and perfect manifestation of the Kingdom, still to come, and their complete
participation in it, come from that same Spirit which they already had received by faith. Paul says that they already were
participants in the Kingdom because they were already "sons"

and "heirs" (4:6-7), because they were "known by God" (4:9),
because the "Jerusalem above" is their "mother" (4:26), because,
instead of "works of the flesh," they bore the "fruit of the
Spirit" (5:16-25), in short, because they were following the
"canon" of the "new creation," which is the only condition of
receiving the blessing of membership in the "Israel of God,"
and its gifts, "peace and mercy" (6:14-16). Paul, therefore,
in the letter to the Galatians, minimizes the distance between
the Kingdom, which is still in the future, and the "last age"
present in the form of the Spirit.[76] Nevertheless, the concept
of the distance between the present and the future, even in the
"last age" as the time of the Spirit, is there. Hints of it
are in 5:5 and 6:8.

The full *disclosure* of the Kingdom, which is the "revelation" of faith with the coming of Christ,[77] awaits its full and
perfect *manifestation* in every life and community. Christian
hope in the *immanence* of the Kingdom in the form of the Spirit
is only partially and imperfectly fulfilled; but when Christian
hope fixes on the *transcendent* character of the Kingdom, it is
always fully and perfectly fulfilled. For the transcendent aspect of the Kingdom is the character of God as the "End" of all
things. The presence and activity of the Spirit is "anticipa-
tory of that End, assuring us of it and uniting us with it."[78]

With Christ and the Spirit, however, God did not *become*
the "End" of all things in the form of the Kingdom. Rather,
in Christ and his Spirit, God as the "End" became the center of
a new structure of existence. Christians in Galatia, for example, gave up their former way of life as a result of experiencing God as the "End," in the form of the presence and activity of the Spirit. They experienced this for the first time on
the occasion of Paul's missionary preaching of the crucified
Christ. It was something new and they recognized in it what
Paul called a "new creation." All this adds up to an experience of the "last age," which is the immanence of God as the
"End."

But, because Christians in the Galatian churches were
religiously (and morally) scrupulous, they were being swept
along by nomists, who had promised them inclusion in God's

kingdom, on the condition that they receive circumcision and
perform other "works of the law," as the eschatological sign
of the people of God. Responding to what he considered a dan-
gerous perversion of the "truth of God," Paul wrote the letter
to the Galatians to remind them of their experiences of the
"last age" already in the presence and activity of the Spirit,
with which they had begun Christian existence. These experiences, which had continued after Paul's departure from Galatia,
Paul argues, were adequate, and in fact the only sufficient,
evidence of participation in the kingdom of God. They should,
therefore, remain steadfast in their faith by which--through
the Spirit, not by circumcision, nor by any of the other "works
of the law"--they already knew God, and were known by God, from
whom they had assurance of righteousness and eternal life.

CHAPTER VI

[1]For a discussion of the eschatological dimension of Paul's "theology" of the possession of the Spirit, see Schweitzer, *Pauline Mysticism*, 160-67. Cf. also Aune, *The Cultic Setting*, 12: "Worship in the Spirit, with all of its ecstatic, charismatic and prophetic manifestations and characteristics," is one major "mode of realizing eschatological salvation in present experience."

[2]Cf. below, pp. 169-71.

[3]Cf. below, pp. 171-72.

[4]Cf. below, pp. 173-74.

[5]Cf. 3:16, 3:19 (ἦλθη) and 3:25 (ἦλθεν is to be supplied after εἰς Χριστόν).

[6]Cf. 3:23a (ἐλθεῖν) and 3:25 (ἐλθούσης). The ἐλθεῖν of "faith" is interpreted in 3:23b as its ἀποκαλυφθῆναι. The use of ἵνα...γένηται with the "blessing of Abraham" in 3:14 is similarly eschatological.

[7]Cf. Johannes Schneider, *TDNT* 2.674; and Delling, *TDNT* 6.305.

[8]Cf. Lightfoot, *St. Paul to the Galatians*, 167; Ellicott, *Paul's Epistle to the Galatians*, 93; Lipsius, *Briefe an die Galater*, 47; Lietzmann, *An die Galater*, 26; Lagrange, *Epître aux Galates*, 101; Oepke, *Paulus an die Galater*, 96; Schlier, *Brief an die Galater*, 194; Bonnard, *Saint Paul aux Galates*, 85; and Betz, *Commentary on Paul's Letter*, on 4:4.

[9]Cf. 1:4, where Paul says that Christ's liberation from the "present evil age" happened κατὰ τὸ θέλημα τοῦ θεοῦ (cf. also 6:9-10 and below, p. 183 n. 46).

[10]Cf. 4:5-6.

[11]Cf. 3:23-25 and 4:1-3.

[12]Cf. 1:4 (πονηρός).

[13]The "works of the flesh" include, for example, εἰδωλολατρία and φαρμακεία (5:20), which recall 4:8-9, where Paul characterizes the Galatians' pagan religion in similar terms, as slavery to beings not by nature gods (idolatry), and as ignorance of God (superstition). Cf. also 3:3.

[14]Cf. 5:22-23 (ἀγάπη, etc.) and 6:9-10 (τὸ καλὸν...τὸ ἀγαθόν). Cf. also 1:3-4, 2:20 and 6:16, 18.

[15]Cf. Burton, *Epistle to the Galatians*, 216.

[16]Cf. Delling (*TDNT* 6.305), who suggests that it means a *qualitative* filling of the "time," i.e., in *content* as well as extent, so that it denotes the coming to completion of God's purpose/s (cf. Mussner, *Der Galaterbrief*, 269). With this interpretation, he contrasts the notion of a span of time that has run its course (cf. Meyer, *Epistle to the Galatians*, 170; and Schlier, *Brief an die Galater*, 194), and that of a divinely ordained point which has been reached (cf. those cited above, p. 179 n. 8).

[17]Cf. Lightfoot, *St. Paul to the Galatians*, 167-68.

[18]Cf. Meyer, *Epistle to the Galatians*, 170; Lagrange, *Epître aux Galates*, 101; and Betz, *Commentary on Paul's Letter*, on 3:19 and 3:22 (although he rejects this interpretation of εἰς Χριστόν in 3:24).

[19]Cf. also 3:25 where ἦλθεν is to be understood after εἰς Χριστόν (cf. above, p. 179 n. 5).

[20]Cf. Burton, *Epistle to the Galatians*, 200; Oepke, *Paulus an die Galater*, 88; Schlier, *Brief an die Galater*, 169-70; Bonnard, *Saint Paul aux Galates*, 76 (cf. also his note on pp. 152-53); and Betz, *Commentary on Paul's Letter*, ad loc. Cf. also Bertram, *TDNT* 5.620-21; Bultmann, *Theology*, 1.266; Conzelmann, *Outline*, 227; and Günther Bornkamm, *Paul* (trans. D. M. G. Stalker; New York: Harper and Row, 1971) 127-28. Bultmann and Conzelmann, however, do not completely relinquish the telic application of the εἰς-clause to the development of the individual. Temporal clauses appear in 3:19 (ἄχρις ἂν ἔλθη τὸ σπέρμα ᾧ ἐπήγγελται); and 3:23b (εἰς τὴν μέλλουσαν πίστιν ἀποκαλυφθῆναι), which corresponds to the πρό-clause in 3:23a, and the genitive absolute in 3:25, which is also a temporal clause.

[21]Cf. Cobb, *The Structure*, 122-23.

[22]Cf. Phil 3:20, 1 Cor 1:7, and Rom 8:19, 23, 25 (cf. also Grundmann, *TDNT* 2.56; Schlier, *Brief an die Galater*, 233 n. 1; and Betz, *Commentary on Paul's Letter*, on 5:5, n. 83).

[23]The content of hope, rather than its source, is identified by δικαιοσύνης, which is an epexegetical genitive (cf. Ellicott, *Paul's Epistle to the Galatians*, 120; Meyer, *Epistle to the Galatians*, 222; Burton, *Epistle to the Galatians*, 278-79; Mussner, *Der Galaterbrief*, 350; Schrenk, *TDNT* 2.207; and Schweizer, *TDNT* 6.426).

[24]The dative is instrumental (cf. Burton, *Epistle to the Galatians*, 278; Bultmann, *TDNT* 2.532; and Robinson, *The Body*, 72 n. 2), and ἐκ πίστεως is the source or origin of the Spirit (cf. 3:2, 5, 14; and Oepke, *Paulus an die Galater*, 119). For the view that ἐκ πίστεως is the origin and source of the *expectation* and *hope*, as a second "principle" alongside of the

Spirit, see Ellicott (*Paul's Epistle to the Galatians*, 120-21),
Meyer (*Epistle to the Galatians*, 222), Lipsius (*Briefe an die
Galater*, 57-58), Burton (*Epistle to the Galatians*, 278),
Lagrange (*Epître aux Galates*, 137), and Bultmann (*TDNT* 2.532).
This view appears to be based on a distinction between the
Spirit as the "objective" basis, and faith as the "subjective"
(cf. Meyer, *Epistle to the Galatians*, 222; and Burton, *Epistle
to the Galatians*, 278; cf. above, Chapter V, p. 155). In any
case, πνεύματι ἐκ πίστεως modifies ἀπεκδεχόμεθα, not ἐλπίδα
δικαιοσύνης, since ἐλπίδα is meant in the objective sense,
rather than in the subjective (cf. Lipsius, *Briefe an die
Galater*, 58; and Burton, *Epistle to the Galatians*, 279).

[25]Cf. Oepke, *Paulus an die Galater*, 119.

[26]For δικαιόω in the present tense, see 2:16 and 3:8, 11
(for δικαιοσύνη, see also 2:21 and 3:6, 21). According to
Bultmann, genuine futures are expressed only in 2:17 (which has
the aorist infinitive with a present participle) and 5:5; so
that he takes the future in 2:16, and the aorist subjunctive in
2:16 and 3:24 as logical or "gnomic," rather than temporal,
just as he calls δικαιοῦσθε in 5:4 a "timeless present" (cf.
Theology, 1.274; and idem, "ΔΙΚΑΙΟΣΥΝΗ ΘΕΟΥ," *JBL* 83 [1964] 15).

[27]Cf. Lipsius, *Briefe an die Galater*, 58; and Lagrange,
Epître aux Galates, 137 (for whom the genitive is subjective).

[28]This interpretation, which takes δικαιοσύνης in an
ethical sense and as an objective genitive, is rejected by
Meyer (*Epistle to the Galatians*, 223).

[29]Cf. below, pp. 173-74.

[30]Cf. 5:6 and 5:13-6:10.

[31]For taking δικαιοσύνη in 5:5 in the forensic sense, see
Meyer, *Epistle to the Galatians*, 222; Bonnard, *Saint Paul aux
Galates*, 104; Schrenk, *TDNT* 2.207; Jeremias, *Parables of Jesus*,
210 n. 1; Bultmann, *Theology*, 1.273; and idem, "ΔΙΚΑΙΟΣΥΝΗ
ΘΕΟΥ," 12-16.

[32]Cf. Bultmann, *Theology*, 1.276, 284, 289.

[33]This is the dialectic between indicative and imperative
according to Bultmann (cf. also Meyer, *Epistle to the Galatians*,
223; and Ernst Käsemann, "The Righteousness of God in Paul,"
pp. 168-82 in *New Testament Questions of Today* [trans. W. J.
Montague; Philadelphia: Fortress, 1969] 170).

[34]As God's eschatological "juridical act," χάρις is virtually synonymous with εἰρήνη and ἔλεος (cf. 1:3, 2:20 and
6:16, 18). Cf. also Bultmann, *Theology*, 1.282.

[35]Cf. Burton, *Epistle to the Galatians*, 278, 471. For a
summary of the German discussion generated by Käsemann's
article ("Gottesgerechtigkeit bei Paulus," *ZTK* 58 [1961]), to

which Bultmann's article "ΔΙΚΑΙΟΣΥΝΗ ΘΕΟΥ" (*JBL* 83 [1964]) is a response, see the "Appendix" by Manfred T. Brauch in Sanders (*Paul*, 523-42).

[36]Cf. 4:17 (ἐκκλεῖσαι), 5:4 (καταργεῖσθαι), and 5:21b (οἱ τὰ τοιαῦτα πράσσοντες βασιλείαν θεοῦ οὐ κληρονομήσουσιν).

[37]In 5:4, ἐν νόμῳ δικαιοῦσθε has to do with "works of the law," particularly circumcision, which is mentioned in 5:2-3, 6 (cf. ἐξ ἔργων τοῦ νόμου εἰσίν in 3:10, and ἐν νόμῳ...δικαιοῦται in 3:11).

[38]Cf. 1:6, 4:17 and 5:4.

[39]Proof (γάρ) of 5:4 is given in 5:5 by means of an argument *e contrario*(cf. Lightfoot, *St. Paul to the Galatians*, 204; Ellicott, *Paul's Epistle to the Galatians*, 119; Meyer, *Epistle to the Galatians*, 222; and Burton, *Epistle to the Galatians*, 278).

[40]The reason (γάρ) for the preceding assertion in 5:5, that the Spirit effects hope of righteousness, is given in 5:6 (cf. Grundmann, *TDNT* 3.397-98).

[41]For the view that the στίγματα τοῦ 'Ιησοῦ (6:17), namely, Paul's "wounds and scars" (cf. 2 Cor 4:10, 12:9-10 and Rom 8:17), are the opposite of circumcision as the eschatological sign, see Otto Betz (*TDNT* 7.663).

[42]Cf. Betz, "The Literary Composition," 377; and idem, *Commentary on Paul's Letter*, on 6:7.

[43]Cf. Hauck, *TDNT* 3.132-33; S. Schulz, *TDNT* 7.546; and Betz, *Commentary on Paul's Letter* , on 6:9.

[44]Cf., for example, Mussner (*Der Galaterbrief*, 403), who calls these "eschatological futures" (cf. also Bonnard, *Saint Paul aux Galates*, 126; and Büchsel, *TDNT* 3.940).

[45]For φθορά, see BAG, 4; Meyer, *Epistle to the Galatians*, 256 (cf. ἀπώλεια); Lipsius, *Briefe an die Galater*, 66; Burton, *Epistle to the Galatians*, 342; Lagrange, *Epître aux Galates*, 160; Oepke, *Paulus an die Galater*, 154; Schlier, *Brief an die Galater*, 277; Bonnard, *Saint Paul aux Galates*, 126; Mussner, *Der Galaterbrief*, 403; Betz, *Commentary on Paul's Letter*, on 6:8, n. 173; and Günther Harder, *TDNT* 9.104. For the view that this sense is secondary to the merely physical and moral sense of decay, corruption, perishability, see Lightfoot (*St. Paul to the Galatians*, 219) and Ellicott (*Paul's Epistle to the Galatians*, 145). For ζωὴ αἰώνιος, see Meyer, *Epistle to the Galatians*, 256; Lipsius, *Briefe an die Galater*, 66; Burton, *Epistle to the Galatians*, 342-43; Lagrange, *Epître aux Galates*, 160; Schlier, *Brief an die Galater*, 277; Bultmann, *TDNT* 2.869, n. 315; and Hermann Sasse, *TDNT* 1.209.

[46]For καιρῷ ἰδίῳ in 6:9 as an eschatological term, see
Meyer, *Epistle to the Galatians*, 256; Lagrange, *Epître aux
Galates*, 161; Oepke, *Paulus an die Galater*, 155; Bonnard, *Saint
Paul aux Galates*, 127; Mussner, *Der Galaterbrief*, 406; Betz,
Commentary on Paul's Letter, ad loc.; and Delling, *TDNT* 3.461
(BAG ["καιρός," 3] translates this "in due time," but in [4]
points out that the concept of a "definite or fixed time"
merges with the eschatological use of the term; Lightfoot
[*St. Paul to the Galatians*, 220], however, does not note this
eschatological sense). For ὡς καιρὸν ἔχομεν in 6:10a, where
ὡς stands for ἕως or ὡς ἄν, see BDF, sec. 455.2, 3; Meyer,
Epistle to the Galatians, 257; Lagrange, *Epître aux Galates*,
161; Oepke, *Paulus an die Galater*, 155; Bonnard, *Saint Paul
aux Galates*, 127; Mussner, *Der Galaterbrief*, 407; Stauffer,
TDNT 1.51; and Delling, *TDNT* 3.460 (BAG ["καιρός," 2] translates κ. ἔχειν "have opportunity," but under "ὡς," [IV, 1, b],
the temporality of this phrase is brought out, "as long as";
Lightfoot [*St. Paul to the Galatians*, 220] and Burton [*Epistle
to the Galatians*, 345], however, lose the eschatological sense
by interpreting the ὡς as "whenever").

[47]Cf. 6:12-13 and 3:3, 5:2-6 and 6:15. In 6:7-10, Paul
provides a conclusion to the *whole* parenetic section (5:1-6:10)
in the form of an eschatological warning (cf. the curse in
1:8-9, and the conditional blessing in 6:16; similarly, 3:1-5,
4:11, 19, 5:2-6 and 6:14-15 express the same note of eschatological warning). As long as 6:7-10 is tied exclusively to
6:1-6, especially v. 6, the sense of 6:8 is understood in terms
of mere selfishness (cf. Lightfoot, *St. Paul to the Galatians*,
219; Ellicott, *Paul's Epistle to the Galatians*, 145-46; Meyer,
Epistle to the Galatians, 255; and Burton, *Epistle to the
Galatians*, 341). But the asyndeton in 6:7 indicates the start
of a new subsection (cf. Oepke, *Paulus an die Galater*, 153;
Schlier, *Brief an die Galater*, 276; Bonnard, *Saint Paul aux
Galates*, 126; and Mussner, *Der Galaterbrief*, 405). The ἑαυτοῦ,
therefore, picks up the motif of circumcision (cf. Lipsius,
Briefe an die Galater, 66), and not selfishness. Cf. also
Betz's discussion of 6:8 (*Commentary on Paul's Letter*, ad loc.).

[48]The εἰς is local (cf. BAG, "σπείρω," 1, b, α; Oepke,
Paulus an die Galater, 157; and Betz, *Commentary on Paul's
Letter*, ad loc.), as well as "ethical" (cf. Ellicott, *Paul's
Epistle to the Galatians*, 145; Burton, *Epistle to the Galatians*,
343; and Oepke, *Paulus an die Galater*, 154).

[49]Cf. Oepke, *Paulus an die Galater*, 154. The flesh is no
less an "objective" power than the Spirit (against Meyer's distinction [*Epistle to the Galatians*, 255]).

[50]Cf. Burton, *Epistle to the Galatians*, 342.

[51]Cf. the "curse" in 1:8-9 (cf. 3:10), which is implicit
in 3:1-5, 5:2-6 and 6:12-16.

[52]Cf. 5:16, 18, 25.

[53]Cf. Meyer, *Epistle to the Galatians*, 256; Lagrange, *Epître aux Galates*, 161; Schlier, *Brief an die Galater*, 277; Bonnard, *Saint Paul aux Galates*, 126; and Mussner, *Der Galaterbrief*, 406 (cf. also Ellicott, *Paul's Epistle to the Galatians*, 146). Although Lipsius (*Briefe an die Galater*, 66) interprets σπείρειν εἰς τὸ πνεῦμα as "einen sittlich guten Lebenswandel," he rejects its identification with τὸ καλὸν ποιεῖν. Burton (*Epistle to the Galatians*, 342–43), on the other hand, understands εἰς τὸ πνεῦμα as referring to the intellectual, religious and moral part of the person, so that σπείρειν εἰς τὸ πνεῦμα denotes "the enrichment of the life of the spirit" (343).

[54]Cf. Lagrange (*Epître aux Galates*, 160), who, however, distinguishes between the "spirit" in εἰς τὸ πνεῦμα and the "Holy Spirit" in ἐκ τοῦ πνεύματος, the former being understood as that part of a person infused with grace. This traditional Thomistic doctrine is presupposed, at any rate, in his explanation of πνεῦμα in εἰς τὸ πνεῦμα, and the "fruit of the Spirit" as "works of grace." But εἰς τὸ πνεῦμα and ἐκ τοῦ πνεύματος are parallel, so that the sphere *to* which one looks for eschatological life is the same πνεῦμα *from* which it comes, which in the letter to the Galatians is not the human spirit (except for 6:18, where πνεῦμα ὑμῶν is virtually synonymous with καρδία, ἔγω, or the center of a person's θέλειν where the divine Spirit does its ἄγειν), but the Spirit of God's "Son" (cf. 4:6; and Lightfoot, *St. Paul to the Galatians*, 218; Meyer, *Epistle to the Galatians*, 256; Lipsius, *Briefe an die Galater*, 66; Oepke, *Paulus an die Galater*, 154–55; and Schweizer, *TDNT* 6.430).

[55]Cf. Bultmann, *TDNT* 2.869 n. 315; and Schlier, *Brief an die Galater*, 277.

[56]Cf. Sasse, *TDNT* 1.209.

[57]Cf. Bultmann, *TDNT* 2.864, 867.

[58]Cf. 1 Thess 4:13-18 and 1 Cor 11:30, 15:29, 51-57.

[59]Cf. 1 Corinthians, which concerns the consequences of "enthusiasm" (especially 1 Corinthians 12-15).

[60]Cf. 1 Corinthians 15 (against Bultmann, *TDNT* 2.864).

[61]Cf. 1 Thess 4:13-18 (against Meyer, *Epistle to the Galatians*, 256; Schlier, *Brief an die Galater*, 277; and Mussner, *Der Galaterbrief*, 407). Cf. also Betz, *Commentary on Paul's Letter*, on 6:10.

[62]Cf. Lagrange, *Epître aux Galates*, 161.

[63]Cf. especially 5:25 (cf. also 3:3).

[64]Cf. Bultmann, *TDNT* 2.865.

[65]For a contrary view, see Pannenberg, *Jesus*, 169-79; "The Working of the Spirit," 13-31; "The Doctrine of the Spirit,"

8-21; *Apostles' Creed*, 128-43; and *Faith and Reality*, 20-38.
He claims that "the biblical" concept of the Spirit as the origin of all life is found in Paul's letters. The result is that
he sees the present activity of the Spirit as merely quantita-
tively different from the past presence and activity of the
Spirit (just as the future work of the Spirit will be quantita-
tively different from the present). Cf. above, Chapter V, p.
167 n. 65.

[66]Cf. Cobb, *Christ*, 262.

[67]Cf. 5:5 and 6:8 (and above, pp. 171-74).

[68]Cf. Gunkel, *Die Wirkungen*, 63-65; Vos, *Traditionsgeschichtliche Untersuchungen*, 32, 76-77; and Cobb, *Christ*,
261-62.

[69]Cf. 5:16, 18, 25.

[70]Cf. 6:1 (cf. also 3:3).

[71]Cf. 6:14-16.

[72]Cf. Cobb, *Christ*, 262. Cf. also Rom 14:17 and 1 Cor
4:20.

[73]Cf. above, pp. 171-74.

[74]Cf. τὸ ἀρραβὼν τοῦ πνεύματος (2 Cor 1:22, 5:5), and
ἡ ἀπαρχὴ τοῦ πνεύματος (Rom 8:23).

[75]For the observation, "that the time of the church between the departure of the resurrected Lord and his future
Parousia is characterized by his absence from the community is
an insight that only begins to develop in Paul's debate with
the Corinthians," see Pannenberg (*Jesus*, 178-79).

[76]In other words, the *causa* of the letter explains the
absence, in the letter to the Galatians, of the expressions
ἡ ἀπαρχὴ τοῦ πνεύματος (Rom 8:23), and τὸ ἀρραβὼν τοῦ πνεύματος
(2 Cor 1:22, 5:5), which indicate the qualitative and quantitative difference between the present and the future.

[77]Cf. 3:23.

[78]Cf. Cobb, *Christ*, 261-62.

PART III

CONCLUSION

INTRODUCTION

The task of the preceding chapters was to understand Paul's
statements about the Spirit in terms of the events that led to
the writing of the letter to the Galatians and the experience
of the Spirit in the churches of Galatia, and in the context of
the letter. Now the task is to understand the Spirit itself
with the aid of Paul's statements in the letter to the Galatians
and the discussion about the Spirit in theology today. This
means we must attempt to speak about the *subject* of Paul's
statements about the Spirit, and not only about his *statements*.
More accurately, the understanding of Paul's statements about
the Spirit is only the beginning of the understanding of the
Spirit itself.

This discussion, therefore, is informed by interpretations
of the Spirit in Bultmann's existentialist theology and in the
theologies of nature of Pannenberg and Pittenger, as well as by
an understanding of statements about the Spirit in Paul's letter to the Galatians. The method or procedure of this discussion is based on the assumption that an understanding of the
Spirit (or any other subject) will be richer the more it is
able to retain, rather than eliminate, the contrasts between
different perspectives. If, however, this is done in such a
way that the contrasts are held in sheer opposition, the resulting understanding would not be richer because of the complexity, but simply incoherent. The next step, therefore, is
to integrate the contrasts by taking account of the major concerns of each perspective and, at the same time, creatively
transforming them.

In this discussion, my own perspective, which is that of
process theology, based on the philosophy of Alfred North Whitehead,[1] plays a necessary role. We all always stand within some
perspective. The alternative, a point of view outside all perspectives, is inherently self-contradictory and, therefore, an
impossibility. The question is whether one's perspective opens
one's perception of the subject to perspectives other than one's
own. Such a broader perception can be achieved by aiming toward

189

integrating the major concerns of different perspectives while
retaining their contrasts. The result is that one's own perspective can be transcended without being eliminated; that is,
it too is creatively transformed. This procedure also avoids,
on the one hand, harmonization and, on the other, the mere
translation of expressions from one language system to another.
Whereas the former eliminates contrasts by denying them, the
latter does this by reducing perspectival contrasts to merely
semantic differences.

We begin with a summary of the understanding of Paul's
statements about the Spirit in the preceding chapters.[2] Next
we turn to the contrast and integration of the major concerns
of Paul's concept of the Spirit in Galatians and of Bultmann's
existentialist interpretation of the Spirit.[3] Then we add to
this discussion the major concerns of the concept of the Spirit
in the theologies of nature of Pannenberg and Pittenger.[4] From
this discussion is derived a concept of the Spirit which takes
account of the major concerns of each perspective, while at the
same time creatively transforming them.

NOTES

PART III. INTRODUCTION

[1]For a general introduction to Whitehead's philosophy,
see Cobb (*A Christian Natural Theology*, 23-46). For an introduction to process theology, see John B. Cobb, Jr. and David R.
Griffin (*Process Theology: An Introductory Exposition* [Phila-
delphia: Westminster, 1976]). For a discussion of "process
hermeneutics," see the essays by John B. Cobb, Jr., William A.
Beardslee, Theodore J. Weeden, Russell Pregeant, and Barry A.
Woodbridge on "New Testament Interpretation from a Process
Perspective" (eds. William A. Beardslee and David J. Lull;
pp. 21-128 in *Journal of the American Academy of Religion* 47/1
[1979]), which also includes Chapter VII of this study in a
revised form.

[2]Cf. below, pp. 193-95.

[3]Cf. below, pp. 195-99.

[4]Cf. below, pp. 199-201.

CHAPTER VII

PAUL'S THEOLOGY OF THE SPIRIT IN
GALATIANS AND THEOLOGY TODAY

Summary

In the letter to the Galatians, Paul speaks about the
Spirit in connection with the proclamation of the crucified
Christ,[1] with beginning a new life,[2] and with ecstatic experiences.[3] He also speaks about the Spirit in connection with
freedom from the law of Moses and from the flesh.[4] The issue
behind these statements about the gift of the Spirit is the
Galatians' consideration of taking up obedience to the law of
Moses, for which circumcision is a symbol and "initiation
rite."[5] What prompted the Galatians to consider going this way
was the charge and promise of Jewish-Christian nomists that
Paul's "anti-nomianism" had made Christ "an agent of sin,"[6] and
that obedience to the law of Moses, including being circumcised,
was the way of righteousness.[7] Statements in the letter to the
Galatians, which probably reflect Paul's own missionary message
to the Galatians, seem to give support to the nomists' charge.[8]
And the Galatians, who were "scrupulous" about religion and
morality,[9] were sensitive to this accusation about Pauline
Christianity and this promise about the way of righteousness
identified with obedience to the law of Moses.

In Paul's rebuttal, he reminds the Galatians of their own
pneumatic experiences, which for Paul exemplify the falsity of
the way of righteousness of obedience to the law of Moses, and
the truth of his own gospel.[10] Their experiences of ecstasy,
which were the result of the incursion of the divine Spirit
into believers' "hearts,"[11] are for Paul evidence of the poverty
and weakness of "human nature." By demonstrating the weakness
of "human nature," their ecstatic experiences prove the falsity
of the way of righteousness of "the works of the law," a way
which Paul argues is based on the assumption that "human nature"
already has the power to be free and to live in accordance with
God's "will"; that is, in Paul's view it is based on confidence
in the flesh.[12]

193

He also reminds the Galatians of the ethical instructions that they had received from him during his missionary visit.[13] Then in 5:13-24, Paul draws anthropological consequences from their experiences of pneumatic ecstasy.[14] Paul argues that human behavior is dominated by "outside" forces that are "at war with each other," namely, σάρξ and πνεῦμα.[15] This means that a person cannot live in accordance with the divine "will," which Paul summarizes in 5:13c, 14,[16] by oneself alone, even if one "wills" to so live,[17] because the human "self" is originally without the help of the divine Spirit and, therefore, can only fulfill the "desires of the flesh." Ecstasy, however, is precisely the incursion of the divine Spirit in the "heart" of the Christian believer that is the necessary prerequisite of doing God's "will." In ecstasy a person's old structure of existence is "shaken up," so that a new structure of existence can take its place; namely, one in which the human "self" can be centered in the "goals and intentions" of the Spirit, rather than in the "goals and intentions" of the flesh.[18] The incursion of the Spirit makes possible a life in accordance with God's "will" because the Spirit brings with it attributes of "the divine life," that is, the "fruit of the Spirit."[19]

Finally, Paul reminds the Galatians of the mythico-historical event, the proclaiming of which was the original Sitz im Leben in which they had received the gift of the Spirit: namely, the crucifixion of Christ.[20] For Paul, in pneumatic ecstasy, Christians in Galatia participated in the death of Christ on the cross. Just as the crucified Christ himself was "raised from the dead,"[21] and now is present in the form of the Spirit, so also does he liberate Christian believers from "the present evil age."[22] For, those who by faith "belong to Christ" put to death "the flesh with its passions and "desires"[23] and "the world,"[24] which Paul interprets as a participation with Christ in his death on the cross. This mythico-historical event also liberates all Christian believers from the law of Moses, precisely through their co-participation in Christ's death on the cross.[25] For the law of Moses does not produce an ecstatic transformation of "sarkic" existence,[26] nor does it have the same relationship to God that the Spirit received by faith does.[27] The Spirit, therefore, is the Galatians' assurance of

the righteousness and eternal life of the "last age," because
the Spirit unites them with the crucified Christ, whom God
"raised from the dead," making the living presence of Christ
the new center of their existence. Obedience to the law of
Moses cannot give them this assurance, because the law of
Moses is completely "outside," spatially as well as temporally,
the framework of the eschatological event of the death of
Christ on the cross.[28]

Section 1. Paul and Existentialist Theology

If theology today is to speak of human existence, and of
God-in-the-world in the light of Paul's message to the Galatians, it must speak of both in a thoroughgoing historical manner. Paul does not think of human existence as if it consisted
of static "human nature." Rather, for Paul, human existence is
genuinely historical, in the sense that mythico-historical
events can and do bring changes in it. The event of the death
of Christ on the cross is one epochal event; and, before it,
the introduction of the law of Moses is another.[29] In Paul's
view, the latter event introduced into human affairs "transgressions" and a new form of "slavery." For the law of Moses
made "sinners" of all who did not perform Jewish national-
ethnic customs,[30] which introduced a division between "Jew and
Greek," and made the latter "sinners" "by nature."[31] Furthermore, by appearing to be the way of righteousness,[32] the law of
Moses prevented one from living by faith; instead, it made
those obedient to it live by "works of the law," which resulted
in placing them under a "curse."[33] Moreover, the law of Moses
introduced into human existence a new form of "slavery."
Originally,[34] everyone was a "slave" to the "weak and beggarly
elements of the world,"[35] and to the "desires of the flesh."[36]
But with the giving of the law of Moses, the Jews were placed
in a new form of slavery under a "pedagogue."[37]

When Christ came, in Paul's view, the changes in human
existence brought by the law of Moses came to an end.[38] No one
any longer was to be a "sinner" or a "righteous one" *by nature*.
All could be righteous by taking in the Spirit of God's "Son"
through faith--and only by this incursion of the divine Spirit.

This meant there were no longer any national-ethnic customs,
the practicing of which made a person righteous, and the not
practicing of which made others sinners. That is to say that,
with the coming of Christ, everyone had been liberated from
"transgressions" that were the basis for dividing Jew from
Greek. It also meant that it was now possible to live by
faith, because when Christ came it was shown[39] that righteousness was from faith, not from "works of the law." In Paul's
view, Gentiles were no longer sinners *by nature*, and Jews were
no longer *by nature* under a slavish "pedagogue"; for both could
take in the Spirit of God's "Son" *by faith*.

For Paul, before the Christ-event and the sending of the
Spirit of God's "Son" into the hearts of Christian believers,
there were at least two different ways of being human, the
Jewish and the Gentile. But, Paul argues, these were really
two variants of human life enslaved to the powers of the
cosmos.[40] To change this human condition of bondage to one of
freedom required nothing short of another act of creation by
divine intervention in the power structure of the world: namely,
the sending of God's "Son,"[41] his death and resurrection,[42] and
the sending of his Spirit into the hearts of believers.[43]

These changes in human existence, brought by mythic-
historical events, cannot be explained simply as changes in
life-styles, nor simply as changes in a person's "self-
understanding." Paul had expected Jewish and Gentile Christians in Antioch to share common meals together;[44] and he warns
the Galatians that their Christian communities would become
discordant and divisive if they practiced obedience to the law
of Moses.[45] When Paul wrote to the Galatians that life in
Christ was a "faith working through love,"[46] that Christian
freedom meant "being servants to one another through love,"[47]
and that they were "to do good to all, especially to those of
the household of faith,"[48] he was not writing mere pious plati-
tudes, nor utopian ideals. Rather, he presupposes the Galatians' structure of existence had been transformed by the
Spirit that they had received by faith, which made them πνευματικοί and made love manifest in their communities a real possibility. That the possibility of making love a social reality

was based on a structural transformation of human existence, by
the incursion of the divine Spirit, is shown by Paul's statement that love is "the fruit of the Spirit,"[49] which is manifest in the lives of those who live in and are guided by the
Spirit.[50]

For Paul, the Spirit is not reducible to a life-style, nor
to an "*understanding* of existence." In Galatians, the Spirit
is not "the new possibility of genuine, human life which opens
up to him who has surrendered his old understanding of himself,"
as Bultmann claims,[51] because for Paul the Spirit is a discrete entity,[52] ingredient in[53] and the source and norm of the
new life in which Christian believers are participants through
faith (that is, by accepting the death of Christ on the cross
as God's act of a "new creation"). For Paul, the Spirit brings
a real *structural* change in the believer's existence, and not
merely a change of "self-*understanding*." For Paul, ecstasy is
an example of the new structure of existence brought by the
Spirit;[54] for in ecstasy the Spirit breaks up the old alignment
of the human "self" with the flesh, and replaces the flesh.
With this new structure of existence, the human "self" has to
take responsibility for its orientation, either toward the
Spirit or toward the flesh; whereas in the old structure of
existence, when the human "self" was enslaved to the flesh, it
had no other orientation from which to choose. The Spirit
creates freedom by creating the possibility of choosing an
alternative orientation.

Paul probably did think of the Spirit as a kind of divine
fluidum, since he had no alternative way to conceptualize an
entity. Because Paul attributes "goals and intentions" to both
Spirit and flesh,[55] however, he does not think of either one as
a mere "substance"; rather, he considers each to be a purposive,
discrete entity. But it is possible to conceive of Spirit and
flesh as purposive, discrete entities without at the same time
treating them as "substances." Flesh, for example, is more
than the "physical substance" making up the outer surface of
the human body; for Paul distinguishes between the *purposes* of
the flesh, which he identifies as the "passions and desires" of
the flesh,[56] and their locus and source, which he thinks of as

the *material* flesh. We can think of the *purposes* of the flesh,
therefore, as "values" whose efficacy is their allurement
toward realization and, therefore, as discrete but nonsubstantial entities, which make up the region at the surface of our
bodies, which is the locus and source of the "desires of the
flesh."

The same can be said, *mutatis mutandis*, of the Spirit as a
discrete, nonsubstantial entity. For Paul, although the Spirit
is no mere aspect of human "nature," it too has purposes, which
he calls "the fruit of the Spirit,"[57] which are distinct from
the "substance" of the Spirit. We can think of these purposes,
whose allurement toward realization is their efficacy, as the
discrete, nonsubstantial entities that make up the Spirit,
rather than thinking of the Spirit as a *fluidum*, which in
Paul's view somehow has these purposes.

Also, Paul probably thought of flesh and Spirit as *coercive*
powers.[58] The compulsive force of the Spirit is demonstrated,
for example, in the ecstatic experiences of Christians in Galatia. This aspect of Paul's concept of the Spirit as a power-
ful, purposive entity is in tension, however, with the concept
of the Spirit as a norm to be followed[59] and as a power that
leads,[60] as Bultmann correctly observed; for the latter concepts portray the Spirit as a power with which human effort is
efficacious. But we cannot say that one set of statements is
determinative for Paul; rather, both seem to be determinative.
The Spirit cannot be manipulated by human effort, and it can
create surprising effects among those in whom its purposes are
realized, as in ecstasy. This aspect of the Spirit is expressed by Paul in terms of its coerciveness. At the same
time, πνευματικοί can drop out of life in the Spirit, as Paul
warns the Galatians they will do if they follow the way of
righteousness of obedience to the law of Moses.[61] Life in the
Spirit is not automatic, but a process depending in part on
human effort.[62] The guidance of the Spirit,[63] therefore, can
be conceived of in terms of *persuasion*, rather than compulsion.
For the concept of persuasion includes real efficacy without
the implication of compulsion. But Bultmann's category of a
"*possibility* of existence" tends to eliminate the notion of

causal efficacy all together, as its reduction in terms of the
decision between alternatives and the dialectic of indicative/
imperative implies.[64] The concept of persuasion, however, expresses the purposiveness of the Spirit. As a power, the
Spirit does not offer possibilities that are neutral toward
their realization; rather, the allurement of its purposes is
weighted toward their fulfillment. This conceptuality gives
expression to Paul's confidence that life in the Spirit is one
in which the purposes of the flesh are not fulfilled.[65] For
the allurement of the goals of the flesh is vivid and immediate, as opposed to the external commandments of the law of
Moses; the Spirit, however, offers alternative, at least as
vivid and immediate, purposes that elicit their fulfillment
instead of the fulfillment of the "desires of the flesh."

Life in the Spirit, therefore, does mean a new "understanding of existence," as Bultmann says. But even at this
level, it entails more than a new understanding of God, the
world and human existence. For life in the Spirit is a "sustained attention to the *Spirit*," "the habitude of *God*-
consciousness," the heightened awareness of the creative
presence of God in human affairs.[66] It is a new "self-
understanding," but only as an understanding of the real presence of *Another*. For Spirit-centered existence is an effective, habitual appropriation of the personal presence of God.

Section 2. Paul and Theologies of Nature

At the beginning of the last section I said, if theology
today is to speak of human existence in the light of Paul's
message to the Galatians, it must speak in thoroughgoing *historical* terms:[67] This is also true when it comes to speaking
about God-in-the-world. For Paul, the Spirit received by
faith is not the *eternal* Spirit, in whom everyone lives, and
in which, with the whole cosmos, everyone has their constant,
creative ground. Pannenberg and Pittenger are quite right,
however, in claiming that the dynamic ground of all life, indeed of the whole cosmos, is the creative presence of God,
which has no beginning or end.[68] But in Galatians, the term
Spirit names the presence of God's "Son" (4:6); that is, the

historical event of the death of Christ on the cross calls
forth sustained attention to the love of God, which is present
in the Spirit.[69] Paul speaks in Galatians of the creative
presence-in-history of God *before* this event in terms of the
divine "will" for the world.[70] But the death of Christ on the
cross is a special event of divine love in history, in the
sense that it decisively elicits the sustained awareness of the
personal presence of God in human affairs, in order to overcome
the obstacles to human freedom; that is, to bring about a "new
creation." As such, Paul's identification of the personal
presence of God in history as the Spirit of Christ points to
the immanence of divine love in the special act of the creation
of a new structure of existence, and to its origin in the death
of Christ on the cross. This enables theology to speak of the
Spirit as a *particular*, but not an exclusive, mode of God's
being-in-the-world. The Spirit known in the new life of faith,
therefore, is the same God that is the constant, creative
ground of all things.[71]

This results in an interesting contrast: on the one hand,
the Spirit experienced when a person accepts the death of
Christ on the cross as God's creative transformation of human
existence is a particular mode of the personal presence of God
in history; on the other hand, the object of God's act of
creating anew is itself not the "world." The Spirit does not
stand in harmony with "nature"; rather, it is at war with it.[72]
Paul does not think of "human nature" as having higher and
lower parts, as if the former were more closely allied with the
divine, and the latter more closely with the "natural world."
Rather, being human for Paul meant being entirely on the side
of "nature." Paul sees nothing redeeming about this
relationship--whether for "nature," or for human life.[73] In
Galatians, the problem is not the "suffering" of creation as
much as it is the suffering of humanity under the slavish
powers of "nature." Redemption, according to Galatians, therefore, is freedom from slavery to the powers of the cosmos:[74]
the law of Moses, flesh, and the world itself.[75] There seems
to be little room in Galatians for divine sympathy for the
"suffering" of creation.

And yet there is in Paul only a "benign neglect" of the
redemption of the body and of creation.[76] Although the problem
of human existence for Paul is how to live *in* the flesh without
living *according* to it, that is, without fulfilling the "desires" of the flesh, living "in" the flesh is a *given* this side
of eternal life in the "last age." For, the new life of faith
is still life *in the flesh*.[77] Furthermore, although Paul lists
"works of the flesh,"[78] from which Christian believers are
liberated by the Spirit, he lists "vices" that are *plainly* destructive.[79] Paul does not present freedom from the flesh as
absolute "apathy"; nor are there any instructions in Galatians
about ascetic practices, nor about the mortification of the
flesh.[80] Paul's approach instead is to push out the "desires
of the flesh" by giving sustained attention to the things of
the Spirit, and by practicing the "fruit of the Spirit" in the
daily life of the community of faith.[81]

As a result, withdrawal from life in the flesh and life
in the world, that is, from "nature," is no longer necessary.
In one sense, the flesh and "nature" as a whole have been
"exorcized." Those who by faith are filled with the sense of
the personal presence of God's power of creative transformation
could then have the courage and wisdom to confront whatever is
destructive in the world, in "nature" as well as in human affairs: that is, to participate in God's creative transformation
in history. Then God's act of re-creation in the mode of the
Spirit, which faith in the crucified Christ receives, would be
joined in human deed with God's primordial act of creative love,
as it is in the unity of the being and activity of God-in-the-
world.

Conclusion

In this study, I wanted to look "ahead," so to speak; to
take up questions from "in front of" the texts, as well as from
"behind" them. For, understanding the activity of the Spirit,
and Christian experience of it, depends in part upon the constant creative transformation of testimonies of early Christians by contrasts with witnesses from theology today. Likewise, the creative transformation of contemporary theological

reflection about the activity of the Spirit can be assisted by
contrasts with such witnesses to early Christian experience of
the Spirit as Paul's message to the Galatians.

The task that remains to complete this process of the
creative transformation of tradition and our contemporary
understanding is the placement of Paul more precisely in his
own history and intellectual culture. Alternative understand-
ings of the questions and answers of human existence contemporary with and preceding Paul provide contrasting views, with
which Paul was in discussion. They also ought to be our dialog partners with Paul. From this discussion, we will learn
more not only about Paul but also about the present activity
of God in the world and human experience of it. The completion
of this task, however, must await another occasion and place.

[1]Cf. 3:1-2.

[2]Cf. 3:3 and 5:25.

[3]Cf. 3:5 and 4:6.

[4]Cf. 5:1-24.

[5]Cf. 1:6-7, 2:15-21, 3:1-5, 4:21, 5:2-12, 18, 23b and 6:12-16.

[6]Cf. 2:17.

[7]Cf. 2:15-16, 21, 3:11, 21, and 5:3-6. Betz conjectures that 6:2, "the law of Christ," might come from the Galatians or Paul's opponents (cf. *Commentary on Paul's Letter*, ad loc.).

[8]For the impression that Christ is "an agent of sin," see, on the one hand, 3:13 and, on the other, 2:19, 3:23-25, 4:5a, 5:1, 13a, 18, 25. Freedom from the law of Moses also is reflected in the popular slogan in 3:28, "neither Jew nor Greek," which Paul's opponents might have interpreted to mean that Pauline Christianity keeps Gentiles "sinners," which they are "by nature" (cf. 2:15), that is, outsiders to the way of righteousness.

[9]At least this is the impression Paul wishes the Galatians to have of themselves (cf. 4:8-10). For Paul this is a negative image, which corresponds to the image of the Galatians in 1:6-7 and 3:1.

[10]For the antithesis between truth and falsity, see 1:6-9, 2:4-5, 13, 5:7-8, and 6:11, 16-17.

[11]Cf. 4:6.

[12]In 3:3, σάρξ (which can refer to the "flesh" of circumcision) refers to "the works of the law," because in Paul's view the latter rely only on the flesh. That this is Paul's view, but probably not his opponents', nor the Galatians', follows from the probability that 3:3 is Paul's reformulation of a phrase which played a role in the Jewish-Christian nomists' propaganda (cf. above, Chapter II, p. 31; Chapter IV, pp. 103-104 and 135 n. 7).

[13]Cf. 5:19-21. In 5:21, καὶ τὰ ὅμοια τούτοις reflects the fact that Paul's parenesis was not something new but was part of common knowledge, which is confirmed by the next clause, which begins with ἃ προλέγω ὑμῖν καθὼς προεῖπον. Betz (*Commentary on Paul's Letter*, ad loc.) conjectures that this refers to "baptismal instruction" from Paul.

[14]Contrary to what Schmithals thinks (cf. *Paul*, 55), in
5:13-24 Paul is on the *defensive* as well as on the offensive
(cf. Schlier, *Brief an die Galater*, 242; and Lietzmann, *An die
Galater*, 39). That an *accusation*, rather than "flagrantly
libertinistic" behavior, lies behind 5:13-24 is shown by 2:17,
which Betz (*Commentary on Paul's Letter*, ad loc.) has demonstrated form-critically, in terms of ancient rhetoric, reflects
the "point of contention," and by 5:18 and 23b, which reflect
that Paul's polemic against the way of righteousness of obedience to the law of Moses is still in view in this section of
the letter.

[15]Cf. 5:17.

[16]Cf. also 1:4, 2:20, 4:4-6 and 5:6, 22.

[17]Cf. 5:17c (ἵνα μὴ ἃ ἐὰν θέλητε ταῦτα ποιῆτε).

[18]Cf. 5:16.

[19]Cf. 5:22-23. Betz (*Commentary on Paul's Letter*, ad
loc.) notes that the first three terms, ἀγάπη, χαρά and εἰρήνη,
denote attributes of the divine. Actually the whole list consists of a mixture of Jewish and Hellenistic attributes of
deity, including the last two, πραΰτης and ἐγκράτεια.

[20]Cf. 3:1-2.

[21]Cf. 1:1.

[22]Cf. 1:4.

[23]Cf. 5:24.

[24]Cf. 6:14-15.

[25]Cf. 2:19-21 and 3:13-14. The concept of the "coming"
and "sending" of Christ or God's "Son" (cf. 3:23-25 and 4:4-5)
does not necessarily include a reference to the crucifixion.
Paul relates the "coming" of Christ as the end of the law of
Moses to Christian baptism (3:26-28), while he relates the
"sending" of God's "Son" as liberation from the law of Moses,
to the "sending" of the Spirit and to the ecstatic Abba-cry
(4:6). When 4:4-5 is set in its context in 4:1-11, the two
sides of Christian liberation are brought together under the
heading of freedom from the στοιχεῖα τοῦ κόσμου. In the parenetic section of the letter, 5:1-6:10, they are brought together
in an anthropological framework (cf. 5:18 = the Spirit opposes
the law of Moses, and 5:24 = Christ opposes the flesh; cf. also
6:14-15, in which Christ opposes the world and circumcision).

[26]Cf. 3:2-5.

[27]Cf. 3:19 and 4:24-25.

[28]Cf. 4:17 (ἐκκλεῖσαι ὑμᾶς θέλουσιν), 5:2 (Χριστὸς ὑμᾶς οὐδὲν ὠφελήσει), and 5:4 (κατηργήθητε ἀπὸ Χριστοῦ..., τῆς χάριτος ἐξεπέσατε).

[29]According to Rom 5:12-21, "the transgression of Adam" is the first such event to change human existence. Paul does not have this event in view, however, in Galatians.

[30]For circumcision, see 2:3-4; 5:2, 3, 6, 11, and 6:12-13, 15; and for its social consequences, see 2:11-14 (cf. also 3:28).

[31]Cf. 2:15.

[32]Cf. 5:4 (cf. also 3:11 and 3:21).

[33]Cf. 3:10-12 (cf.also 3:22).

[34]We are not told how in Galatians; but for Paul's view in Rom 5:12-21, see above, n. 29.

[35]Cf. 4:3, 8-9.

[36]This is the presupposition of 5:13-24.

[37]Cf. 3:23-25.

[38]Cf. 3:6-29.

[39]Cf. 3:23 (πίστιν ἀποκαλυφθῆναι).

[40]Cf. 4:3, 8-9.

[41]Cf. 4:4-5.

[42]Cf. 1:1, 4, 2:21, 3:13, 5:24, 6:14-15.

[43]Cf. 3:2, 3, 5, 14, 4:6, 5:16, 18, 25.

[44]Cf. 2:11-14.

[45]Cf. 5:15 (cf. also 5:19-21). For the contrast, see 3:28.

[46]Cf. 5:6.

[47]Cf. 5:13c.

[48]Cf. 6:9-10.

[49]Cf. 5:22-23.

[50]Cf. 5:16, 18, 25.

[51]Cf. Bultmann, *Theology*, 1.336. Cf. also 1.335: "everything indicates that by the term 'Spirit' he means the eschatological existence into which the believer is placed by having

appropriated the salvation deed that occurred in Christ."
Bultmann's statements about "walking in the Spirit" (1.330,
337) also indicate that he takes this to mean a change of one's
"understanding of existence."

[52]For Bultmann's comments on the concept of the Spirit as
a discrete entity, see *Theology* (1.333-34). When he criticizes
Paul's substantialist concept of the Spirit as a "non-worldly
material," Bultmann is correct; but he need not thereby eliminate all speaking of the Spirit as an entity, unless entities
are by definition "substances" for Bultmann.

[53]For Bultmann's comments on the immanence of the Spirit,
that is, its "indwelling" as an ingredient in Christian existence, which Bultmann considers mythological because, again,
it is bound up in Paul with substantialist thinking, see
Theology (1.333-34).

[54]For Bultmann's comments on the ecstatic effects of the
Spirit, see *Theology* (1.335-36). His objection here is both to
the notion of real structural change, and to that of compulsion; but the latter is not necessary for the former.

[55]Cf. 5:13b (ἀφορμή τῆς σαρκός), 5:16-17, 24 (ἐπιθυμίαι,
παθήματα, ἐπιθυμεῖν τῆς σαρκός, and ἐπιθυμεῖν τοῦ πνεύματος);
cf. also Rom 8:5-7, 27 (φρόνημα and φρονεῖν τῆς σαρκός or τοῦ
πνεύματος). Bultmann thinks these concepts are mythological
(cf. *Theology*, 1.336).

[56]Cf. 5:16-17, 19-21, 24 (cf. τὰ τῆς σαρκός in Rom 8:5).

[57]Cf. 5:22-23 (cf. also τὰ τοῦ πνεύματος in Rom 8:5).

[58]Cf. 5:17, especially the ἵνα-clause.

[59]Cf. 5:16, 25; and 6:1 (dative of means or manner).

[60]Cf. 5:18.

[61]Cf. 3:3 (cf. also 1:6-7, 4:8-11, 12-20, and 5:1-7).
In 4:30, Paul tells the Galatians what will happen to them if
they follow the nomists (cf. Betz, *Commentary on Paul's Letter*,
ad loc.).

[62]Cf. the imperatives in 5:16, 25; and the concept of
"sowing to the Spirit" in 6:8.

[63]Cf. 5:18 (πνεύματι ἄγεσθαι).

[64]Cf. Bultmann, *Theology*, 1.332, 336, 337-38.

[65]Cf. 5:16.

[66]Cf. Albert C. Outler, "Veni, Creator Spiritus: The
Doctrine of the Holy Spirit," *PSTJ* 19 (1966) 31-40, especially
39. Cf. Rom 12:1-2 and Phil 4:8.

[67]Cf. above, p. 195.

[68]Cf. Pannenberg, "Working of the Spirit," "Doctrine of the Spirit," *Apostles' Creed* (128-43), and *Faith and Reality* (20-38); and Pittenger, *Life in Christ* (35-46, 62-73) and *The Holy Spirit*.

[69]Cf. 2:20 and 5:22 (cf. also 5:6, 13-14). This is the meaning of the connection between the proclamation of the crucified Christ and receiving the gift of the Spirit in 3:1-5.

[70]Cf. 1:4 (τὸ θέλημα τοῦ θεοῦ), which is also expressed in 3:8 (προϊδοῦσα δὲ ἡ γραφὴ...προευηγγελίσατο), and 4:2, 4 (ἡ προθεσμία τοῦ πατρός...τὸ πλήρωμα τοῦ χρόνου).

[71]Cf. Rom 8:18-39.

[72]Cf. 5:17 (cf. also 1:4 and 6:14-15).

[73]Cf. Rom 8:18-23.

[74]Cf. 4:3, 8-9.

[75]Cf. 1:4, 3:6-29, 4:21-31, and 5:1-6:10, 14-15.

[76]Cf. 1 Cor 15:35ff.; Rom 8:11, 23.

[77]Cf. 2:20.

[78]Cf. 5:19-21.

[79]Φανερὰ δέ ἐστιν τὰ ἔργα τῆς σαρκός (5:19a).

[80]Paul's statements in Phil 1:21-24 are remarkably similar to Stoic writings about suicide (cf. Betz's comments, in "Paul's Concept," 11-12).

[81]Cf. 5:13-24 and 5:25-6:10 (cf. also 5:6).

BIBLIOGRAPHY

A. COMMENTARIES ON THE LETTERS OF PAUL

1. Romans

Barrett, Charles K. *The Epistle to the Romans*. Harper's New Testament Commentaries. New York: Harper & Row, 1957.

Dodd, Charles Harold. *The Epistle of Paul to the Romans*. Moffatt New Testament Commentary 6. New York: Harper & Bros., 1932.

Gaugler, Ernst. *Der Römerbrief*. Part 1: *Kapitel 1-8*. Prophezei: Schweizerisches Bibelwerk für die Gemeinde. Zürich: Zwingli-Verlag, 1958 (orig. 1945).

Käsemann, Ernst. *An die Römer*. 2nd ed. Handbuch zum Neuen Testament 8a. Tübingen: J. C. B. Mohr (Paul Siebeck), 1974.

Kuss, Otto. *Der Römerbrief*. 1st fasc.: *Röm. 1,1-6,11*; 2nd fasc. *Röm. 6,11-8,19*. 2nd ed. Regensburg: Friedrich Pustet, 1963.

Lietzmann, Hans. *An die Römer*. 5th ed. Handbuch zum Neuen Testament 8. Tübingen: J. C. B. Mohr (Paul Siebeck), 1971.

Michel, Otto. *Der Brief an die Römer*. 11th ed. H. A. W. Meyer, Kritisch-exegetischer Kommentar über das Neue Testament 4. Göttingen: Vandenhoeck & Ruprecht, 1957.

Sanday, William, and Headlam, Arthur C. *A Critical and Exegetical Commentary on the Epistle to the Romans*. 2nd ed. International Critical Commentary 32. New York: Scribner's Sons, 1896.

Schelkle, Karl Hermann. *The Epistle to the Romans. Theological Meditations*. Trans. Brian Thompson. New York: Herder and Herder, 1964.

Weiss, Bernhard. *Der Brief an die Römer*. 9th ed. H. A. W. Meyer, Kritisch-exegetischer Kommentar über das Neue Testament 4. Göttingen: Vandenhoeck & Ruprecht, 1899.

Zahn, Theodor. *Der Brief des Paulus an die Römer*. 1st and 2nd ed. Kommentar zum Neuen Testament 6. Leipzig: A. Deichert (Georg Böhme), 1910.

2. 1 and 2 Corinthians

Lietzmann, Hans. *An die Korinther* I-II. 4th ed. Supplemented
     by W. G. Kümmel. Handbuch zum Neuen Testament 9.
     Tübingen: J. C. B. Mohr (Paul Siebeck), 1949.

Meyer, Heinrich August Wilhelm. *Critical and Exegetical Hand-
     Book to the Epistles to the Corinthians.* Trans. D. Douglas
     Bannerman. Rev. and ed. William P. Dickson. New York:
     Funk & Wagnalls, 1884.

Wendland, Heinz Dietrich. *Die Briefe an die Korinther.* 10th
     ed. Das Neue Testament Deutsch 7. Göttingen: Vandenhoeck
     & Ruprecht, 1964.

3. 1 Corinthians

Allo, E.-B. *Saint Paul première épître aux Corinthiens.*
     2nd ed. Paris: J. Gabalda, 1956.

Bachmann, Philipp. *Der erste Brief des Paulus an die Korinther.*
     4th ed. Supplements by E. Stauffer. Kommentar zum Neuen
     Testament 7. Leipzig: A. Deichert, 1936.

Barrett, Charles K. *A Commentary on the First Epistle to the
     Corinthians.* Harper's New Testament Commentaries. New
     York: Harper & Row, 1968.

Conzelmann, Hans. *A Commentary on the First Epistle to the
     Corinthians.* Hermeneia--A Critical and Historical Commen-
     tary on the Bible. Trans. James W. Leitch. Ed. George W.
     MacRae, S.J. Philadelphia: Fortress, 1975.

Héring, Jean. *The First Epistle of Saint Paul to the Corinthi-
     ans.* Trans. A. W. Heathcote and P. J. Allcock. London:
     Epworth, 1962.

Moffatt, James. *The First Epistle of Paul to the Corinthians.*
     Moffatt New Testament Commentary 7. London: Hodder and
     Stoughton, 1938.

Robertson, Archibald, and Plummer, Alfred. *A Critical and
     Exegetical Commentary on the First Epistle of St. Paul to
     the Corinthians.* 2nd ed. International Critical Commen-
     tary 33. Edinburgh: T. & T. Clark, 1914.

Weiss, Johannes. *Der erste Korintherbrief.* 10th ed. H. A. W.
     Meyer, Kritisch-exegetischer Kommentar über das Neue
     Testament 5. Göttingen: Vandenhoeck & Ruprecht, 1925.

4. 2 Corinthians

Allo, E.-B. *Saint Paul seconde épître aux Corinthiens.*
2nd ed. Paris: J. Gabalda, 1956.

Barrett, Charles K. *A Commentary on the Second Epistle to the Corinthians.* Harper's New Testament Commentaries. New York: Harper & Row, 1973.

Heinrici, C. F. Georg. *Der zweite Brief an die Korinther.*
8th ed. H. A. W. Meyer, Kritisch-exegetischer Kommentar über das Neue Testament 6. Göttingen: Vandenhoeck & Ruprecht, 1900.

Héring, Jean. *The Second Epistle of Saint Paul to the Corinthians.* Trans. A. W. Heathcote and P. J. Allcock. London: Epworth, 1967.

Plummer, Alfred. *A Critical and Exegetical Commentary on the Second Epistle of St. Paul to the Corinthians.* International Critical Commentary 34. Edinburgh: T. & T. Clark, 1915.

Windisch, Hans. *Der zweite Korintherbrief.* 9th ed.
H. A. W. Meyer, Kritisch-exegetischer Kommentar über das Neue Testament 6. Göttingen: Vandenhoeck & Ruprecht, 1924.

5. Galatians

Betz, Hans Dieter. *A Commentary on Paul's Letter to the Churches in Galatia.* Hermeneia--A Critical and Historical Commentary on the Bible. Ed. Helmut Koester. Philadelphia: Fortress, 1979.

Bonnard, Pierre. *L'Epître de Saint Paul aux Galates.* 2nd ed. Commentaire du Nouveau Testament 9. Neuchâtel: Delachaux et Niestle, 1972.

Burton, Ernest de Witt. *A Critical and Exegetical Commentary on the Epistle to the Galatians.* International Critical Commentary 35. Edinburgh: T. & T. Clark, 1921.

Ellicott, Charles J. *A Critical and Grammatical Commentary on St. Paul's Epistle to the Galatians.* Andover: Warren F. Draper, 1884.

Lagrange, Marie Joseph. *Saint Paul épître aux Galates.* Paris: J. Gabalda, 1950.

Lietzmann, Hans. *An die Galater.* 4th ed. Handbuch zum Neuen Testament 10. Tübingen: J. C. B. Mohr (Paul Siebeck), 1971.

Lightfoot, Joseph Barber. *The Epistle of St. Paul to the Galatians.* Grand Rapids, MI: Zondervan, 1957 (orig. 1865).

Lipsius, R. A. *Briefe an die Galater*, *Römer*, *Philipper*.
    Vol. 2, Part 2. 2nd ed. Handkommentar zum Neuen Testa-
    ment. Freiburg: J. C. B. Mohr (Paul Siebeck), 1892.

Meyer, Heinrich August Wilhelm. *Critical and Exegetical Hand-
    Book to the Epistle to the Galatians*. Trans. G. H.
    Venables and Henry E. Jacobs. New York: Funk & Wagnalls,
    1884.

Mussner, Franz. *Der Galaterbrief*. Herders theologischer
    Kommentar zum Neuen Testament 9. Freiburg/Basel/Wien:
    Herder & Herder, 1974.

Oepke, Albrecht. *Der Brief des Paulus an die Galater*. 2nd
    ed. Theologischer Handkommentar zum Neuen Testament 9.
    Berlin: Evangelische Verlagsanstalt, 1957.

Schlier, Heinrich. *Der Brief an die Galater*. 14th ed.
    H. A. W. Meyer, Kritisch-exegetischer Kommentar über das
    Neue Testament 7. Göttingen: Vandenhoeck & Ruprecht,
    1971.

6. 1 and 2 Thessalonians

Best, Ernest. *A Commentary on the First and Second Epistles
    to the Thessalonians*. Harper's New Testament Commentar-
    ies. New York: Harper & Row, 1972.

Dibelius, Martin. *An die Thessalonicher I-II, An die
    Philipper*. 2nd ed. Handbuch zum Neuen Testament 11.
    Tübingen: J. C. B. Mohr (Paul Siebeck), 1925.

Dobschütz, Ernst von. *Die Thessalonicher-Briefe*. 7th ed.
    H. A. W. Meyer, Kritisch-exegetischer Kommentar über das
    Neue Testament 10. Göttingen: Vandenhoeck & Ruprecht,
    1909.

Ellicott, Charles J. *A Critical and Grammatical Commentary on
    St. Paul's Epistles to the Thessalonians*. 2nd ed.
    Andover: Warren F. Draper; Boston: W. H. Halliday;
    Philadelphia: Smith, English, 1872.

Frame, James E. *A Critical and Exegetical Commentary on the
    Epistles to the Thessalonians*. International Critical
    Commentary 38. Edinburgh: T. & T. Clark, 1912.

Lünemann, Gottlieb. *Critical and Exegetical Hand-Book to the
    Epistles to the Thessalonians*. Trans. Paton J. Gloag.
    New York: Funk & Wagnalls, 1885.

B. ALL OTHER WORKS

Aristotle. *De Partibus Animalium*. Trans. A. L. Peck.
Rev. ed. Loeb Classical Library 12. Cambridge: Harvard
University; London: William Heinemann, 1945.

_____. *De Sensu et Sensili*. Trans. W. S. Hett. Rev. ed.
Loeb Classical Library 8. Cambridge: Harvard University;
London: William Heinemann, 1957.

Aune, David Edward. *The Cultic Setting of Realized Eschatology in Early Christianity*. Novum Testamentum, Supple-
ments 28. Leiden: E. J. Brill, 1972.

Barrett, Charles K. "The Allegory of Abraham, Sarah, and
Hagar in the Argument of Galatians." Pp. 1-16 in *Recht-
fertigung. Festschrift für Ernst Käsemann zum 70.
Geburtstag*. Ed. Johannes Friedrich, Wolfgang Pöhlmann,
and Peter Stuhlmacher. Tübingen: J. C. B. Mohr (Paul
Siebeck); Göttingen: Vandenhoeck & Ruprecht, 1976.

Bauer, Walter. *A Greek-English Lexicon of the New Testament
and Other Early Christian Literature*. Trans. W. F. Arndt
and F. W. Gingrich. Chicago: University of Chicago, 1957.

_____. *Orthodoxy and Heresy in Earliest Christianity*.
Trans. by a team from the Philadelphia Seminar on Chris-
tian Origins. Ed. Robert A. Kraft and Gerhard Krodel.
Philadelphia: Fortress, 1971.

Beardslee, William A. and David J. Lull (eds.). "New Testament Interpretation from a Process Perspective." *Journal
of the American Academy of Religion* 47/1 (1979) 21-128.

Betz, Hans Dieter. *Lukian von Samosata und das Neue Testament:
Religionsgeschichtliche und paränetische Parallelen. Ein
Beitrag zum Corpus Hellenisticum Novi Testamenti*. Texte
und Untersuchungen zur Geschichte der altchristlichen
Literatur 76 (5th series, vol. 21). Berlin: Akademie,
1961.

_____. *Nachfolge und Nachahmung Jesu Christi im Neuen
Testament*. Beiträge zur historischen Theologie 37.
Tübingen: J. C. B. Mohr (Paul Siebeck), 1967.

_____. *Der Apostel Paulus und die sokratische Tradition:
Eine exegetische Untersuchung zu seiner "Apologie"
2 Korinther 10-13*. Beiträge zur historischer Theologie
45. Tübingen: J. C. B. Mohr (Paul Siebeck), 1972.

_____. "2 Cor 6:14-7:1: An Anti-Pauline Fragment?" *Journal
of Biblical Literature* 92 (1973) 88-108.

_____. "Spirit, Freedom, and Law: Paul's Message to the
Galatian Churches." *Svensk exegetisk årsbok* 39 (1974)
145-60.

Betz, Hans Dieter. "The Literary Composition and Function of
    Paul's Letter to the Galatians." *New Testament Studies* 21
    (1975) 353-79.

_____. "In Defense of the Spirit: Paul's Letter to the
    Galatians as a Document of Early Christian Apologetics."
    Pp. 99-114 in *Aspects of Religious Propaganda in Judaism
    and Early Christianity*. University of Notre Dame Center
    for the Study of Judaism and Christianity in Antiquity 2.
    Ed. Elisabeth Schüssler-Fiorenza. Notre Dame, IN:
    University of Notre Dame, 1976.

_____. "Galatians, Letter to the." Pp. 352-53 in *The
    Interpreter's Dictionary of the Bible* (Supplementary
    volume). Ed. Keith Crim, Lloyd R. Bailey, Sr., Victor P.
    Furnish and Emory S. Bucke. Nashville: Abingdon, 1976.

_____. "Eine judenchristliche Kult-Didache in Matthäus 6,
    1-18: Überlegungen und Fragen im Blick auf das Problem
    des historischen Jesus." Pp. 445-57 in *Jesus Christus in
    Historie und Theologie. Neutestamentliche Festschrift für
    Hans Conzelmann zum 60. Geburtstag*. Ed. Georg Strecker.
    Tübingen: J. C. B. Mohr (Paul Siebeck), 1975.

_____. "Paul's Concept of Freedom in the Context of
    Hellenistic Discussions About Possibilities of Human
    Freedom." Pp. 1-13 in *Protocol Series of the Colloquies
    of the Center for Hermeneutical Studies in Hellenistic
    and Modern Culture* 26. Ed. W. Wuellner. Berkeley, CA:
    The Graduate Theological Union and the University of
    California, 1977.

Bieder, Werner. "Gebetswirklichkeit und Gebetsmöglichkeit bei
    Paulus. Das Beten des Geistes und das Beten im Geiste."
    Theologische Zeitschrift 4 (1948) 22-40.

Blass, F., and Debrunner, A. *A Greek Grammar of the New
    Testament and Other Early Christian Literature*. 10th ed.
    Trans. and rev. Robert W. Funk. Chicago: University of
    Chicago, 1961.

Boers, Hendrikus. *Theology out of the Ghetto: A New Testament
    Exegetical Study Concerning Religious Exclusiveness*.
    Leiden: E. J. Brill, 1971.

Bonner, Campbell (ed.). *The Homily on the Passion by Melito,
    Bishop of Sandis, and Some Fragments of the Apocryphal
    Ezekiel*. Studies and Documents 12. London: Christophers;
    Philadelphia: University of Pennsylvania, 1940.

Bornkamm, Günther. *Early Christian Experience*. Trans. Paul L.
    Hammer. New York: Harper & Row, 1969.

_____. *Paul*. Trans. D. M. G. Stalker. New York: Harper &
    Row, 1971.

Bousset, Wilhelm. *Kyrios Christos: A History of the Belief in Christ from the Beginnings of Christianity to Irenaeus.* Trans. John E. Steely. Nashville: Abingdon, 1970.

Brandenburger, Egon. *Fleisch und Geist: Paulus und die dualistische Weisheit.* Wissenschaftliche Monographien zum Alten und Neuen Testament 29. Neukirchen-Vluyn: Neukirchener Verlag, 1968.

Bruce, F. F. "Galatian Problems, 3. The 'Other' Gospel." *Bulletin of the John Rylands University Library of Manchester* 53 (1970-71) 253-71.

Büchsel, Friedrich. *Theologie des Neuen Testaments: Geschichte des Wortes Gottes im Neuen Testament.* 2nd ed. Gütersloh: C. Bertelsmann, 1937.

Bultmann, Rudolf. *The History of the Synoptic Tradition.* Rev. ed. Trans. John Marsh. New York: Harper & Row, 1968.

_____. "The Problem of Ethics in the Writings of Paul." Pp. 7-32 in *The Old and New Man in the Letters of Paul.* Trans. Keith R. Crim. Richmond, VA: John Knox, 1967.

_____. "Paul." Pp. 111-46, 307 in *Existence and Faith: Shorter Writings of Rudolf Bultmann.* Trans. Schubert M. Ogden. New York: World, 1960.

_____. *Theology of the New Testament.* 2 vols. in 1. Trans. Kendrick Grobel. New York: Scribner's Sons, 1951, 1955.

_____. "Ursprung und Sinn der Typologie als Hermeneutischer Methode." Pp. 369-80 in *Exegetica, Aufsätze zur Erforschung des Neuen Testaments.* Ed. Erich Dinkler. Tübingen: J. C. B. Mohr (Paul Siebeck), 1967.

_____. "ΔΙΚΑΙΟΣΥΝΗ ΘΕΟΥ." *Journal of Biblical Literature* 83 (1964) 12-16.

_____. *The Gospel of John: A Commentary.* Trans. G. R. Beasley-Murray (gen. ed.), R. W. N. Hoare, and J. K. Riches. Philadelphia: Westminster, 1971.

Burton, Ernest de Witt. *Syntax of the Moods and Tenses in New Testament Greek.* 3rd ed. Edinburgh: T. & T. Clark, 1955 (orig. 1898).

Cobb, John B., Jr. *A Christian Natural Theology Based on the Thought of Alfred North Whitehead.* Philadelphia: Westminster, 1965.

_____. *The Structure of Christian Existence.* Philadelphia: Westminster, 1967.

_____. *Christ in a Pluralistic Age.* Philadelphia: Westminster, 1975.

Cobb, John B., Jr., and David R. Griffin. *Process Theology: An Introductory Exposition*. Philadelphia: Westminster, 1976.

Conzelmann, Hans. *Outline of the Theology of the New Testament*. Trans. John Bowden. New York: Harper & Row, 1969.

Crownfeld, Frederic R. "The Singular Problem of the Dual Galatians." *Journal of Biblical Literature* 64 (1945) 491-500.

Cullmann, Oscar. *Baptism in the New Testament*. Studies in Biblical Theology 1. Trans. J. K. S. Reid. London: SCM, 1950.

_____. *Early Christian Worship*. Studies in Biblical Theology 10. Trans. A. Stewart Todd and James B. Torrance. Chicago: Henry Regnery, 1953.

_____. *The Christology of the New Testament*. Rev. ed. Trans. Shirley C. Guthrie and Charles A. M. Hall. Philadelphia: Westminster, 1963.

Deissmann, Adolf. *The Religion of Jesus and the Faith of Paul*. 2nd ed. Trans. William E. Wilson. New York: George H. Doran, 1926.

_____. *Paul: A Study in Social and Religious History*. 2nd ed. Trans. William E. Wilson. New York: Harper & Row, 1927.

Delling, Gerhard. *Worship in the New Testament*. Trans. Percy Scott. Philadelphia: Westminster, 1962.

Dibelius, Martin. *Paulus und die Mystik*. München: E. Reinhardt, 1941.

Dodd, C. H. *The Interpretation of the Fourth Gospel*. Cambridge: Cambridge University, 1970.

Dodds, Eric Robertson. *The Greeks and the Irrational*. Berkeley, CA: University of California, 1971.

Dunn, James D. G. *Baptism in the Holy Spirit: A Re-examination of the New Testament Teaching on the Gift of the Spirit in Relation to Pentecostalism Today*. Studies in Biblical Theology 15 (2nd series). London: SCM, 1970.

_____. *Jesus and the Spirit: A Study of the Religious and Charismatic Experience of Jesus and the First Christians as Reflected in the New Testament*. Philadelphia: Westminster, 1975.

Duprez, Antoine. "Note sur le rôle de l'Esprit-Saint dans la filiation du chrétien, à propos de *Gal.* 4:6." *Recherches de science religieuse* 52 (1964) 421-31.

Epictetus. *The Discourses as Reported by Arrian, The Manual, and Fragments*. Loeb Classical Library 1. Trans. W. A. Oldfather. London: William Heinemann; New York: G. P. Putnam's Sons, 1926.

Fuller, Reginald H. *The Foundations of New Testament Christology*. New York: Scribner's Sons, 1965.

_____. *The Formation of the Resurrection Narratives*. New York: Macmillan, 1971.

Gager, John G. *Kingdom and Community: The Social World of Early Christianity*. New Jersey: Prentice-Hall, 1975.

Georgi, Dieter. *Die Gegner des Paulus im 2. Korintherbrief. Studien zur religiösen Propaganda in der Spätantike*. Wissenschaftliche Monographien zum Alten und Neuen Testament 11. Neukirchen-Vluyn: Neukirchener Verlag, 1964.

Gunkel, Hermann. *Die Wirkungen des heiligen Geistes, nach der populären Anschauung der apostolischen Zeit und der Lehre des Apostels Paulus: Eine biblisch-theologische Studie*. 2nd ed. Göttingen: Vandenhoeck & Ruprecht, 1899.

Güttgemanns, Erhardt. *Der leidende Apostel und sein Herr: Studien zur paulinischen Christologie*. Forschungen zur Religion und Literatur des Alten und Neuen Testaments 90. Göttingen: Vandenhoeck & Ruprecht, 1966.

Haenchen, Ernst. *The Acts of the Apostles: A Commentary*. Trans. Bernard Noble, Gerald Shinn, Hugh Anderson and R. McL. Wilson. Philadelphia: Westminster, 1971.

Hahn, Ferdinand. *The Titles of Jesus in Christology: Their History in Early Christianity*. Trans. Harold Knight and George Ogg. New York: World, 1969.

Hanson, Anthony T. *Studies in Paul's Technique and Theology*. London: SPCK, 1974.

Hengel, Martin. *Judaism and Hellenism: Studies in their Encounter during the Early Hellenistic Period*. 2 vols. Trans. John Bowden. Philadelphia: Fortress, 1974.

Hercher, R. *Epistolographi Graeci*. Paris: Didot, 1873.

Hodgson, Peter C. *New Birth of Freedom: A Theology of Bondage and Liberation*. Philadelphia: Fortress, 1976.

Hommel, Hildebrecht. "Das 7. Kapitel des Römerbriefes im Licht antiker Überlieferung." Pp. 90-116 in *Theologia Viatorum*. Vol. 8. Jahrbuch der kirchlichen Hochschule Berlin, 1961/1962. Ed. Fritz Maass. Berlin: Walter de Gruyter, 1962.

Isenberg, Sheldon R. "Millenarism in Greco-Roman Palestine." *Religion* 4 (1974) 26-46.

_____. "Power Through Temple and Torah in Greco-Roman Palestine." Pp. 24-52 in *Christianity, Judaism and Other Greco-Roman Cults: Studies for Morton Smith at Sixty*. Part 2: *Early Christianity*. Studies in Judaism in Late Antiquity 12. Ed. Jacob Neusner. Leiden: E. J. Brill, 1975.

218   The Spirit in Galatia

Jaeger, Werner. *Paideia: The Ideals of Greek Culture.* Vol. 3: *The Conflict of Cultural Ideals in the Age of Plato.* Trans. Gilbert Highet. New York: Oxford University, 1944.

Jeremias, Joachim. *The Prayers of Jesus.* Studies in Biblical Theology 6 (2nd series). Trans. John Bowden, Christoph Burchard and John Reumann. London: SCM, 1967.

_____. *New Testament Theology: The Proclamation of Jesus.* Trans. John Bowden. New York: Scribner's Sons, 1971.

_____. *The Parables of Jesus.* 2nd rev. ed. Trans. S. H. Hooke. New York: Scribner's Sons, 1972.

Jewett, Robert. *Paul's Anthropological Terms: A Study of Their Use in Conflict Settings.* Arbeiten zur Geschichte des antiken Judentums und des Urchristentums 10. Leiden: E. J. Brill, 1971.

_____. "Agitators and the Galatian Congregation." *New Testament Studies* 17 (1971) 198-212.

Josephus, Flavius. *Jewish Antiquities. Books XVIII-XX.* Loeb Classical Library 9. Trans. Louis H. Feldman. Cambridge: Harvard University; London: William Heinemann, 1965.

Kamlah, Ehrhard. *Die Form der katalogischen Paränese im N. T.* Wissenschaftliche Untersuchungen zum Neuen Testament 7. Tübingen: J. C. B. Mohr (Paul Siebeck), 1964.

Käsemann, Ernst. "Formeln II. Liturgische Formeln im N. T." Pp. 993-96 in *Religion in Geschichte und Gegenwart.* Vol. 2. 3rd ed. Ed. Kurt Galling. Tübingen: J. C. B. Mohr (Paul Siebeck), 1958.

_____. "Geist." Pp. 1272-79 in *Religion in Geschichte und Gegenwart.* Vol. 2. 3rd ed. Ed. Kurt Galling. Tübingen: J. C. B. Mohr (Paul Siebeck), 1958.

_____. "The Righteousness of God in Paul." Pp. 168-82 in *New Testament Questions of Today.* Trans. W. J. Montague. Philadelphia: Fortress, 1969.

_____. *Perspectives on Paul.* Trans. Margaret Kohl. Philadelphia: Fortress, 1971.

Kittel, G., and Friedrich, G. (eds.). *Theological Dictionary of the New Testament.* 9 vols. Trans. and ed. G. W. Bromiley. Grand Rapids, MI: William B. Eerdmans, 1964-1974.

Baumgärtel, Friedrich and Behm, Johannes. "καρδία, κτλ." 3 (1965) 605-14.

Bertram, Georg. "ἔργον, κτλ." 2 (1964) 635-55.

Betz, Otto. "στίγμα." 7 (1971) 657-64.

Büchsel, Friedrich. "κρίνω, κτλ." 3 (1965) 921-23, 933-54.

Büchsel, F. and Rengstorf, K. H. "γεννάω, κτλ." 1 (1964) 665-75.

Bultmann, Rudolf. "ἐλπίς, κτλ." 2 (1964) 517-23, 529-35.

_____. "ζάω, κτλ." 2 (1964) 832-43, 849-51, 855-75.

_____. "πιστεύω, κτλ." 6 (1968) 174-82, 197-228.

Delling, Gerhard. "καιρός, κτλ." 3 (1965) 455-64.

_____. "λαμβάνω, κτλ." 4 (1967) 5-15.

_____. "πλήρης, κτλ." 6 (1968) 283-311.

_____. "στοιχέω, κτλ." 7 (1971) 666-87.

Fitzer, Gottfried. "σφραγίς, κτλ." 7 (1971) 939-53.

Friedrich, Gerhard. "εὐαγγελίζομαι, κτλ." 2 (1964) 707-37.

Goppelt, Leonhard. "τύπος, κτλ." 8 (1972) 246-59.

_____. "ὕδωρ." 8 (1972) 314-33.

Grundmann, Walter. "δέχομαι, κτλ." 2 (1964) 50-59.

_____. "δύναμαι, κτλ." 2 (1964) 284-317.

_____. "ἰσχύω, κτλ." 3 (1965) 397-402.

_____. "κράζω, κτλ." 3 (1965) 898-903.

_____. "χρίω, κτλ." 9 (1974) 493-96, 527-80.

Harder, Günther. "φθείρω, κτλ." 9 (1974) 93-106.

Hauck, Friedrich. "θερίζω, θερισμός." 3 (1965) 132-33.

_____. "μένω, κτλ." 4 (1967) 574-88.

Kittel, Gerhard. "ἀββᾶ." 1 (1964) 5-6.

_____. "ἀκούω, κτλ." 1 (1964) 216-25.

Kuhn, Karl Georg. "προσήλυτος." 6 (1968) 727-44.

Lohse, Eduard. "χείρ, κτλ." 9 (1974) 424-37.

Oepke, Albrecht. "βάπτω, κτλ." 1 (1964) 529-46.

_____. "λούω, κτλ." 4 (1967) 295-307.

Procksch, Otto. "ἅγιος, κτλ." 1 (1964) 88-97, 100-15.

Rengstorf, Karl Heinrich. "ἀποστέλλω, κτλ." 1 (1964) 398-447.

Sasse, Hermann. "αἰών, αἰώνιος." 1 (1964) 197-209.

Schneider, Johannes. "ἔρχομαι, κτλ." 2 (1964) 666-84.

Schrenk, Gottlob. "δίκη, κτλ." 2 (1964) 178-225.

_____. "πατήρ, κτλ." 5 (1967) 945-59, 974-1022.

Schulz, Siegfried. "σπέρμα, κτλ." 7 (1971) 536-38, 543-47.

Schweizer, Eduard. "πνεῦμα, κτλ." 6 (1968) 389-455.

_____. "σάρξ, κτλ." 7 (1971) 98-105, 108-10, 119-51.

_____. "υἱός, υἱοθεσία." 8 (1972) 354-57, 363-92, 399.

Stauffer, Ethelbert. "ἀγαπάω, κτλ." 1 (1964) 35-55.

_____. "ἵνα." 3 (1965) 323-33.

Strathmann, Hermann. "πόλις, κτλ." 6 (1968) 516-35.

Kramer, Werner. *Christ, Lord, Son of God*. Studies in Biblical
    Theology 50. Trans. Brian Hardy. London: SCM, 1966.

Lampe, Geoffrey W. H. *The Seal of the Spirit: A Study of the
    Doctrine of Baptism and Confirmation in the New Testament
    and the Fathers*. London: Longmans, Green, 1951.

Lloyd, G. E. R. *Greek Science After Aristotle*. Ancient Cul-
    ture and Society. New York: W. W. Norton, 1973.

Lütgert, Wilhelm. *Gesetz und Geist: Eine Untersuchung zur
    Vorgeschichte des Galaterbriefes*. Beiträge zur Forderung
    christlicher Theologie I/22/6. Gütersloh: C. Bertelsmann,
    1919.

Lutz, Cora E. *Musonius Rufus. "The Roman Socrates."* Yale
    Classical Studies 10. New Haven, CT: Yale University,
    1947.

Luz, Ulrich. "Der alte und der neue Bund bei Paulus und im
    Hebräerbrief." *Evangelische Theologie* 27 (1967) 318-36.

Malherbe, Abraham J. "'Gentle As A Nurse': The Cynic Back-
    ground to I Thess ii." *Novum Testamentum* 12 (1970) 203-17.

Meeks, Wayne A. "The Image of the Androgyne: Some Uses of a
    Symbol in Earliest Christianity." *History of Religions* 13
    (1973) 165-208.

Moore, George Foot. *Judaism in the First Centuries of the
    Christian Era, the Age of the Tannaim*. 2 vols. New York:
    Schocken, 1927.

Moule, C. F. D. *An Idiom Book of New Testament Greek*. Cam-
    bridge: The University Press, 1953.

_____. "2 Cor 3,18b, καθάπερ ἀπὸ κυρίου πνεύματος." Pp.
    231-37 in *Neues Testament und Geschichte: Historisches
    Geschehen und Deutung im Neuen Testament*. O. Cullmann zum
    70. Geburtstag. Ed. Heinrich Baltensweiler and Bo Reicke.
    Tübingen: J. C. B. Mohr (Paul Siebeck); Zürich: Theolog-
    ischer Verlag, 1972.

Munck, Johannes. *Paul and the Salvation of Mankind*. Trans.
    Frank Clarke. Richmond, VA: John Knox, 1959.

Mussner, Franz. *Theologie der Freiheit nach Paulus*. Quaes-
    tiones Disputatae 75. Freiburg/Basel/Wien: Herder &
    Herder, 1976.

Niederwimmer, Kurt. *Der Begriff der Freiheit im Neuen Testa-
    ment*. Theologische Bibliotek Töpelmann 11. Berlin:
    Alfred Töpelmann, 1966.

Ogden, Schubert M. *Christ Without Myth: A Study Based on the
    Theology of Rudolf Bultmann*. New York: Harper & Row,
    1961.

Ogden, Schubert M. *The Reality of God, and Other Essays*.
New York: Harper & Row, 1963.

Outler, Albert C. "Veni, Creator Spiritus: The Doctrine of
the Holy Spirit." *Perkins (School of Theology) Journal* 19
(1966) 31-40.

Pannenberg, Wolfhart. *Jesus--God and Man*. Trans. Lewis L.
Wilkins and Duane A. Priebe. Philadelphia: Westminster,
1968.

_____. "The Working of the Spirit in the Creation and in
the People of God." Pp. 13-31 in *Spirit, Faith, and
Church*. Ed. Edward P. Echlin, S.J. Philadelphia: Westminster, 1970.

_____. "The Doctrine of the Spirit and the Task of a
Theology of Nature." *Theology* 75 (1972) 8-21.

_____. *The Apostles' Creed in the Light of Today's Ques-
tions*. Trans. Margaret Kohl. Philadelphia: Westminster,
1972.

_____. *Faith and Reality*. Trans. John Maxwell. Phila-
delphia: Westminster, 1977.

Paulsen, Henning. *Überlieferung und Auslegung in Römer 8*.
Wissenschaftliche Monographien zum Alten und Neuen Testament 43. Neukirchen-Vluyn: Neukirchener Verlag, 1974.

Perrin, Norman. *Rediscovering the Teaching of Jesus*. New
York: Harper & Row, 1967.

_____. *The New Testament, An Introduction: Proclamation
and Parenesis, Myth and History*. New York: Harcourt,
Brace, Jovanovich, 1974.

Peterson, Erik. ΕΙΣ ΘΕΟΣ. *Epigraphische, formgeschichtliche
und religionsgeschichtliche Untersuchungen*. Forschungen
zur Religion und Literatur des Alten und Neuen Testaments
(n.f.) 24. Göttingen: Vandenhoeck & Ruprecht, 1926.

Philo. *Quis Rerum Divinarum Heres sit*. Loeb Classical Library
4. Trans. F. H. Colson and G. H. Whitaker. Cambridge:
Harvard University; London: William Heinemann, 1932.

_____. *De Specialibus Legibus*, I-III. Loeb Classical
Library 7. Trans. F. H. Colson. Cambridge: Harvard
University; London: William Heinemann, 1937.

Pittenger, W. Norman. *Life in Christ*. Grand Rapids, MI:
William B. Eerdmans, 1972.

_____. *The Holy Spirit*. Philadelphia: United Church, 1974.

Plato. *Respublica*, VI-X. Loeb Classical Library 6. Trans.
    Paul Shorey. Cambridge: Harvard University; London:
    William Heinemann, 1935.

_____. *Ion*. Loeb Classical Library 8. Trans. W. R. M.
    Lamb. Cambridge: Harvard University; London: William
    Heinemann, 1925.

Plutarch. "De sera numinis vindicta." *Moralia* 548A-568A.
    Loeb Classical Library 7. Trans. Phillip H. De Lacy and
    Benedict Einarson. Cambridge: Harvard University; London:
    William Heinemann, 1959.

_____. "Maxime cum principibus philosopho esse disserendum."
    Moralia 776A-779B. Loeb Classical Library 10. Trans.
    H. N. Fowler. Cambridge: Harvard University; London:
    William Heinemann, 1936.

Pohlenz, Max. *Freedom in Greek Life and Thought: The History
    of an Ideal*. Trans. Carl Lofmark. Dordrecht-Holland:
    D. Reidel, 1966.

Ridderbos, Herman. *Paul, An Outline of His Theology*. Trans.
    John R. DeWitt. Grand Rapids, MI: William B. Eerdmans,
    1975.

Rivkin, Ellis. "The Internal City: Judaism and Urbanization."
    Journal for the Scientific Study of Religion 5 (1966)
    225-40.

Robinson, James M. *A New Quest of the Historical Jesus*.
    Studies in Biblical Theology 25. London: SCM, 1959.

_____. "Regeneration." Pp. 24-29 in *The Interpreter's
    Dictionary of the Bible*. Vol. 4. Ed. George A. Buttrick.
    Nashville: Abingdon, 1962.

Robinson, John A. T. *The Body. A Study in Pauline Theology*.
    Studies in Biblical Theology 5. London: SCM, 1952.

Ropes, J. H. *The Singular Problem of the Epistle to the Gala-
    tians*. Harvard Theological Studies 14. Cambridge:
    Harvard University, 1929.

Sanders, E. P. "Patterns of Religion in Paul and Rabbinic
    Judaism: A Holistic Method of Comparison." *Harvard
    Theological Review* 66 (1973) 455-78.

_____. *Paul and Palestinian Judaism: A Comparison of Pat-
    terns of Religion*. Philadelphia: Fortress, 1977.

Schmidt, Wilhelm (ed.). *Heronis Alexandrini opera quae super-
    sunt omnia*. Vol. 1: *Pneumatica et automatia*. Leipzig:
    B. G. Teubner, 1899.

Schmithals, Walter. *The Office of Apostle in the Early Church.*
Trans. John E. Steely. Nashville: Abingdon, 1969.

_____. *Gnosticism in Corinth: An Investigation of the
Letters to the Corinthians.* Trans. John E. Steely.
Nashville: Abingdon, 1971.

_____. *Paul and the Gnostics.* Trans. John E. Steely.
Nashville: Abingdon, 1972.

Schnackenburg, Rudolf. *Baptism in the Thought of St. Paul:
A Study in Pauline Theology.* Trans. G. R. Beasley-Murray.
New York: Herder and Herder, 1964.

Schoeps, Hans Joachim. *Paul. The Theology of the Apostle in
the Light of Jewish Religious History.* Trans. Harold
Knight. Philadelphia: Westminster, 1961.

Schweitzer, Albert. *The Mysticism of Paul the Apostle.* Trans.
William Montgomery. New York: Seabury, 1931.

Schweizer, Eduard. "Zur Herkunft der Präexistenzvorstellung
bei Paulus." *Evangelische Theologie* 19 (1959) 65-70.

_____. "Zum religionsgeschichtlichen Hintergrund der
'Sendungsformel' Gal. 4.4f; Röm. 8.3f; Joh. 3.16f; 1 Joh.
4.9." *Zeitschrift für die neutestamentliche Wissenschaft*
57 (1966) 199-210.

Stalder, Kurt. *Das Werk des Geistes in der Heiligung bei
Paulus.* Zürich: EVZ, 1962.

Stendahl, Krister. *Paul Among Jews and Gentiles, and Other
Essays.* Philadelphia: Fortress, 1976.

Tannehill, Robert C. *Dying and Rising With Christ: A Study in
Pauline Theology.* Beihefte zur Zeitschrift für die neutestamentliche Wissenschaft 32. Berlin: Alfred Töpelmann,
1967.

Taylor, T. M. "'Abba, Father' and Baptism." *Scottish Journal
of Theology* 11 (1958) 62-71.

Theissen, Gerd. "Legitimation und Lebensunterhalt: Ein Beitrag
zur Soziologie urchristlicher Missionare." *New Testament
Studies* 21 (1974/75) 192-221.

Thornton, Lionel Spencer. *Confirmation, Its Place in the
Baptismal Mystery.* London: Dacre, A. & C. Black, 1954.

Turner, Nigel. *A Grammar of New Testament Greek.* Vol. 3:
Syntax. Edinburgh: T. & T. Clark, 1963.

Unnik, W. C. van. "Reisepläne und Amen-Sagen, Zusammenhang und
Gedankenfolge in 2. Korinther i 15-24." Pp. 144-59 in
Sparsa Collecta: The Collected Essays of W. C. van Unnik.
Part 1: *Evangelia, Paulina, Acta.* Novum Testamentum, Sup-
plements 29. Leiden: E. J. Brill, 1973.

Vielhauer, Philipp. "Paulus und das Alte Testament." Pp. 33-
    62 in *Studien zur Geschichte und Theologie der Reforma-
    tion. Festschrift für Ernst Bizer*. Ed. Luise Abramowski
    and J. F. Gerhard Goeters. Neukirchen-Vluyn: Neukirchener
    Verlag, 1969.

Vos, Johannes Sijko. *Traditionsgeschichtliche Untersuchungen
    zur paulinischen Pneumatologie*. Assen: Van Gorcum, 1973.

Weber, Max. *The Theory of Social and Economic Organization*.
    Trans. A. M. Henderson and Talcott Parsons. Ed. Talcott
    Parsons. New York: Free Press; London: Collier-Macmillan,
    1947.

Wegenast, Klaus. *Das Verständnis der Tradition bei Paulus und
    in den Deuteropaulinen*. Wissenschaftliche Monographien
    zum Alten und Neuen Testament 8. Neukirchen-Vluyn:
    Neukirchener Verlag, 1962.

Wikenhauser, Alfred. *Pauline Mysticism: Christ in the Mystical
    Teaching of St. Paul*. Trans. Joseph Cunningham. New
    York: Herder & Herder, 1960.

INDEX OF PASSAGES